AUCTION!

Among the books, magazines, tape-recording transcriptions, catalogues, sale lists, interoffice memoranda, and other reference sources which have been consulted, particular acknowledgment is gratefully made to Frank Arnau's *The Art of the Faker,* Dusseldorf, 1959; Gerald Reitlinger's *The Economics of Taste,* London, 1961; Maurice Rheims's *The Strange Life of Objects,* London, 1961; Richard Rush's *Art as an Investment,* Englewood, New Jersey, 1961; Aline B. Saarinen's *The Proud Possessors,* New York, 1958; Francis Henry Taylor's *The Taste of Angels,* Boston, 1948; and the pages of *The New York Times.*

Of the many people who donated time, advice, and encouragement, special thanks are said to I. O. Chance; Peter Wilson; Leslie Hyam and his associates; Irma Ritter, who typed the manuscript; and the colleague who contributed the research and expertise,

Jerene Jones

JAMES BROUGH

AUCTION!

RELEASE 85271

THE **BOBBS-MERRILL** COMPANY, INC.
A SUBSIDIARY OF HOWARD W. SAMS & CO., INC.
Publishers · INDIANAPOLIS · NEW YORK

To the company of men, from
Fra Angelico to John Zoffany,
who made it all possible.

"Tea with Mrs. Erickson" appeared in *McCall's*
in slightly different form.

FIRST PRINTING, 1963
COPYRIGHT © 1963 BY JAMES BROUGH
ALL RIGHTS RESERVED
LIBRARY OF CONGRESS CATALOG CARD NUMBER 63-11637

PRINTED IN THE UNITED STATES OF AMERICA

CONTENTS

I

TEA WITH MRS. ERICKSON

W HEN Mrs. Anna Erickson invited any art dealer or museum curator to take tea with her, nothing short of sudden, crippling injury could keep him away. If necessary, most of them would have contrived to arrive, punctual to the minute, on crutches or stretcher outside her brownstone house at 110 East Thirty-fifth Street in the Murray Hill section of New York City, to be carried up the four steep steps to her black-painted, double entrance doors.

It would be hard to imagine anyone less peremptory than the tall, gray-haired, gentle-mannered old woman, yet invitations to visit her carried the weight of royal command, not to be refused. A visitor could forgive himself for admiring her generosity in asking him around, while he wondered whether she might be epicurean, and understandably so, in the exercise of her power.

In her quiet sitting room, he somehow had to manage the delicate task of balancing his china teacup, paying suitable court to his soft-spoken hostess and keeping his eyes from straying avariciously to the large painting in the thick, gilt-crusted frame that dominated both the room and the conversation. It was impossible to ignore it. It was the cause and the curse of such social occasions.

Its size alone, four feet eight and one-half inches by four feet five and three-quarter inches, made it impressive, but there was more to it than that. Sharing somewhat crowded wall space with a Frans Hals, a Holbein and two lesser Rembrandts, this was the glory of Mrs. Erickson's small but magnificently choice collection, numbering twenty-four pictures in all, which she inherited from her late husband.

It depicts a sunken-cheeked, bearded man with a look of brooding sadness in his lustrous eyes, which are the focal point of composition. In a dark robe with huge ruffed golden sleeves, he stands with his right hand resting on a battered plaster bust. Though it had as many titles as previous owners, it was known generally by now as "Aristotle Contemplating the Bust of Homer," a Rembrandt masterpiece. It was to become the world's costliest and, contemporarily, most celebrated painting when it came up for auction in the fall of 1961, stirring feeling of kinship to greatness in everyone who had ever set foot inside the lowliest auction house from Monterey to Kennebunkport and bid for a box of broken china or a dented pewter tankard, possibly Georgian.

Anna Erickson, an old-fashioned woman, knew that it was the picture and not her hospitality alone that made her the candle around which the cognoscenti fluttered like moths. One visitor, Theodore Rousseau Jr., who is a curator of European paintings at the Metropolitan Museum of Art, has recalled, "I first saw it in Mrs. Erickson's sitting room after the last war. It jumped out of its frame. It gripped me. I would have tea with her, and I could not take my eyes off it."

Like other callers, he lived in constant, calculating hope that by some magic word or ineffable charm he might one day succeed in persuading her that only the Met was worthy of being named in her will to inherit the resplendent Rembrandt. Neither Rousseau nor his rivals for her posthumous favor could be regarded as ghoulish, but they were sharply aware that Anna Erickson's years were piling up and time grew shorter every birthday.

James J. Rorimer, director of the Metropolitan, made no bones about it. "I first saw it at the Century of Progress Exposition in Chicago in 1933," he related. "It was hanging in the Chicago Art Institute. I just stood and looked at it and was overwhelmed. I can't honestly say if I knew at that precise moment that it must someday be in the Metropolitan, but I thought about that picture over the years more and more. The more Mrs. Erickson aged, the more interested I became."

She refused, politely but pointedly, to be parted from the painting in her lifetime or to contemplate bequeathing it to anybody. The "Aristotle" had always been the particular pride of her husband, Alfred W. Erickson, who was born of Swedish descent at Farmers Mills, New York, in 1876. By nature, he was shy and retiring; by profession he was a high-principled, pioneering huckster who landed in the advertising business at the turn of the century, when that business was in its cradle. He made a comfortable fortune from his own company, the Erickson Advertising Agency, which in 1930 joined with the W. H. K. McCann Company, forming McCann-Erickson Incorporated, with himself as chairman of the board.

Eight years before the merger, he had enough ready cash to start buying pictures, prompted by that combination of acquired good taste and innate good business that impelled many men in similar circumstances to emulate somewhat the

On this epic evening, "Aristotle" found a new home

Mellons and the Kresses and the Fricks, who were building up the great collections of America. Erickson's taste and his cash outlays expanded with the years, which is not unusual.

One of his first purchases, Raeburn's "Captain David Kinloch, R.N.," cost him $22,000 in 1922; it went for a cut price $7,500 in 1961 in the auction that saw "Aristotle" sell for $2,300,000. Holbein's portrait of "Sir George Nevill, Fifth Lord Bergavenny," for which the neophyte collector paid $130,000 in 1926, was knocked down that same evening for a mere $35,000, and a Thomas Gainsborough for which Erickson had forked out $300,000 in 1928 was sold for $35,000, too.

The big Rembrandt was the most expensive painting that the art-struck advertising man ever bought. It also had the most checkered career of anything in his collection, and he had for it the feelings of a father for a prodigal son. Its history dates to 1652, when a Sicilian nobleman, Don Antonio Ruffo, commissioned Rembrandt van Rijn to paint a portrait of a philosopher—any philosopher—to hang in his palace near the harbor of Messina.

The commission, the only one Rembrandt received from a noteworthy foreign collector, could not have reached him at a more convenient time. Though he was painting better than ever before or again in his life, he was close to bankruptcy. He was forty-six years old, and his reputation was in decline, largely as a result of antagonizing the complacent burghers of Amsterdam with his huge group portrait of one of their officer's guilds, "The Nightwatch," which they had commissioned. Instead of following convention, he had crowded most of the figures in the background and allowed a cloud to shadow their faces. His clients decreased. He was compelled to sell canvases along with his household linens to meet his creditors.

Don Antonio was a rich art lover, whose palace, a meeting place for artists, writers and scientists, was laden with sculpture, tapestries, busts of Greek and Roman heroes. His collection of paintings already included works by Lucas van Leyden, Titian, Van Dyck, Poussin and Reni. The masters of the past and the leaders of his own day interested him equally—he was an ideal collector from an artist's point of view.

His original instructions asked only for a philosopher; painting him an Aristotle was Rembrandt's idea, so far as existing documents indicate. The picture has had several titles over the centuries—a Philosopher, a Savant, a portrait of the Italian poet Torquato Tasso or the Dutch historian Van Hooft. Theodore Rousseau believes, "The presence of the bust of Homer, however, and of the medal with a profile of Alexander hanging on the figure's elaborate golden chain are enough to indicate that a representation of Aristotle is intended."

There are two other bits of conclusive evidence in this not unusual dispute about the identity of the subject of an Old Master. In an inventory of his possessions made by Rembrandt himself, he listed a plaster bust of Homer. And when the finished painting arrived in Messina in 1654 aboard the ship *Bartolommeus,* Don Antonio, a meticulous record-keeper, described it as *Aristotele che tinen una mano sopra una statua*—"Aristotle holding one hand on a statue."

Ruffo had some misgivings about the picture at first. It was too big, he complained, and it looked unfinished. The price, not including crating and lading charges, ran to 500 florins, which was four times as much as he was used to paying the best Italian artists for similar work. But he paid up—$7,800 in present currency—and once he was accustomed to it, he rated "Aristotle" one of the most important items in his expanding collection.

It was one of the approximately one hundred pictures which his will directed should be forever inherited by the eldest son in future generations of the family. Fortunately for dealers, curators and auctioneers, "forever" stretches far beyond anyone's control. God's disposal of man's proposals is a stark necessity to the art business. In 1743 the plague, endemic in Europe at the time, struck down the eldest Ruffo and each of his brothers. The paintings passed into the hands of a cadet branch of the Ruffos; Don Antonio's will was broken; and some of the hundred were sold.

Whether "Aristotle" was among them is unknown. For roughly fifty years, no records exist to tell its story. Early in the nineteenth century, it turned up in England, the property of Sir Abraham Hume, Baronet, Fellow of the Royal Society, amateur painter and intimate of Sir Joshua Reynolds. Hume didn't try to reach beyond his grave with any fine phrases about "forever" or "in perpetuity." Possibly the descendant of his felt no qualms when he disposed of the Rembrandt toward the close of the Victorian era.

The new owner was Rodolphe Kann, who had made his millions in South Africa in association with Cecil Rhodes, the diamond-digging founder of scholarships. Kann was partial to Rembrandts. He collected eleven of them, which after his death were bought by Joseph Duveen, the English dealer who appointed himself a transatlantic arbiter of good taste, and shipped from France to storage in London and New York.

Duveen included among his steady patrons Arabella Huntington, the widow of Collis P. Huntington, one of the promoters of the Central Pacific Railroad. Arabella accepted Duveen's advice on everything from hats to art to hairdos. She bought paintings from him in whole batches—Hals, Velázquez, van der Weyden, Bellini and "Aristotle."

When Arabella had departed the earthly scene, her son Archer gave two lesser Rembrandts and a Hals to the Metropolitan as a memorial to his father, whose reputation needed embellishment with those who'd done railroad business with him. Archer Huntington restrained his generosity when it came to "Aristotle," for which he used one of its earlier, alternative titles. "To avoid any confusion," he wrote to the Met, "I will state that I do not include the painting by Rembrandt known as Portrait of a Savant . . . as this I shall retain for my own home at a future date."

Theodore Rousseau has noted sadly, "It is tantalizing to think that the picture might have come to the museum at that time as a gift." If the Metropolitan wasn't spared the future need to scrape up more than two million dollars, neither did Archer's thought for adorning his home with a masterpiece come to anything. He allowed Duveen to buy back the Rembrandt and employed the proceeds in building the American Academy of Arts and Letters, a case where one picture was worth uncounted thousands of words.

Alfred Erickson was a customer to gladden the heart of Duveen, who could make the biggest titan feel honored to buy from him. Alfred was no titan but a mild, plump-faced bourgeois who favored pince-nez and high collars. To Duveen, he was small fry, permitted only to feel privileged in picking up "Aristotle" for $750,000 in November, 1928. His discrimination was unquestionable, but his timing was off. Within a year of his purchase, the stock market collapsed. Two years and one week after he bought it, he was forced to sell his favorite picture. Duveen was happy to pay him half a million dollars for it.

Duveen could detect the sentiments Erickson felt for the picture. He held on to it until February, 1936, when Alfred's business had picked up to the point where he could buy the Rembrandt a second time, with a check to Duveen for $590,000. His devotion deserved better, but he had only nine months in which to live in the presence of a painting that hints at immortality. Alfred Erickson died on November 2, 1936, at the age of sixty, long before art as a commodity began its present boom.

Mrs. Erickson was loyal to her husband's memory and his prize. She added one or two pictures to their collection, no more alert than he could have been to currently popular arrangements by which collectors can give works of art to public institutions and museums to save on Federal taxes. She believed in liquidating real property and putting the money into legacies. An invitation to tea meant a chance to look at "Aristotle," nothing more than that.

She died on February 7, 1961. Her will provided that her estate be divided into ninety equal parts. It amounted to an implicit order that the collection would have to be sold. As soon as the word was out, the museum wrote off their hopes of picking up the Rembrandt as a gift and began to make other plans.

Now it was the turn of the dealers to press for an advantage. Some of the niceties were forgotten in their approaches to her executors. The dealers were in for some swift disappointments. The besieged executors—the Bankers Trust Company and a firm of attorneys—hesitated to contemplate the law suits Mrs. Erickson's heirs might bring if the paintings were sold privately. Trouble could brew over whether a dealer had been allowed to buy too cheaply. Judges might have to rule whether an heir had been cheated on a subsequent sale. A public auction would assure the best possible price being obtained under the circumstances. Then, too, at public auction in New York and London the buyer has no recourse if his purchase turns out to be an inauthentic work. *Let the buyer beware* is timeless advice at an auction; you pay your money and you take your chances.

Four months after Mrs. Erickson died, never imagining the sensational future of her pictures, it was announced that dealers were out; it was time for the auction houses to fight to corner the collection. The siege of the executors was continued with all the wiles at the houses' command.

The foremost of them, Sotheby & Company of London, had its lofty, impeccable chairman, Peter Wilson, make at least three trips to New York to bid for the opportunity to stage the Erickson sale. His counterpart at Christie's, also of London, I. O. Chance, crossed the Atlantic an equal number of times on the same mission. Already on the scene in New York, the Parke-Bernet Galleries Incorporated, under the formidable direction of Leslie A. Hyam, mustered its forces.

The executors carefully explained that there would be no playing of favorites. "We would take the paintings to Togoland and sell them there," a spokesman said unabashedly, "if we thought we could get more money for them there than anywhere else. Our job is to get the most money we can for our clients."

It was a situation that spawned superlatives, though just how superlative the bids would be had yet to be seen. The Rembrandt, James Rorimer judged, was "the most important single painting available on the market in decades." Leslie Hyam rated the Erickson pictures "the greatest collection of Old Masters to be sold in the twentieth century." If he neglected to add "at public auction" the omission was attributable to enthusiasm, but Andrew Mellon had paid the Soviet government eight million dollars for the Hermitage treasures and then handed over to Duveen three times that sum for a collection on which the National Gallery was founded in Washington, D.C. Mellon paid for the building and threw in a $5,000,000 endowment fund, too.

Later, as the "Aristotle" fever mounted, there were chauvinistic rumors, recorded by the *Washington Post,* that the Soviets were out to carry off the Rembrandt at any price for the depleted Hermitage collection in Leningrad, presumably to get back at Mellon for wresting Raphael's "Alba Madonna" from the Hermitage when they were down and out in 1931. "The Justice Department," the *Post* noted, "has been asked whether there is any statute that could be used to save the Rembrandt if it is sold to a foreign bidder." The existence or otherwise of any such law never came to light. The Russians bid not a single kopeck when "Aristotle" was put on the block.

The persuasions that Peter Wilson lavished on Mrs. Erickson's executors appeared to be making very little impression. His strategy was an Anglicized version of a political candidate's plea, "Let's look at the record." He argued, "In recent years, all the most important sales of paintings have been at Sotheby's. We had nine of the ten highest prices ever paid for pictures." On the basis of his firm's two centuries of experience and expertise, he made his case for London and Sotheby's as "the natural place" for the Erickson sale. When those arguments faltered, he offered the executors a guaranteed minimum figure from the sale of the entire collection. They remained noncommittal. I. O. Chance echoed Wilson's plea for London to get the executors' nod, speaking perhaps less impressively than his competitor, since Christie's was obviously operating at some disadvantage, a middleweight among the heavies.

Back at Parke-Bernet, Leslie Hyam was applying his resourceful self to garnering the mouth-watering collection for his own house. Something more than the desire for international prestige was urging him on. His galleries' gross sales were down approximately $800,000 from the previous year's $9,200,000. This was half of what Sotheby's took in during the same period and about one million dollars less than the business done by Christie's.

Hyam let his emphasis fall on money, a persuasion to be depended upon in the circumstances. "Seventy-five per cent of the great world fortunes are in the United States," he declared. "It's Americans who buy the great paintings in London and who set the prices. The idea that sellers get higher prices in London is British propaganda. The Erickson sale will demonstrate to the world that the art market is *here*."

American museums, avid for the Rembrandt and most of the twenty-three other pictures, fell in with that argument for reasons of their own. They would stand a much better chance of picking up the prizes if the collection were to be auctioned close to home rather than abroad. Hyam in all likelihood found a vocal ally in James Rorimer, who had never allowed himself to forget the "Aristotle" from the first sight of it nearly thirty years earlier. The Metropolitan, where he has worked since 1927, already owned thirty-one Rembrandts, half a dozen of them, incidentally, from Rodolphe Kann's former treasure trove. But in terms of Rembrandts, Rorimer considered it impossible to have too much of a good thing. He was determined to lay hold of "Aristotle," a move that he called "playing for strength" in numbers. In his philosophy, a museum has a public obligation to "make every effort to acquire great examples of the world's artistic heritage."

The pressure of two minds, Hyam's and Rorimer's, with a single thought convinced the executors that the United States and Parke-Bernet were the natural places for the auction. How did Parke-Bernet win the day after four months of dickering? C. Russell Sigler, an attorney for the Erickson estate, answered in four simple words: "They were very competitive."

Unquestionably, Hyam surrendered a considerable part of his galleries' usual commission, which would otherwise have amounted to a staggering twenty per cent of the $4,679,250 which the collection brought under the hammer. In London, aggrieved national pride led one national newspaper to speculate that Hyam had sacrificed every dime in commissions and was willing to carry out the job for the sake of prestige alone. When confronted with this, Hyam snapped, "Nonsense!"

Whatever the terms, the working population of Parke-Bernet was elated over its victory, from Hyam down to the youngest office girl. Louis J. Marion, the chief auctioneer, in the manner of a man who knows his words are beyond dispute, acknowledged, "In twenty-five years of auctioneering, selling that Rembrandt will be the highlight of my career."

Shortly after Mrs. Erickson's death, the pictures had been trucked for safekeeping to the warehouse of Day & Meyer, Murray & Young on Second Avenue and Sixty-second Street. The place served as a kind of redemption center for Hyam and Marion, who, by appointment only, escorted some sixty interested museum directors, curators and trustees there to take a preliminary peek at the riches before their removal for display at the auction galleries. The only American museums wealthy enough to be in the running each sent representatives to this series of pre-views—the Metropolitan, the Cleveland Museum of Art, the Carnegie Institute of Pittsburgh, the Toledo Museum and the William Rockhill Nelson Gallery in Kansas City.

Reassured now the ceremony of finding a new proprietor for "Aristotle" would be staged in America, Rorimer, who became the Met's director in 1955 after serving six years in a similar capacity at the museum's uptown medieval branch, the Cloisters, laid detailed plans to accomplish his heart's desire. What the Metropolitan buys is decided by majority vote of its purchasing committee of nine, all of them museum trustees, including the president, Roland L. Redmond. A few days before the date set for the auction, Rorimer had the committee in his office for a long strategy conference.

The key question was not whether the museum wanted "Aristotle" but how much, in terms of money and desire. Rorimer's plump face and imperturbable manner effectively conceal his professional passions. Ideally, he said, he wanted to spend no more than $1,500,000—"a nice price," in his words. But that sensibility about the market place which is a prime requirement for a successful museum director warned him that the "likely" price would be $2,300,000. The fact that events proved he hit the figure on the nose affords him no more than modest satisfaction.

After that assessment, the committee fell to debating what else the Met might do with that amount of money. In its financial statement for the year ending June 30, 1961, its endowment funds were valued at $118,353,826, but they represent the museum's entire working capital, to be conserved at the highest possible level. The committee, however, had no reservations about pushing the boat out to catch the Rembrandt. They set a ceiling price considerably above the $2,300,000 figure, perhaps as high as $2,500,000, though the Met and Rorimer, like all such places and their men, are close-mouthed about money.

Georges Wildenstein, a celebrated dealer, had offered to do the actual bidding on the big night free of charge. He had recommended himself highly as a dependable hand two years earlier by whisking an important Georges de La Tour out of France and selling it to the museum for something in the region of $750,000; the precise figure was not disclosed for reasons touched on above. But the committee pinned its faith on Rorimer. He was chosen without a dissenting voice to handle the bidding at Parke-Bernet's soirée.

The money, it was decided, was to be raised in the simple fashion of passing round the hat, rather than by following big-business practice in mortgaging purchasing power for two or three years to come. No borrowing proved necessary. "As it developed," Rorimer confided, "I think the purchasing committee could have done it out of purchase funds, but we might have had to get permission from the trustees to use some capital."

The metaphorical hat was passed around among more than one hundred friends, trustees and well-endowed art lovers, among them Robert Lehman, Mrs. Charles B. Payson and Charles B. Wrightsman, who turned out to have an interest, too, in acquiring the second highest-priced painting of the Ericksons, Fragonard's fragile, glowing picture of a young girl reading, "La Liseuse." Rorimer, in the democratic tradition, also mentions that a Brooklyn workman contributed a day's wages and a young girl donated $35 saved in pennies.

The Cleveland Museum was also in the throes of plotting how to buy "Aristotle," uncomfortably aware that the Met must be busy in the same endeavor. Cleveland's director, Sherman E. Lee, had nursed a longing akin to James Rorimer's since 1941, when Lee saw the Rembrandt on exhibition. Cleveland's curator of paintings, Henry S. Francis, shared his senior's enthusiasm for a picture he describes as "a great experience." In August, weeks before the Met's decisive conference, Lee and Francis had won their trustee's agreement that a healthy chunk of the museum's $80,000,000 endowment could be devoted to bidding for "Aristotle." The big question again was, "How much?" A lesser question was, "Who should do the bidding?"

An answer to the second problem was swiftly found. Lee, lacking experience in the spine-tingling craft, bowed out and telephoned an old and trusted friend who had helped the museum in the past, Saemy Rosenberg, of Rosenberg & Stiebel, art dealers, 32 East Fifty-seventh Street. He was on his way to Rotterdam, so though he consented to act as professional bidder for Cleveland, the agonizing question of "how much" would have to wait until his return to the United States.

It was nearly three months before he could lunch with the museum group at Cleveland's Union Club. By then, the auction was a matter of seven days away. Lee reported subsequently to Milton Bracker of *The New York Times*:

"Mr. Rosenberg said that in his opinion a bid of $1,500,000 had no chance; a bid of under $2,000,000 might have a very remote chance; $2,000,000 would have an outside chance; $2,250,000 was a good, respectable bid that might well get the picture—but it might go higher. We told him we would notify him on the morning of the sale."

Cleveland's strategists endured a brain-racking week pondering such puzzles as whether the painting was worth its probable price, what kind of reputation did the museum want for itself, would it be better to fight for "Aristotle" with the risk of losing than not fight at all. The museum finally girded its loins to do battle up to a limit of $2,250,000. On the morning of the sale, November 15, 1961, Sherman Lee and Harold Terry Clark, the museum president, met Saemy Rosenberg in New York and handed him written authority with that limit attached. The dealer was blunt: it was a good bid, with a chance of success, but it might be too small.

"Well," Lee said, "the die is cast, and that's it."

Parke-Bernet had been living through equally trying days ever since the collection was brought in from the warehouse under heavy guard, to be hung for display on the dun-colored velvet walls of the galleries. Judicious, jubilant publicity from Leslie Hyam's public-relations staff was whipping up interest in the world's

Aristotle Onassis (third from left) and friends

press and public like a Mixmaster beating cream. The "Aristotle" had been labeled "the million-dollar Rembrandt," and overnight every television watcher and news-paper and magazine reader became an art lover. Museum curators, dealers and experts with varying degrees of qualification for the name vied with each other in estimating what the painting would bring in. With nothing yet disclosed about behind-the-scenes arithmetic, the best guesses for public consumption were that the Rembrandt might go to $1,800,000 and the collection to perhaps $3,000,000.

On the three public inspection days, crowds milled through the Parke-Bernet establishment on Madison Avenue at Seventy-sixth Street, trampling the plum-colored carpeting, pestering the armed Pinkerton guards with unanswerable ques-tions, surrendering their umbrellas grudgingly at the check rooms—the weather was mostly wet, but the guards hated umbrellas. "You never know what a fanatic might do," said one Pinkerton man. "Imagine some nut poking a hole in that picture!"

The rumors, inspired or otherwise, were flying again. A namesake of the sub-ject, Aristotle Onassis, the Greek shipping magnate, was anxious to acquire the painting at any price, according to some whispers. A syndicate of Texans was going to buy the whole blamed shooting match to start a new museum down there. The Netherlands government was willing to go to any price to bring Rembrandt back to his native land. James Rorimer had a private word or two to say about that. The Rijksmuseum in Amsterdam had once tried to buy the picture direct from Mrs. Erickson, he said, but she had declined, because she would rather see it in the Met. Nothing was heard at the sale from Onassis, the Lone Star State or Amsterdam.

Out in Pittsburgh, however, another aging woman was out to get the trophy for the Carnegie Institute. Mrs. Sarah Mellon Scaife, widow of Alan M. Scaife and a niece of Andrew Mellon, was willing to spend "a little over $2,000,000." On the night, she had her bidding on the Institute's behalf performed by an attorney, Eli Whitney Devevoise, of 320 Park Avenue. He fell out at $2,200,000 but picked up Frans Hals' "Man With a Herring" for $145,000 and Perugino's "St. Augustine" for $125,000, so his work was not entirely wasted.

One other collector was prepared for heavy action, Baron Heinrich von Thyssen-Bornemisza, a Dutch-born naturalized Swiss whose collecting includes a third wife, the former Fiona Campbell-Walters, a British magazine cover girl before he married her in 1956. His father, who was partial to the Dutch school of painters, started collecting when he resided at Castle Rohoncz, Hungary. The family collection still bears that name, though it is housed nowadays in a museum at Lugano, Switzerland. The young baron—he was born in 1921—happens also to be the nephew of the late Fritz Thyssen, the German industrialist who brought something less than luster to the family name by his devoted support of Adolf Hitler.

The old baron wanted to buy "Aristotle" in the Thirties, when it lodged with Duveen. Now the son was desperately anxious to acquire it in memory of his father to the tune of more than $2,000,000, a sum he authorized to be bid for him. Had he succeeded, his identity would have been concealed. Some of his German associates shuddered at the thought of what publicity would do to draw attention to the Thyssen name, which is not yet completely deodorized of Uncle Fritz's Nazi taint.

The young baron brought his beautiful baroness to the galleries on the night that turned out to be the glossiest art auction America had seen to date. She wore an imposing array of jewels and a twenty-five-dollar bouffant hairdo. They were each armed with the necessary white ticket that gained them admission to the principal salesroom. White was the elite color among the 1,800 passes printed for the occasion—pink was good only for lesser galleries, where the proceedings could be watched on closed-circuit television screens, with an aide sitting by them to relay bids by microphone to the main salesroom.

Tickets had been carefully parceled out to well-known collectors, including relatives and representatives of the Mellons, the Rockefellers, the Woolworths, the Whitneys, the Gimbels, the Lehmans, the Cartiers and the Fords. Tickets had gone to dealers, museum curators and celebrated bystanders from most major cities of the United States and virtually every country of Western Europe. Billy Rose was there, Perle Mesta, Arlene Francis, and Mrs. William Woodward with a broken leg in a cast. The five hundred people, squeezed onto rented chairs in the main gallery, squirmed in the heat of television lights and the stare of network cameras.

The tickets had become status symbols. Scalpers were selling any they could lay hands on for $50 apiece and more. Some disappointed applicants tried forging these passports to the velvet-hung arena and were even more disappointed to find that every ticket was double-checked by gray-uniformed guards. It was harder to slip in uninvited to see the next chapter in the life of "Aristotle" than to wangle an invitation to tea with Mrs. Erickson.

Madison Avenue was aswirl with furs, fancy coiffures and diamonds from Seventy-sixth to Seventy-ninth Street. The crowd, doing its best to look simultaneously important, rich and knowledgeable, stood in line for an hour and more to get inside. There, the truly knowing spotted Leslie Hyam wearing a pale blue shirt for benefit of the television cameras, a dark blue suit and a white carnation. Louis Marion was wearing a distinctly harassed look beneath his bright red hair.

Gavel in hand, he stepped up to the little rostrum that stood immediately in front of the stage where the paintings were carried on and off for brief inspection. At the first sight of the Rembrandt, with the spotlights turning "Aristotle's" sleeves a glowing gold, the crowd burst into applause. Marion told his audience, "I've never said a million dollars in twenty-five years up here, but tonight I hope to say it." He hadn't long to wait. For "Aristotle," the seventh picture brought swiftly into view by sweating gallery assistants, he had in his pocket a sealed opening bid of one million passed to him less than an hour earlier by a clergyman acting for an aspiring private collector.

In jumps of $100,000 at a time, the auction of the century was under way. Rorimer, seeming bland to the point of disdain, held his hand until $1,500,000 had been reached. That came within the first minute. The four leading contenders— the Metropolitan, the Carnegie Institute, Cleveland, and Baron Thyssen—were finding the field thinning. Three bids had come in over the microphones from outsiders sitting in the lesser galleries—for $1,110,000, then $1,300,000 and $1,600,-000. "In the future," Marion quipped, "they'll get tickets to the main salesroom."

The bids clicked on, and the minutes ticked by to two. At $1,800,000 the baron's bidder, Harry Brooks of M. Knoedler & Company, who sat at a discreet distance from his still-secret principal, dropped out. He had sensed that the race would outdistance him. The wife of a Met trustee was panic-stricken by what she saw: Rorimer's eyes appeared to be drooping. She nudged her husband. "He's asleep, for God's sake," she whispered frantically. "Bid another $100,000 before it's too late."

The contest had come down to two contenders—Rorimer for the Met and Saemy Rosenberg for Cleveland. Marion's eyes flickered between them. Rorimer fingered his lapel to let the auctioneer know it was his bid. Then he gazed fixedly to his right to indicate, by prearranged signal, the size of his bid: $2,300,000, topping Rosenberg's last call as determined by the directions in his pocket. Marion stared hard at the sixty-nine-year-old dealer, but Rosenberg's eyes remained steady and expressionless. "I had no particular feeling," he said quietly later. "After fifty-four years in the business, I never have feelings any more. But I was sorry I couldn't get it for Cleveland."

Marion's voice rose a tone or two in the ritualistic "Fair warning." Then his ivory gavel pounded the sale to a close. From start to finish, four minutes had elapsed.

In the often absurd secrecy of the game, the first announcement declared that "Aristotle" was now the property of "an Eastern museum," but the anonymity was untenable for longer than a few minutes. It was New York's venerable, vaunted Metropolitan that had bought what auctioneers and buyers alike agreed contentedly was the world's most expensive painting, and everybody could read about it in massive headlines in the morning.

By all accounts, Mrs. Erickson, venerable and vaunted herself in her day, would have been contented with that, too.

II

A MAN WITHOUT CUNNING

Losing "Aristotle" and the rest of the Alfred Erickson collection to a rival gallery was probably the biggest professional disappointment ever to come the way of Peter Cecil Wilson, who up to that time had been much better acquainted with success than setbacks as the chairman, brightest star, and empire builder of the world's most eminent auction house, Messrs. Sotheby & Company, of 34 New Bond Street, London, W. 1.

Since he makes a point of avoiding grand pronouncements about anything at all and clings to the English sporting tradition of losing gracefully, his public comments on the defeat were only mildly acidic.

"On the record, we thought we might have been the natural place for the Erickson sale," he said.

In private, over the teacups which he and his eight fellow directors raise together every Monday afternoon in the austere white board room on the top floor of their cluttered premises, he was more emphatic. He conceals a healthy share of proper pride and passion behind an exterior of calm charm. It would have been surprising if that pride, which was hurt, did not lead to intensified rivalry between the great houses on each side of the Atlantic.

In appearance, he is well equipped to do battle, being of the tall, cool, impos-

Peter Wilson (right): the tall, cool, imposing breed

ing breed that produces Guards officers. His father was, in fact, a baronet and cavalry officer, his grandfather a baron. Wilson is competitive by nature as well as by profession. He has made a point of visiting the United States four or five times a year in his constant search for grist for his special kind of mill. After the Erickson drubbing, he was more than ever ready to catch a jet flight to New York at the drop of a hat, to bring in the treasures of the world to redress the cash balance of the old. It was his readiness to travel fast in 1957 that started Sotheby's reputation soaring after a single hour of auctioneering.

Wilhelm Weinberg was a German Jew who had made his fortune as a banker in the Netherlands. When the Germans invaded his adopted homeland in 1941, he fled to the United States, but his wife and three children fell victim to the Nazis. Weinberg settled in Scarsdale, New York, in a house teeming with works of art, including paintings by Cézanne, Degas, Gauguin, Manet, Monet, Pissarro, Renoir, Redon, Seurat, Sisley, Utrillo, and Van Gogh, with some bronzes by Maillol, Degas, Daumier, and Picasso thrown in for good measure. His will directed that most of his two-million-dollar estate was to go to charity, together with the proceeds from the sale of his collection.

At the news of Weinberg's death, Wilson was off as soon as you could say "Vincent van Gogh," taking with him to Scarsdale Mrs. Carmen Gronau, the only member of her sex among the directors, a slender, mild woman who handles Old Masters and Old Master drawings for the firm. He went through the Weinberg house from one direction and she from another, each jotting down valuations of the pictures and sculpture, which remained there for inspection.

This grand tour was, and is, an essential part of Wilson's method of operation wherever possible. As he did for the executors of Mrs. Erickson's estate, he likes to support his claim that Sotheby's can obtain the highest prices anywhere in the world by throwing in a quick estimate, usually conclusive, of just how much cash may be expected. Nowadays, he can enhance the arithmetic with the prestige of his company's name, but in Weinberg days that reputation had to be built.

The tour of the Scarsdale house brought the not unusual result. "When we compared our totals," Mrs. Gronau said later, "they were less than ten per cent apart. The price we eventually got for the collection topped our adjusted estimate by ten per cent."

As arranged and presented by Wilson, the Weinberg sale was the first really big postwar auction in its category. Among the several high marks it established was the first use of closed-circuit television for simultaneous bidding from three galleries—a fellow director sat at a rostrum in each of the two smaller ones, which are done in pool-hall green, to telephone bids to the main room, papered a plum red, where Wilson officiated.

Two days before the sale, Queen Elizabeth, the Duke of Edinburgh, and Princess Margaret took an after-hours peek at the collection, escorted by the directors. While the presence of British and European royalty is not exceptional at Sotheby's, this particular visit set the cherry on the sundae so far as public interest and excitement were concerned. Mollie Panter-Downes of *The New Yorker,* a knowing commentator on the British social scene, noted that the evening excursion "would seem to be significant as an indication of the extent to which art . . . has become big news," since the Queen's tastes admittedly run more to race horses than Rembrandt and the Duke's to polo rather than Picasso.

Early arrivals among the crowd, which totaled some three thousand before the doors were closed, began gathering in New Bond Street soon after breakfast on sale day. The scholarly young women among the eighty or so staff members, who normally spend their time helping in cataloguing, acted as whippers-in. In the big gallery, workmen were hauling at the heavy tarpaulin that covers the massive skylight. A legion of press photographers fired away at every recognizably famous or noticeably attractive female face in sight. From the back of the room, television cameras of the British Broadcasting Corporation and the National Broadcasting Company stared impassively at the melée.

Shortly after ten o'clock, with nearly an hour to go before Peter Wilson gaveled the sale to a start, every rented gilt chair was taken, and standees were crammed at the rear of the gallery. Front-row seats had been allotted to the dealers of London, New York, and Paris, who whispered together in a dozen accents, from Mayfair to Mittel Europe. At eleven o'clock, Wilson mounted the rostrum and stood for a moment like the rector of a fashionable church surveying his Sunday-morning congregation. A smattering of applause from the front row spoiled the Episcopalian impression, and he smiled deprecatingly.

Three small Daumier bronzes were up first and sold for $3,920. The rest of the bronzes and some Lautrec and Delacroix drawings prepared the way for Wilhelm Weinberg's pictures, the heart of the collection. The Cézannes came and went, the Corot, two Degas, two Fantin-Latours, a Gauguin. The crowd was eager and willing, the dealers were shaking their heads over the prices, and Wilson looked more impenetrable than ever.

The size of the bids was only one indication that something was stirring. A second portent of the shape of things to come was provided by a London businessman, a Mr. Bright, hitherto unknown as a collector. By paying $61,600 for Renoir's not especially remarkable "Jeune Femme au Corsage Rouge," Mr. Bright identified himself as one of the postwar rich whose willingness to pay exceedingly well for pictures they want for pleasure or profit supports the present boom in art.

The Renoir ranked third in the day's arithmetic. Second place was won by a Van Gogh, "La Tête de l'Ange," painted in his madness from an engraving sent him while he was in the St. Rémy asylum. M. Knoedler & Company bought it, along with the highest-priced painting in the collection, another Van Gogh, "Les Usines à Clichy"—red-roofed factories with belching smokestacks—which had gone for the equivalent of roughly $5,000 in 1928 and now, nineteen years later, sold for $86,800.

By the time the throng had filed down the stairs into the street again, the estate of Wilhelm Weinberg was $914,256 better off; Sotheby's was well on its way to becoming the premier auction house in London, and London the hub of the international market. Peter Wilson remained as remote as a visiting bishop waiting for the collection to be taken up.

He is the very image of Sotheby's. No Madison Avenue brain trust could conceive a figure more appropriate to the product, unless it might be Commander Edward Whitehead for Schweppes. Sotheby's man is pink-skinned and, on duty, splendidly dressed in dazzling white shirt and navy blue suit or morning coat and striped trousers. He hints unmistakably of a good barber, good wine and a good London club, which in his case is the St. James's.

"Selling pictures," he has said, in something approaching self-justification, "is not like selling boots."

To a considerable degree, the leader of a successful auction house must invent himself, like an actor casting himself for life in a particular role. He is forced to combine in his person the dual personalities of connoisseur and businessman, qualified to identify his raw material and then sell it at the best possible price. He is compelled to be concerned equally with art and money, to the point where there is no distinction between them in his thinking. Wilson is the archetype of his kind, recognizable as something of a masterpiece of the eighteenth-century English school.

He was born on March 8, 1913, at the family home, Eshton Hall, Gargrave,

Yorkshire, and attended the expected public school, Eton, and New College, Oxford. His height, six feet four inches, makes him an easy mark for any dealer, customer or curiosity seeker who wants a word with him on his way to his office, which is tucked away in a corner overlooking a triangular courtyard down one of the labyrinthine corridors in which Sotheby's premises abound. He has a soft, clear, only slightly pear-shaped voice in which to conduct his duties as chief auctioneer of paintings—another director looks after rare books, a second is responsible for chinaware, a third attends to jewelry and silver, and so on.

Wilson's manner is distinctly twentieth century, though his tastes date back a couple of hundred years, as shown by the furniture and furnishings of his own country house and London home. In the days when Sotheby's was founded—in 1744—it was customary for the man with the gavel to keep a stream of extravagant praises flowing around whatever was up for bidding, like a present-day peddler of watches hypnotizing a carnival crowd. Wilson's unrivaled ability to conjure bigger and bigger bids from his audiences rests on an imperturbable air plus a handful of phrases carefully chosen and enunciated to arouse the last ounce of acquisitiveness in his listeners' souls: "At eight thousand, eight thousand then . . . ," or more pointedly, "It's against you now, sir, the gentleman on the aisle," or with a kind of aggrievement, "Will *nobody* offer more?"

It is hard to imagine him outside the gilded frame of his calling, but in pre-Sotheby days, after coming down from Oxford, he held what he calls "a terribly humble job, a hopeless kind of job" as editorial factotum and assistant circulation manager of *Connoisseur,* an art magazine. A year later, he decided that he had picked up enough of the vocabulary and enough knowledge of antiques to go to work in the three-story dingy white stucco building where he has reigned ever since. He must also have gone to work immediately on establishing his own personal style, the unruffled look, the relaxed elegance, the understatement. "The cunning of Wilson," one colleague has noted, "is that there is no cunning."

Before he mounted the dark birch rostrum for the first time in 1938 to sell the first of the nearly 30,000 pictures which have since gone under his gavel, he practiced at home all weekend. In a mock auction, he knocked down every bit of furniture they owned to his young wife and their baby son's nurse. Another son was born before the marriage was dissolved; Wilson has not remarried.

According to friends, he still spends a sleepless night before any big sale. His outward calm, which is the envy of his colleagues and competitors, hides a nervous digestion revolving like a carousel. The only signs of emotion which his intimates can recognize, however, are two patches of white which appear in the pink of his cheeks.

When Wilson joined up, Sotheby's ranked second, behind Christie's. The firm was actually founded by a bookseller, Samuel Baker of Russell Street, Covent Garden, who numbered Benjamin Franklin among his customers, and its catalogues still bear the legend, "Auctioneers of Literary Property and Works illustrative of the Fine Arts." In 1744, Baker held the first of the continuous series of sales, for a

Samuel Baker: "That he who Bids most is the Buyer . . ."

twelve-month turnover of £826, on which Sotheby's stakes its claim to be the oldest auction house in the world. Turnover for the 1960–1961 season, incidentally, was $23,634,100, nearly half of which was accounted for by Wilson's department alone.

Baker's portrait, by Grignor, hangs in the offices today, picturing a sedate but determined old gentleman in a white bob-wig and plum-colored coat. His original ivory gavel has only recently been retired, to attain the status of an *exhibit*. He drew up a set of five conditions of sale which, his successors rather smugly declare, "suggest that if the price-escalator has changed during two centuries, the principles have not." Substituting the modern "s" for the archaic "f", those conditions read:

I.   That he who Bids most is the Buyer, but if any Dispute arises, the Book or Books to be put to Sale again.

II. That no Person advances less than Sixpence each bidding, and after the Book arises to One Pound, no less than One Shilling.

Sotheby's in the Eighteenth Century

III. The Books are in most elegant Condition, and supposed to be Perfect, but if any appear otherwise before taken away, the Buyer is at his Choice to take or leave them.

IV. That each Person give in his Name, and pay Five Shillings in the Pound (if demanded) for what he Buys, and that no Book be deliver'd in Time of Sale.

V. The Books must be taken away at the Buyer's Expence, and the Money paid at the Place of Sale, within Three Days after each Sale is ended.

Any Gentleman who cannot attend the Sale, may have their Commissions receiv'd and faithfully executed,

By their most Humble Servant,

Samuel Baker.

The first Sotheby, Leon, joined the business in 1778, one of three generations which carried on the firm for nearly one hundred years, after substituting their name on the door for Baker's. The last Sotheby, Samuel Leigh, who died in 1861, was a zealous bibliographer whose mark endures in a series of "Hints for a young auctioneer of books," drawn up for him by his friend Joseph Halewood, a founder of the Roxburghe Club. Particular respect is still paid by Peter Wilson and his partners to Hint Number One: "Consider your Catalogue as the foundation of your eminence and make its perfection of character an important study." The catalogues, now priced at sixpence, are themselves collected avidly, since they often contain more information about an artist than can be found in any readily available reference book.

Picasso *verso:* "Woman Seated in a Garden"

Fine art, on which the firm's international reputation as a record breaker is based nowadays, didn't appear in any significant amount in the catalogues until the advent of the First World War, a few years after Sotheby's had moved into its present unassuming quarters among the more resplendent art galleries and shops of New Bond Street. The Black Horse Inn once stood on the site; its wine cellars, unspoiled by the centuries, turned out to be ideal for storing paintings and works of art unharmed by bleaching sunlight or temperature variations.

The firm—which set at least three records in four recent years by garnering $2,186,800 for the Jakob Goldschmidt collection, $364,000 for a Gainsborough and $244,000 for Picasso's double-sided "Death of Harlequin" and "Woman Seated in a Garden"—will sell anything that comes in, provided the proceeds are likely to cover processing costs. In the case of Old Masters, meaning pictures painted before 1800, the necessary minimum valuation is a modest $80.

An inevitable result of this open-door policy has been to strain storage space beyond capacity and compel Sotheby's to spread out into next-door basements, where there may be found some 60,000 paintings, suits of armor, china, silver salvers, walking sticks, statuary, and, indeed, just about anything man ever made. Pictures are stacked ten deep against the walls, rolled-up rugs line the corridors. Priceless furniture stands beside pieces so battered they seem scarcely worth carting away. Every desk, table top, bureau, *secrétaire,* vitrine, or cabinet has something sitting on it, usually generously coated with dust.

On the street floor there are two entrances, one for goods and one for people, on either side of a W. H. Smith & Company newsstand. The inside seethes with both people and goods. All day long the hopefuls arrive at the worn oak counter

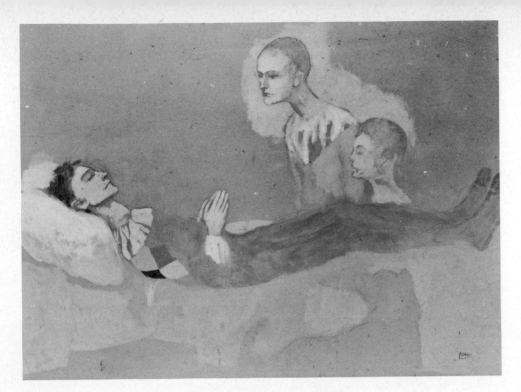

Picasso *recto:* "Death of Harlequin"

in the basement den illuminated by a row of green-shaded lamps, where a staff of solemn young women venture a preliminary appraisal of the contents of the battered suitcases or shapeless brown-paper parcels. More often than not, the response is inevitably negative, but never automatically so.

A local postmistress once came in carrying a roll of worthless prints, from the middle of which fell a Watteau drawing lost since it was engraved by Jullien in the eighteenth century. An agent brought an undistinguished scrapbook of unknown provenance; it contained a Rembrandt drawing, for which the British Museum paid $8,400, and an even rarer drawing by Roger van der Weyden. A retired colonel arrived with a little white owl, a knickknack, so he thought, that might get broken if it remained much longer on his mantelpiece; it turned out to be a hitherto un-known sample of the earliest Chelsea porcelain, and it sold for $8,400. A turquoise glass beaker weighing less than an ounce was a $13,440 Venetian masterpiece, now on exhibit in the Victoria and Albert Museum. A set of drawings, bought for a song in Ireland, proved to be the work of Fra Bartolommeo, and Sotheby's sold them for $310,800.

For reasons apparent above, house rules insist upon courtesy to all callers. If there are grounds for hope wrapped up in brown paper, then the practice is to in-vestigate. Only directors may accept items for auction. Though they all share some-thing of Wilson's half-amused manner, they are experts in their fields, who can often assess at a glance the worth of the book, the diamond, the figurine put on their desks, which would be respectively the directorial concern of Anthony Hobson, Frederick Rose, and Jim Kiddell.

During the 1961 season, a French nun sent in a portrait bust of a broad-nosed

A French nun sent in this Gauguin carving

young Tahitian girl, carved in wood with polychrome decoration, wearing a necklace of coral and little sea-snail shells. It was, declared the nun, the work of Paul Gauguin. Because Gauguin sculpture is exceedingly rare, expert authentication was necessary. The ten-inch carving was shipped off to the Royal Botanical Gardens at Kew. Three slivers of the wood were examined and found to be Solomon Islands cedarwood, a tree common on Tahiti. Sotheby's was satisfied.

"Carved probably from life during Gauguin's first visit to Tahiti from 1891 to 1893," said the note in the catalogue, living up to the reputation of that volume as an instrument of precision. "It was formerly the property of the daughter of a friend of Gauguin's. In either 1894 or 1895 when she was a small child Gauguin gave her this sculpture instead of the doll he had promised her." For this precious plaything the London dealers, Frank Partridge & Sons, with premises across the street, were content to pay $32,200.

No house can afford to rely on chance callers for its livelihood. One of Wilson's daily chores is to read the obituary columns of the London *Times,* which Sotheby secretaries clip and distribute among the appropriate directors so that they may estimate the possibilities of the deceased's estate as a source of auction material. Wilson has the macabre reputation of being able to hear a death rattle before the priest is called.

There is only one way to become a partner, and that is by buying your way in. The current nine directors own the business, though at least one of them, Rose of jewelry and silver, borrowed the admission fee to the ranks. Lord Rothschild was glad to put up $10,000 for the purpose when he learned that Rose was no more than an employee. Each partner has wide leeway in running his department, but on retirement, he has to relinquish his stock. Since this is a personal partnership, no profit figures are published, but commissions average ten per cent of the annual turnover, which in round figures amounted to $19,000,000 in the 1959–1960 season, $16,000,000 for the previous period, and $9,000,000 for the one before that.

Wilson began to enjoy his share of the bonanza in 1938, when he joined the partnership. He has been buying driblets of stock ever since, mostly from retiring partners, and he now owns the control as well as much of the prestige, thereby drawing considerably more than his director's salary of approximately $18,000 a year. His colleagues bear him no discernible envy, however, since his reputation and ability to divine marketable material much as a dowser detects water make him the Midas of the auction marts, able to turn most of what he touches into gold.

The year following the Weinberg auction, his fellow directors were sufficiently impressed with Wilson's talents to elect him chairman of the company. He repaid

A gala night at Sotheby's

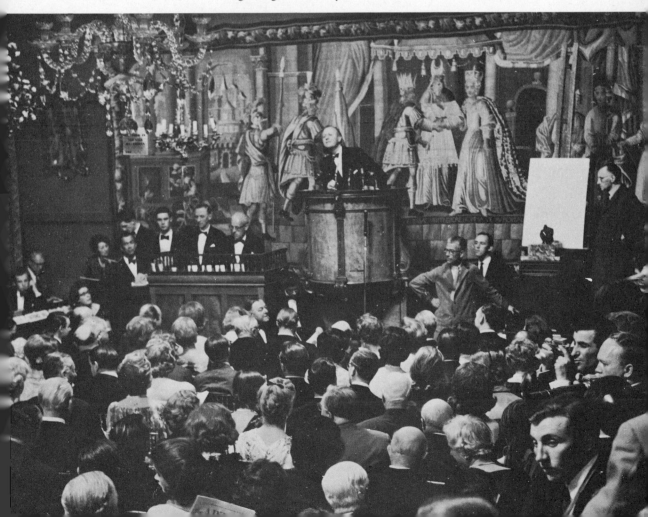

them for their confidence in him very soon thereafter by pulling off the second in the golden series of sales that pushed Sotheby's to the top. The Goldschmidt sale of October, 1958, where seven paintings brought $2,186,800, still brings a gleam to the chairman's pale blue eyes. Until the Erickson Rembrandt removed some of the gilt from the gingerbread, the disposal of Jakob Goldschmidt's mighty collection was acknowledged as "the sale of the century" wherever dealers and collectors met.

There were three Manets, two Cézannes, a Van Gogh, and a Renoir. These were the gems of a collection which Goldschmidt, a leading banker and financier in pre-Hitler Germany, had been permitted to take with him when he left the country in 1933. In passing, it must be noted that perhaps the only group of the world's inhabitants with a remaining debt to Nazi terror are the art collectors. Not since the social upheavals of the eighteenth century had there been such a wholesale movement of great pictures as in the Second World War, with the consequent opportunity for new collectors to lay hold of them.

Except for charity affairs, the Goldschmidt landmark was the first evening sale London had seen. To heighten the opening-night atmosphere, Wilson had a candy-pink awning hung from Sotheby's dingy walls. The closed-circuit television cameras, an indispensable part of these big-money festivals, were installed wherever there was room to set up a few rented chairs, even down in the basement.

Among the favored ticket-holders was actor Burt Lancaster, in sunglasses, trying to shoulder his way through the jam of onlookers outside. Somerset Maugham smiled bonily as he was swept along. There was Lady Violet Bonham-Carter, who is sometimes charged with trying to run the British Liberal party; Lady Churchill; Sir Simon Marks, who runs Britain's most spectacular chain of department stores; Charles Clore, the financier; Garfield Weston, the biscuit king; Sir John Rothenstein, director of the Tate Gallery; Basil Goulandris, the Greek shipowner, who the previous year had captured Gauguin's "Still Life With Apples" for $297,142 in a spirited battle with a fellow Greek shipping tycoon, Stavros Niarchos, at the Galerie Charpentier auction rooms in Paris.

Among the less-favored members of the public in attendance was a guest in white tie and tails who was barred from the main gallery. "I spent ten thousand pounds here in one year," he complained shrilly to a Sotheby hostess, "and now they accuse me of gate crashing. There'll be a letter. I shall write a stinking letter to the directors."

Inside Sotheby's, where the customary controlled chaos prevailed, Dame Margot Fonteyn stood on her celebrated prima ballerina's toes for a better look at the scene. "I haven't a collection," she explained. "I can't afford one." At 9:37 P.M., Wilson climbed on to the rostrum and tapped lightly with his ivory palm gavel to bring the meeting as close to order as possible on this momentous night. Two elderly attendants in Confederate-gray uniforms lifted a Manet "Self-Portrait" on to the tall easel. "Lot Number One," Wilson announced, "what am I bid?" Queen Elizabeth's dressmaker, Hardy Amies, scrambled up onto his chair to improve on his view.

Stavros Niarchos fought and lost . . . Lady Churchill waxed enthusiastic

"Five thousand pounds," Wilson was articulating softly into his microphone, "eight thousand, ten thousand. . . ." The bids whizzed in from all quarters, rather like arrows from Cheyennes besieging the wagon train, until the auctioneer called, "Sixty-five thousand, the bid is in the front." His cool eyes swung to and fro across the warm room, then his gavel sounded gently. "Yours, sir, in the fourth row." He wrote down the price in his fawn-colored record book.

That evening, another Manet, "La Rue de Berne," fetched $316,400, and Van Gogh's "Public Garden at Arles," thought to be one of the four pictures he painted for Gauguin's room before that good companion arrived in Arles in 1888, sold for $369,600. A Renoir entitled "La Pensée"—a title which the artist could never understand because, as he said, "that girl never thought; she lived like a bird and nothing more"—went under the hammer for $201,600. Cézanne's "Still Life With Apples" brought $252,000, its reputation evidently undamaged by a Cockney barrow boy whom a London newspaper had previously quoted as sneering, "I wouldn't sell them apples for eighteenpence a pound."

In the furious twenty minutes of sale, all the time it took to find buyers for everything in Sotheby's greatest sale to date, Cezanne's glowing "Boy in a Red Waistcoat" commanded the top price and top honors. George Keller, a New York dealer, went to $616,000 for it, more than doubling the previous record price at auction for an Impressionist painting, the $297,142 paid in Paris by Goulandris for the Gauguin from the late Mrs. Margaret Thompson Biddle's collection. For the Renoir, Wilson, looking pale in the glare of lights, had even missed one bid, which is as rare as Arnold Palmer fluffing a putt. He didn't spot a London dealer, Stanley Wade, signaling him from the back row. "I couldn't do much about it," Wade admitted afterward, "and short of making a scene, I had to let it go. What a disappointment!"

By that time, Wilson had confessed himself overwhelmed by it all. "I have never before sold so fast, and I don't think I ever shall again. I am absolutely done," he added in a unique admission of frailty, "I really can't stand any more." In a tradition of the house, he retired with some of the more distinguished members of the audience across the street to a champagne party in the elegant galleries of the dealer Frank Partridge, a customer of long standing.

One advantage Wilson has over rivals in his trade is the apparent omniscience that comes from his social background, the fact that he can talk as one upper-class Englishman to another upper-class Englishman who may have the odd Gainsborough hung over the dining-rooom sideboard or a Zoffany adorning the servants' hall. "He knows every picture in every manor in England," one London dealer has said, but Wilson himself is more modest.

"Our work," he avers, "is simple compared to the way a dealer like Wildenstein works. We couldn't hope to compete with his spy network in the field. But people come to us because they know we can usually get what we estimate the pictures will fetch."

The process by which an important painting changes hands at auction is somewhat akin to procreation, in that the beginning is customarily a discreet duet whereas the outcome demands public notice. A collector can't call his broker and order a worthwhile picture; Wilson by the same set of rules does not tout for sales, and it would be unthinkable for him brazenly to suggest that a picture should be consigned to the block. But he does have a world-wide circle of friends and acquaintances; he does get around; and when he weekends at a country house, castle, or château in England or elsewhere, he does keep his eyes peeled for what hangs on the walls.

Precisely how he persuaded the executors of Hugh Arthur Richard Grosvenor, second Duke of Westminster, to allow Sotheby's to handle some "items termed surplus to family requirements" is not recorded. His social charm, knowledgeability, and expertise all contributed something to the result, which amounted to another triumph for the business, since included in the surplus property was Rubens' masterpiece, "Adoration of the Magi," which the family had bought from the Marquis of Lansdowne in 1806; two exceptional landscapes by Claude, "The Golden Calf" and "The Sermon on the Mount"; fifteen other paintings; the staggering Westminster tiara; and assorted furniture and silver.

The Duke was every bit as fantastic as the fortune he inherited from his forebears, who had the sense to hold on to the farm which the family acquired in Elizabethan times, comprising some six hundred acres of what are now the Mayfair,

A Sunday painter on
the island of Madeira

Belgravia, and Westminster districts of London. His heirs still own the Grosvenor
Square property on which the United States Embassy stands, making it the only
establishment of its kind standing on "foreign soil"; the lease, signed in 1950, runs
for 999 years. During the war, the Duke, the largest landowner in London, had
rented his town house in the same square as a service club for GIs at a rental of
one pound a year. He also donated a corner of his property as the site on which
the British government erected a statue of Franklin Delano Roosevelt.

When he died in 1953 of a heart ailment at the age of seventy-four, he left a
widow, the thirty-nine-year-old former Anne Sullivan, who was his fourth wife. All
her predecessors had divorced him after sampling the high style which provided him
with a four-masted, ocean-going yacht; 30,000 acres of British countryside; a pack
of 400 boar hounds and a château in Normandy to which he once invited 600
sportsmen for a single hunt; a string of race horses; and Eaton Hall, Cheshire,
which has its own miniature railroad running to the nearest main-line terminal.

He sold the old family home in London, Grosvenor House, several decades
ago—it is now one of the town's more distinguished hotels—some time after his
first Duchess had returned there one night from a Buckingham Palace party and
found the great wrought-iron gates locked against her, an early intimation that
separation was in the making.

Wife Number Three received the celebrated Porter-Rhodes diamond as a
wedding present in 1926, and Sir Winston Churchill, a commoner then, was best
man at the ceremony. The Duke spread the joy by sending neat cards to 1,000 of
his well-to-do London tenants, announcing that he was graciously remitting one
week's rent in honor of his marriage.

A Sunday painter at home

There was a duel in the sun for Rubens' "Adoration"

When Sotheby's was invited to help raise the wind to meet death duties amounting to eighty per cent of his Grace's worth, it was not the first time that the Grosvenors had sold off some of their treasures. In 1921, when the Duke found himself short of ready cash, he was stalked by Duveen and separated from Gainsborough's "The Blue Boy," Gainsborough's "The Cottage Door," and Reynolds' "Sarah Siddons as the Tragic Muse" for something in excess of $600,000. Duveen promptly sold all three of them to H. E. Huntington, renowned equally for helping build up the Southern Pacific Railroad and for marrying his aunt, the indomitable Arabella Huntington.

Wilson's enterprise in garnering the Westminster trove was a triumph for everyone concerned, but the actual structure of Sotheby's suffered some minor knocking about. "Adoration of the Magi" comprises eighty-five square feet of canvas, 12 by 6 feet, and a hole had to be sawed in the floor of the main auction room so that the massive altarpiece could be hoisted up from the basement. It was painted in Antwerp in 1634 for the Convent of the Dames Blanches, eleven days' work for Peter Paul Rubens, which brought him 920 florins, or $208 at current rates. Upon the suppression of the convents in the late eighteenth century, the "Adoration" was auctioned in Brussels for 8,511 florins. It arrived in England in 1788 and latterly had hung in the entrance hall at Eaton Hall, surviving the company of Allied forces during the war years when they were in peaceful occupation of the place.

The June day of the auction was hot and muggy, typical big-sale weather at Sotheby's, which takes advantage of that peak month of the London season, when garden parties burgeon and the Queen haunts Ascot races. Once again Wilson and the Sotheby staff put on an elegant show in coaxing $1,299,788 from buyers' wallets for the eighteen Westminster paintings up for sale. He had knocked down thirteen previous lots—other things besides the Westminster "surplus items" were up that day—before reaching the fourteenth, the "Adoration."

He asked for an opening bid of $56,000. Immediately a voice from the rear called $280,000. "It was unnerving," said Wilson later, though not even the telltale white patches appeared on his cheeks. Up to $336,000 went the prices, and then a barely perceptible nod from rumpled Leonard Koetser, a London dealer in Old Masters for thirty years, signaled that he was in the play. There followed a duel that converted the shabby gallery into something like an archery green, with Koetser and Geoffrey Agnew of Bond Street's Thomas Agnew & Sons loosing bids like arrows in flight toward a target, while the sun blazed down through the open skylight.

Wilson's eyes went from Koetser, halfway back in the room, to Agnew, down front; from Agnew, in conservative dark suit, to Koetser, in a casual sports jacket. At $14,000 a bid, each tried to force the other out of the contest. Then Koetser went to $770,000—3,600 times more than Rubens was paid—and Agnew shook his head forlornly. Koetser smiled; his unidentified client, he said, had authorized him to go higher if he had to.

The client turned out to provide a further surprise. Alfred Allnut, a British building contractor, virtually unknown as a collector, had formerly owned race

Peter Wilson at work: cool eyes in a warm room

horse's. He wanted the "Adoration" to hang in some deserving place of public worship and presented it to Cambridge University, where in King's College Chapel temperature and humidity controls were laid on to accord the altarpiece optimum living conditions. The Duke's estate was diminished but not entirely denuded; it still had a little museum's worth of Rembrandts, Hogarths, Stubbs, Gainsboroughs, Lelys, Pietro da Cortonas, and Panninis.

Wilson is an expert in relations with the public and in the commercial version of much the same thing which is called public relations. He lets pompous visitors know he appreciates the trouble they put upon themselves to act that way. He treats the simple, unsophisticated caller with something like a bedside manner. The day-to-day practice of public relations he has put into the hands of Brigadier Stanley Clark, a cheerful, square-shaped former newspaperman who spends a good part of his time wandering through Sotheby's maze of backrooms and basements with a modified walkie-talkie hung around his neck so that the office can find him wherever he may be.

Though communication on the premises is haphazard and a visitor is constantly bumping into girls calling to each other rather plaintively down the corridors, communication with the press is constant and professional. Wilson's willingness to court publicity and give newspaper interviews whenever he has the time certainly helped the firm to eclipse its competitors; Sotheby's chalked up another "first" in hiring a public-relations man. Wilson welcomes the newspaper headlines the big sales bring, and the staff is encouraged to talk freely and informatively to anybody.

One plum to fall into the lap of the publicity people bears the name Elizabeth Taylor. In 1961, she consigned a Matisse, "Femme Couchée sur une Chaise-

Longue," to Wilson's department and collected $33,000 minus commission for it. Soon afterward, she sent along a Frans Hals portrait, also from the stock assembled by her late husband, Michael Todd, but that transaction came unstuck. In prior instructions to Wilson, she had set her own reserve price on the picture, in the knowledge that he had knocked down a similar Frans Hals to a London dealer for a healthy $509,000 only six months earlier.

Wilson has explained his sense of timing, which can usually be depended on to keep the pot aboiling, only in the most general terms. "Sometimes," he told one inquisitive American, "you just look round the room, and your eye falls on someone who's about to bid, and you can squeeze a bid out of them." Unhappily, this power failed to stir his audience the night Miss Taylor's Frans Hals came up. The crowd watched the bidding climb sluggishly to $44,800, considerably short of the reserve figure, and then everyone sat on his hands, seeing the rare spectacle of Wilson visibly shaken. There was nothing for him to do but follow approved, emergency procedure and knock down the portrait to a nonexistent bidder. For this buying in by the house, Miss Taylor, according to custom, was charged two-and-a-half per cent of the last genuine bid.

With another famous name, though of different vintage, the gallery did much better. For some time, Wilson had been aware that for Somerset Maugham the joys of his collection of thirty-five Impressionist and Modern canvases were beginning to pall, mainly because of the trouble he was put to in protecting them from theft. It was "an irksome business," Maugham found, having to lock them up in a strong room every time he left his Villa Mauresque in St. Jean-Cap Ferrat for a few days, and by the summer of 1961, when some light-fingered Riviera types stole eight million dollars' worth of art from museums, galleries, and private homes on the Côte d'Azur, he had made up his mind to dispose of the lot. "Even if I were only going out to dinner," he wrote, "I could not be sure that a thief would not take the opportunity to steal one or two of my pictures."

Wilson, true to form, made no mention of his advance knowledge when he

Somerset Maugham at
the Villa Mauresque

first called on the old literary gentleman, who found the auctioneer so impressive that he invited him for a second, business visit. "Once we know a collection is going on the block," Wilson has said, "getting the sale is high-pressure business." There was no sign of such pressure, however, in his talks with Maugham. After two days of quiet negotiating, Maugham himself said, "I wouldn't trust my pictures with anyone else." As the sale date approached, he helped things along by releasing for newspaper publication excerpts from a chatty little book entitled *Purely For My Pleasure,* which he had written about the paintings and his experiences in collecting them.

The collection was a decidedly mixed bag, most of the pictures being, in Wilson's judgment, far from first rate and not exactly "life-enhancing," which was the fulsome description supplied by one British journalist. But Maugham's name could be relied on to strengthen the prices, as collectors on both sides of the Atlantic developed the itch of ownership. Sotheby's touted the sale as expected to bring in $2,240,000.

There were Renoirs, Gauguins, Monets, Matisses, and others. Of the Picassos, one was the double-header, which for inspection at the gallery was fixed in a special stand so that both sides were on view. On the night of the auction, when the usual scene of cash and glamour was set under the glittering chandeliers with the usual catalogue price tags dangling from them, it was knocked down for $244,000 to a shy woman in a large white hat, Miss Charlotte Ramus, who works for a London art-packing firm and was bidding for Henri Lyon, a Paris stockbroker.

The evening began mildly, according to script. Wilson plans his effects carefully, like a play in three acts, the first being gentle but stimulating, the second concluding with the real climax, the third bringing the curtain down with another bang "but not as big a bang." Lot One on this occasion was mild indeed—"Still Life with Vegetables," by Roderick O'Conor, who met Maugham in Paris around the turn of the century and took an instant dislike to him, though he was willing enough to sell him three of the few still lifes O'Conor ever painted.

Maugham reciprocated the feeling by modeling Clutton in *Of Human Bondage* after O'Conor, who was depicted in after years as "bitter, lonely, savage and unknown . . . at war with himself and the world, producing little in his increasing passion for perfection he could not reach." There was some speculation that the five hundred paintings O'Conor left might become fashionable, bringing him fame from the writer he disliked, but the three auction pictures went for something under $3,000.

Wilson had said a little earlier, "I can't say I know much about O'Conor. I believe we did once sell one of his paintings for $420 or so. I must say they look a bit out of place in this company."

The big bang of the evening was provided by the double-sided Picasso—the gouache on board, "Death of Harlequin," and on the verso side the less important "Woman Seated in a Garden." The bangs then diminished by way of another Picasso, two Pissarros, and two Renoirs, until Lot Thirty-five, an unexceptional

Utrillo, was sold for $30,800. The adding machines totted up the night's take: roughly $28,000 for each minute of sale, making a total of $1,466,864.

Maugham stayed at the Villa Mauresque. When his secretary (and adopted son), Alan Searle, telephoned the news, he sighed, "It is a lot of money for a single gentleman to get rid of." The money was to be used to help struggling elderly writers, through a fund to be administered by a British literary society. He expressed no disappointment over the fact that the figure fell short of the $2,240,000 Sotheby's had anticipated. Neither was there any public expression of disappointment from Peter Wilson. "I'm sorry the newspapers published those big estimates beforehand," he said disarmingly in his office, separated from the auction rooms by a hall with a service stairway leading to the rabbit warren in the basements.

He had one residual problem on his hands, arising from Maugham's tangled relationship with Lady John Hope, whom the octogenarian author disowned. She claimed that nine of the paintings sold at Sotheby's had previously been deeded to her.

Wilson was not unduly alarmed. He recalled that Lady Hope's solicitor had once drawn up a trust fund whereby Maugham, supposedly to minimize death duties, would make over his estate to her, retaining an allowance for his own needs. After several letters, the solicitor finally received a reply from the old man. "I, too," Maugham declared, "have read *King Lear*."

Mr. James Christie by Sir Joshua Reynolds

III

DAYS OF PURPLE, DAYS OF GOLD

I N 1776, in the Great Auction Rooms of Mr. James Christie in Pall Mall, London, the genial, rosy-cheeked proprietor had decided, with the approach of middle age, to devote less time to Jacobite politics and concentrate instead on business, for which he had a natural talent—the gift of gab. He had inherited good looks from both the English and Scottish sides of his family, but his politics he owed largely to his mother, a Macdonald and close kin to Flora, the savior of Bonnie Prince Charlie. Anyone interested in pictures had reason to sympathize with the lost cause of the Stuarts. King Charles I assembled his country's most important collection of paintings—and a notable one—before the axman took off his head.

Christie's aquiline nose smelled opportunity before he was twenty, when he resigned his commission in the Royal Navy, left his native town of Perth, where he was born in 1730, and rode down to London, to work as assistant to a Covent Garden auctioneer. At the age of thirty-three or thereabouts, he took over the Pall Mall rooms formerly occupied by a printmaker and went into auctioneering for himself, in competition with at least sixty other London establishments of the same kind, selling anything from art to hay.

His timing was impeccable. The forces of change which were building everywhere were on the point of making London, in place of Paris, the principal art market of the world. The first golden era of British collecting was dawning.

43

A pre-sale exhibition at Christie's

Christie appears to have been more a man of words than of action. He was on to good business, and he didn't let politics stand in the way.

Charles I employed a network of agents—William Petty and Balthazar Gerbier are two names on record—to scout Europe, buying for him at sales in the Netherlands or from poverty-stricken Italian noblemen like the Duke of Mantua. Charles owned three Correggios, a painter rated the most potent influence on Italian art of the day. He had Raphaels, who had inspired the entire contemporary Italian school. He'd commissioned Van Dyck portraits of himself as monarch at fees of two hundred guineas, which would have to be translated at perhaps $10,000 today.

One swing of the ax put an end to the glory. The collection was forcibly sold in London during 1650 and the two years following by order of Charles's temporary successor, the self-appointed Cromwell. The still-intact crowned heads of Europe wasted no time weeping for their decapitated cousin but whipped off envoys and couriers to the British capital to buy up everything they could. Don Antonio Cardenas was glad to buy Raphael's madonna, "La Perla," for £2,000, at least $100,-000 in modern values. Eberhard Jabach, a banker from Antwerp and one of the new bourgeois collectors, picked up the three Correggios for £1,000 apiece; by

A golden age dawned
with Charles I

labyrinthine turns of fate and avarice, the three now rest in the Louvre.

There were no auction rooms as such in London to accommodate the Crom-wellian sale, but by the time Charles's son came to a natural end of his years in 1685, they had become a recognized part of London life. Christie didn't get around to selling pictures until he had broken his teeth on less glamorous items. His first catalogue listed wines, plate, china, and jewels, on the last of which he could always be relied upon to let the rhetoric flow. He had a reputation as "The Specious Ora-tor," and it was well founded.

"Let me entreat you, ladies and gentlemen—permit me to put this inestimable piece of elegance under your protection," he would thunder in the purple customary to his calling. "Only observe, the inexhaustible munificence of your superlatively candid generosity must harmonize with the refulgent brilliancy of this little jewel."

A cartoon of the day catches him in full flight, a commanding figure with steel-rimmed spectacles pushed up on his forehead, declaiming, "Will your ladyship do me the honor to say £50,000—a mere trifle—a brilliant of the first water, an unheard-of price for such a lot, surely."

In a good month, a country estate or a town house might come his way. In

David Garrick:
the Great Auction Rooms
were a social rendezvous

between times, he'd settle, quoting an early catalogue, for such treasures as "two Nankeen chamber-pots; Sir Isaac Newton, Pope, and Handel in bronze, finely repaired by the late ingenious Mr. Robiliac . . . four flat irons, a footman, a gridiron trivet, two brass candlesticks, snuffers, hanging iron, ladle; etc." He had standards, however, beneath which he refused to stoop. At various times, he politely declined to accept "a hoof of the ass that our Savior rode into Asia on" and "a pedigree bedstead suitable for accouchements," which the contented owner wished to pass on to someone else since he held it "twice responsible for twins." Not even passing consideration would Christie give to a "cat with eight legs, two tales *(sic)*, dog's head, and cat's smellers, which lived fifteen minutes." Until he got pictures to sell, he rubbed along with a steady traffic in wine and chamber pots, with and without lids.

Pictures sales started the year after he opened shop in Pall Mall. At first, it must have been poor stuff, the usual overpainted, dishonestly pedigreed daubs that brought the prices they deserved when they arrived in the salesrooms; more important work was still sold privately. A "Moonlight" allegedly by Aelbert Cuyp, the Dutchman, went for £3 11 shillings. A reputed Titian brought all of two guineas. A "Holbein" was knocked down for less than £5. Michelangelo, Andrea del Sarto, Tintoretto, and Rembrandt—all turned up in the catalogue, but if there was a masterpiece among them, it went unnoticed. There were no experts to authenticate pictures, and forgers flourished. "Let the buyer beware" was the only rule. There were no long-established auction houses that would stand behind what they sold. If a painter had pictures to sell, he worked through an agent. If a collector had

Lord Chesterfield: he turned
up in a coach-and-six

paintings to dispose of, he resorted to a middleman, often a clergyman, sometimes even a valet. With few public auctions, there had been accumulated no reliable records of prices, which were therefore haphazard and arbitrary.

But as his chamber pots made way for better-priced chinaware, James Christie prospered and in 1770 moved to a new Pall Mall address, No. 125, next door to Schomberg House, into which Thomas Gainsborough moved as his neighbor and friend. Every afternoon, beginning at one o'clock, Christie's organ tones resounded in his octagonal main room, where pictures could be hung four tiers deep before they reached the domed ceiling.

To bolster prices, James resorted to advertising and press notices. He regularly placed announcements in *Lloyd's Evening Post* to extol the virtues of such objects as "a collection of Italian, French, and Flemish pictures of great value, belonging to a person of quality, and all in an excellent state of repair." Two years after his change of address, he joined with a syndicate of businessmen to found a morning newspaper of their own, the *Morning Post,* though it didn't amount to much in their hands and was later sold at a loss, though not under Christie's hammer.

His energetic methods were rapidly making his Great Auction Rooms a social rendezvous. The circle included Gainsborough, David Garrick, Sir Joshua Reynolds, and even the awesome Earl of Chesterfield, who took time off from writing to his son to turn up for one major sale in a coach-and-six.

Gainsborough was impressed by James to the point where he painted his portrait and presented it to the auctioneer as a sample, to be "hung in the great sale room, avowedly for the purpose of drawing public attention to the artist's name as a portrait painter." The painter at the time was charging 160 guineas for whole lengths and forty guineas for heads. The Christie portrait, a half length with a commissionable fee of eighty guineas, also included in the lower left-hand corner a fragment of landscape, to indicate a further Gainsborough skill; his landscapes ran to about the same price as whole lengths. Christie's successors weren't shrewd enough to hold on to the portrait either for prestige or sales propaganda. The Gainsborough is owned today by J. Paul Getty. The painting of the founder that hangs on the walls of the modern premises is a vastly inferior work by Vanderguvht.

Two separate though interrelated revolutions, the French and the Industrial, combined to put profits in the original Christie's pockets. Commissions for sales one year amounted to £16,000, which comes close to $1,000,000 by present-day reckoning. The age of machines was creating a new moneyed class eager to lay hands on the fine things of life. Empire building in the Indies was pouring gold into the counting houses in London, where the Royal Academy had been founded in 1769. And, in counterpoint, terror by guillotine in France was driving art treasures by the shipload out of the country.

In spite of what his friends called a "very good head for scheming," James's plans occasionally came unstuck. He had heard, for instance, that the debt-ridden Philippe, Duke of Orleans, was out to sell his collection of 400 pictures. The proceeds were to finance a plot to restore Philippe as Regent of France by deposing his uncle, Louis XIV. It was a truly fantastic collection. Ostensibly it included twelve Raphaels, nine of which are now recognized as such; twenty-seven Titians, of which eighteen have failed to stand the more expert scrutiny of modern times; four Veronese allegories; Rubens' "Judgment of Paris"; Tintoretto's bovinely beautiful "Origin of the Milky Way"; and Rembrandt's "Mill," now in the National Gallery of Washington. Some of the pictures, which were turning up in batches in London, were making a return trip across the Channel—they'd once been the property of King Charles before banker Evrard Jabach bought and subsequently sold them.

In 1790, the asking price for the lot was 100,000 guineas, and a London syndicate, including the Prince of Wales, was set up to make the purchase. But Christie sent an agent, Philippe Tassaert, to Paris to assess the collection. On the basis of his reports, James decided that the price was too high. His word carried weight; the syndicate deal fell through.

The duke's negotiators then divided the collection in two, the Dutch and Flemish pictures on one hand, the French and Italian on the other. The first lot got clean away from Christie. They were smuggled out of Paris and put on show at the original modest quarters of the Royal Academy in Pall Mall, between Carlton House and the Haymarket, at an admission charge of one shilling a head. The French and Italian paintings, more than 300 of them, were carried out of France later, when the Terror was at its height, and wound up in the hands of Noel Desanfans.

Desanfans turned down all offers, confident that the Empress Catherine of

Du Barry escaped with fistfuls of jewels

Russia, an enthusiastic newcomer to collecting, would buy him out. But the lady was fickle, and the opportunist was stuck. He consigned part of his collection to Christie, for a four-day sale which should have been the sensation of London, with Murillo, Reynolds, and Poussin among the painters represented.

But the international art market had been established only shakily in London at this time. The guillotine, plus the iron law of supply and demand, was creating a situation where Old Masters could be picked up in the courtyard of the Louvre at ten francs each. Christie's sale was a flop, with prices down fifty per cent and more below levels of a decade earlier. None suffered the ultimate ignominy of a Ludovico Caracci, "Christ Crowned with Thorns," which tumbled then and went on tumbling until, when last seen at Christie's in 1913, it went to the Duke of Sutherland for a flat two guineas, including the frame.

The advent of Napoleon knocked the bottom out of the world art market, and it stayed out for roughly fifty years. Kings and merchant princes were too concerned about their fates to buy many pictures. Loot from Versailles remained unsold in London salesrooms. With only an occasional picture sale worth talking about, Christie's trade flourished in something more readily transportable than pictures in troubled times—jewelry.

The Countess Du Barry had escaped from France with a considerable part of the treasure she had piled up as the favorite of Louis XV, including fistfuls of pearls and uncut diamonds. She collected £8,791, 4 shillings, and ninepence when Mr. Christie put her property under his gavel. Possibly encouraged by this venture, she stole back to her château in the hope of picking up more of her valuables. But a Negro servant betrayed her, and the guillotine was waiting.

The sale of jewels owned by the famous, infamous, royals, and disreputables is a Christie tradition. The Russian crown jewels, mostly of eighteenth-century origin, were put on the block in 1927 for a total of nearly a quarter of a million dollars. Twenty years later, the Duchess of Kent collected some $15,000 for silver from her late husband's estate, part of the $261,560 windfall garnered for her by the auction house. Mrs. Michael Wilding didn't fare badly in 1959, either, when a record per-caret price for a single diamond brought her $156,000, minus commission, for a 23.7-caret, step-cut ring.

For one crowned head, King Edward VII, the house performed a more unusual service by disposing of his collection of sherry for a staggering £18,311. As one historian of the galleries observed, "Sherry, like certain pictures, went out of fashion for a while after that."

Three years after the nineteenth century arrived, James Christie died in the Pall Mall house where he had lived and worked for nearly forty years. In his lifetime of jovial eloquence, he had personally conducted more than 1,200 sales. He left another milestone behind him—the sale of Raphael's miniature masterpiece, "The Vision of a Christian Knight," to Sir Thomas Lawrence, a high-fee portraitist of the day and a collector of distinction. Sir Thomas paid £409 10 shillings for a painting which is conservatively estimated to be worth $1,500,000 today.

The same year, a modest but much more romantic picture came up. The collection of Sir William Hamilton, one of history's most celebrated cuckolds, contained a portrait of his wife, Emma, by Madame Vigée le Brun. Nelson's sentiments for Lady Hamilton compelled him to buy the thing from Christie for £300, then dash off a letter to Emma. "My dearest friend," her hero wrote, "I have bought your picture, for I could not bear it should be put up at auction, and if it had cost me 300 drops of blood I would have given it with pleasure."

The original Christie was succeeded by two more generations of his family and a variety of partners. The constantly expanding business moved into premises in King Street, St. James's, where carriages would stand double-parked on important sales days, unloading dukes, marquises, earls, old dowagers, young heiresses, clergy, cavalry officers, Parliamentarians.

A magazine writer of the era turned in some paragraphs about the place that, with minor changes of detail, could as well describe a big modern sale: "There was my Lord So-and-So calling his Grace of Such-and-Such, and there was the gallant Colonel Somebody shaking hands with the Hon. Major Nobody, while old Lady Asterisk, with a fat poodle under her arm which she would not resign, made way after her fair daughter, who was leaning on a gay Captain of the Guards. . . . The noble crowds broke into groups; there was a truce to the levelling of glasses, and the buzz and murmur—the 'beautiful!' 'superb!' 'unique!' 'unquestionable!'—died away as the auctioneer mounted the rostrum . . . His commendations of the various lots were delivered with courteous intonations of voice and measured cadences, and seemed to pay deference to the judgement of the company, while in fact they did much to direct it."

The social set had to take a drive out of town for the main event of 1848. The journey to Stowe, the Duke of Buckingham's country seat, was well worth the trouble and the bumpy roads because there was a touch of scandal to shorten the miles. The auction, which lasted forty days before the last bit of porcelain had been disposed of, was a forced sale of an old family collection, the first of a continuing series which became a familiar spectacle under pressure of later wars and taxes. Buckingham needed money, not for the first time. In the 1830's, approximately 1,000 pictures had been shipped off from Stowe to Christie's, where they sold for less than one pound apiece, "filling the junkshops of Wardour Street for months and years to come."

The sale at Stowe itself rang no bells, even though the duke had steeled himself to put some portraits of his forefathers on the block. The cult of worshiping somebody else's ancestors, provided they were painted by an eighteenth- or nineteenth-century English portraitist, had scarcely begun. There was a little competitive bidding on behalf of several branches of the Rothschild dynasty, who were in the market for antecedents, yet the forty days produced a total of only £77,562, 4 shillings, and sixpence.

Lord Ellesmere picked up a literary bargain for £72 15 shillings in a portrait of William Shakespeare, which has been attributed to the actor John Taylor and to Will's companion at the Mermaid, Richard Burbage. Ellesmere enjoyed it in private for eight years, then handed it on to Britain's National Portrait Gallery.

The son of a gamekeeper who had been brought up at Stowe went to work at Christie's and stayed there for more than half a century, as a partner and an institution in his own right. Thomas Woods put his stamp on the business and his name on the door of Christie, Manson & Woods Limited, which remains its official title today. (William Manson was another partner who is similarly commemorated.) Mr. Woods's keen, bespectacled eyes resulted in two pictures multiplying their value by 30,000 per cent over a span of fifty-one years.

Frans Hals, who was popular enough with his Dutch patrons during his lifetime, has had his ups and downs in the salesroom. At the time that Christie's was founded, Hals was decidedly down, with his "Laughing Cavalier" sold at The Hague for a piffling £15. Two Hals portraits in the Buckingham collection, one a lady and the other a gentleman, fared even less nobly at the Stowe sale, when they were hammered down at seven guineas and ten and a half guineas respectively. When they showed up again at Christie's in 1899, Woods spotted them for what they were. He made sure they were accurately catalogued and, as auctioneer, sold the gentleman for £3,150, and the lady for two thousand guineas.

By the time Woods reached his prime, the raffish ways of the Regency had been replaced by Victorian respectability. The Christie crowds, be-bustled and top-hatted, still represented the cream of society and still clapped with delight at the big sales as bids leapt up by a thousand guineas a time. "The Christie audience," the London *Graphic* noted somewhat loftily, "revels in high prices simply for money's sake, though of course some of the applause is meant for the picture."

The applause rang out as a matter of course one day in 1876 when Thomas Gainsborough's "Duchess of Devonshire" was lifted onto the easel for an opening bid of one thousand guineas and an immediate second offer of three times that sum. The portrait had been part of the collection of literally hundreds of pictures gathered by Wynn Ellis, a rich silk manufacturer who had died the year before. It had been bought a generation earlier from a picture-restorer for £63, which was considerably more than a schoolmistress had paid for the original massive canvas at auction in 1839; she had it cut down to fit over her mantelpiece.

By Gerald Reitlinger's expertly documented account, authentication of this picture was doubtful at best. When Sir John Millais, who had been making a study of Gainsborough, laid eyes on the dubious duchess in the salesroom, he took off down Christie's staircase, shouting, "I don't believe Gainsborough ever saw it."

But by this time, competition among buyers for ancestral portraits, preferably ducal, was on the boil. Baron Ferdinand Rothschild, who was hot after Gainsboroughs like the rest of his family, lusted after the duchess. The Earl of Dudley craved her to the extent of ten thousand guineas. But his bid was topped by that of Morland Agnew, of the art-dealing clan, who bought it for stock for one hundred guineas more. It was, observed the knowledgeable Mr. Woods, "the highest price paid at Christie's for any picture." But in the great boom in prices that was in the making, the record was soon shattered.

Woods was not always so well pleased. The verification of paintings is a subject to which Christie's made an important contribution. In general, their catalogues were the pride of Mr. Woods. When the Henry Doetsch collection of 448 pictures were prepared for the block in 1899, the house had all of them repedigreed. Some of those pedigrees were, in one expert's subsequent judgment, "more or less imaginary." Thomas Woods suspected as much and couldn't contain his suspicions. In the middle of the sale, he turned to take a final look at the imposturing pictures, snorted audibly and stepped down from the rostrum. Another partner had to pick up the gavel and finish the sale.

The last Christie to be connected with the business had long since retired when Woods handled his own last sale in the early years of this century, but golden days continued for the house. From the collection of Charles Frederick Huth, it sold for five thousand guineas a Primus vase that had been picked up in Wardour Street for $1.50 at current rates, in a transaction that highlights the surprise turn of fortune which is a favorite theme nowadays with Christie's staff.

They like to recall the water color by Thomas Rowlandson of Vauxhall Gardens, the eighteenth-century stamping ground for rakes and doxies, which turned up in an East End of London junk shop. It was bought there for one pound; it sold for £2,730. Then there was the British soldier who brought in a picture he had unearthed in his father's workshop, hoping to pick up perhaps $50. At auction it realized $5,880—"Seneca and Nero" by Peter Paul Rubens.

One of Christie's folk heroines is a Mrs. P. Jones, of Queen's Place, Southsea, Hampshire, who arrived with a George I coffee pot, for which she was promptly paid $1,960 (£700). "Some weeks ago a Brighton dealer came to my house," she reported, "and asked if I had any silver. He saw my coffee pot and offered me £45. A week later, he came back and offered me £80. Thank goodness, I held out!"

In the same struck-by-fortune category must be named Mrs. K. F. Finch, of Shanklin, Isle of Wight. She had a teapot which her mother had used every day until she died. Christie's current Silver, Arms & Armour man, A. G. Grimwade, recognized it as a George I, seven-sided teapot by Isaac Ribouleau. Put up for sale in 1952, it fetched $4,960.

The venerable firm today describes itself as "the oldest fine-arts auctioneers in the world," justifying the claim on the grounds that Sotheby's, though senior by twenty-two years, started by selling books. In recent years, Sotheby's has outmatched its rival by doing business at roughly double the rate.

Christie's occupies a three-story gray stone pile at No. 8 King's Street, a mixture of Georgian and neo-Renaissance, which had to be rebuilt almost entirely after it was blitzed by the Luftwaffe in 1941. The firm, which has cultivated friends in important places as a matter of policy all its life, was promptly offered accommodation by Lord Derby in his house in Stratford Place, from which he moved out all his furniture to make room for the auctioneers.

Six years later, with the war over, a second nobleman, Lord Spencer, gave Christie's the use of his home in St. James's Place while the King Street headquarters were being put together again. Only the façade remained, and it was taken down brick by brick, each ticketed and numbered in the process, so that the old building could be reconstructed exactly as it used to be, as a kind of talisman of the good old days.

A visitor to King Street finds himself afoot on a dignified thoroughfare which accommodates a number of expensive dealers in art, antiquities, and fine silver. The perpetually green trees of St. James's Square provide the backdrop. Beyond the portico of Christie's itself, the entrance hall is paneled in light, waxed oak, with an imposing staircase leading up to the auction rooms.

The flavor is *ancien régime*. A handful of people wander around peering at the objects on display for future sales with the same respectful air to be found in, say, the Frick or the reading room of the British Museum. A few regular customers keep an eye on whatever sale the day provides. An appointed routine prescribes the disposal of china and porcelain on Mondays; jewelry, musical instruments, and objects of virtu on Tuesdays; silver and books on Wednesdays; furniture, rugs, and objects of art on Thursdays; pictures on Fridays.

Between the two World Wars, the tide began to flow against Christie's. No precise date or single sale marks the turn that saw the house lose its place as the preeminent picture mart in the world, but as collectors' tastes moved toward the

The Gainsborough portrait that needs no title

Impressionists and Post-Impressionists, Christie's remained conservative, Victorian, and most particularly Barbizon, that faded French school of landscape, named after a village in the Forest of Fontainebleu. Its first Picasso didn't reach the house until 1937, when it was knocked down for less than $1,000. In the same year, with similar portents of decline, six Braque and Juan Gris canvases sold for less than $5,000 in all.

Shortly before the turn, there were some years of particular glory. When the John Singer Sargent collection arrived on offer in 1925, it brought close to a million dollars in the currency of the times. The following year, M. Knoedler & Co. paid £60,900 for Romney's "Portrait of Mrs. Davenport"—another "highest ever" price—and sold it for about £70,000 to Andrew Mellon for the National Gallery in Washington; an equivalent price today would be some $500,000. It was Christie's who, with Duveen, negotiated the private sale of the Duke of Westminster's "Blue Boy" by Gainsborough, "The Tragic Muse" and "The Cottage Door" by Reynolds.

The Wall Street disaster that began in 1929 clobbered all the salesrooms, but none harder than Christie's. The era of partial recovery that followed in the late Thirties didn't do much to help, because it coincided with the swing in taste away from the English eighteenth- and nineteenth-century painters, which had been the stock in trade of the house, toward the Moderns. While skirts and hair grew as short as ready cash, the Barbizon pictures, which American collectors had once clamored for, became a barbiturate on the market after the United States had been flooded with forged Corots.

Out of step with the times, an apologist for Christie's was complaining as late as 1932 that "the comparative scantiness of woman's costume and the vogue of short hair are considered to lack that flowing grace which characterized the fashions of an earlier day." With an almost audible sigh, he added, "It may be that, in the course of time, opinions will change and that, when viewed dispassionately from a distance of years, the fashions of this age may be considered to possess attractions which at present escape us. If it should prove so, then the work of the neo-Georgian portrait painters may fetch their own high prices in the auction rooms."

Of course, it didn't prove so. Christie's, instead of riding on a flood tide of prosperity, drowsed along in a backwater. The place was no longer a "must" on the calling list for a tour of the town. Instead of such glory as the Holford sale, when a collection that included six Rembrandts was sold in a single afternoon for well over $1,000,000, business went more to such rewarding items as a Fabergé cigarette case ($3,220), a Bustelli porcelain figurine ($12,880), or the journal and log of Captain James Cook, who discovered Australia ($148,400).

On a foreboding February 22 in 1957, Christie's put up for sale a portrait of George Washington attributed to Gilbert Stuart. The seventy-three-year-old head of the picture department, Sir Alec Martin, handled the gavel for the sale, but more than 250 bidders stared back coldly as he pleaded, "Only 800 guineas? But this, as you know, is Washington's birthday." They still sat on their hands. What was intended to be the star attraction in a group of old and modern pictures had to be bought in by the house.

I. O. Chance conducts a sale

There is no reason for supposing it to be a consequence of that day, but four-teen months later the company was reorganized, Sir Alec was replaced, and a new chairman was found in Ivan Oswald Chance, an old Etonian who had started working part time for Christie's when he was eighteen years old.

Subsequently, as part of the same program to update the firm and catch up with its rivals, a full-time representative was engaged to work in New York and was in-stalled in an office with a teleprinter to facilitate transatlantic bidding. The interior walls at King Street were repainted a creamy white, and a series of board-room luncheons were instituted for partners, collectors, museum officials, politicians, and members of the press.

Chance, who is closely related to the art-dealing Agnew clan, is a big man with blue eyes, graying hair, and a cordial handshake. He is cut from the same bolt of cloth as his competitor at Sotheby's, Peter Wilson, in having a good war record (Coldstream Guards), a fashionable address, and superior clubs (Brook's, White's and Pratt's). As a collector of sorts he, too, likes the eighteenth century, but his purchases are modest. He is nicknamed "Peter." He has a deserved repu-tation for courtesy and total honesty.

Working under less pressure than Wilson, Chance is fond of taking time to have a philosopher's look at the market. "Art auctions," he said, "have always been fashionable, attracting the rank, fashion, and beauty of the day. But only in

"Encampment on Dartmoor" by Augustus John

the past ten years did auctions become front-page news for modern media, starting right after the Second World War."

A new generation came into the market, he found. "There were a great number of people with money who were willing to spend up to £10,000 backing their own judgment on furniture, silver plate, and so on. There was a sociological change, with more people living in the same amount of space in new apartment houses. Where twenty-five pictures might have hung before in a private home, there would be 150 hanging in an apartment house."

Chance believes that "we can see the present only in terms of the past. Remember the drop in prices of the eighteenth-century English portraitists. The escapism of today, the concern about The Bomb and destruction, makes people want anything that's light and pretty—the paintings of Boucher, Watteau, Fragonard."

What kind of sale gives him the most satisfaction? "Selling something difficult to sell, to somebody who really needs the money. I like competition, the close finish. I get more satisfaction from that than out of a safe ride."

At least one sale in 1962 brought back a bit of the former glory, though Americans were noticeably absent from the crowded salesrooms. Augustus John, the graybeard who had died the previous October at the age of eighty-three, was a painter in the British taste whose reputation scarcely extended overseas. He was probably the last Bohemian by "La Bohème" definition, a romantic who traveled with gypsies in his younger days, in old age a Rabelaisian presence who allowed his incontinence to flow unheeded when he sat at table in London cafes.

Bidding from the crowd of almost a thousand people was "fantastic" in the adjective of Mr. Chance. Most of the pictures were unfinished, many of them previously unknown. But one, "The Little Concert, or the Tinkers," found rolled up and infested with cockroaches at John's studio in Fordingbridge, near Salisbury, sold for $4,480. A self-portrait, dominated by beard and hungry eyes, sold for $24,990, destined for Lord and Lady Cowdray.

The excitement on days like this is always infectious. One bidder forked out $15,288 for a portrait that had failed to make $2,380 when it was exhibited at a London gallery earlier in the year. And John's paint-encrusted easel earned $294, adding a mite to the total $278,712.

There is an apparent law of life which stipulates that by the time a business achieves suitably impressive accommodations, a smooth-running organization, and superior personnel, it is inevitably past its prime. A "growth" concern, by contrast, is required to labor with a helter-skelter table of management and in inadequate quarters, according to the rule.

If this is true, then Christie's may have lost its old prestigious magic forever. But the art market has some of the characteristics of an esthetic lottery. Sotheby's backed the winners with the Impressionists and Moderns. I. O. Chance has many well-wishers, even among his competitors, who hope that it will be Christie's turn next.

IV

THE PROPER PARENTS OF AN ART

A T the Parke-Bernet Galleries on that epic evening when "Aristotle" found a new home, two weary employees, sipping cold coffee from paper cups, hashed over the significance of the event in which they had been involved, while they watched the still dazed crowds waiting for "down" elevators to restore them to earth and the realities of Madison Avenue.

"One thing you can be sure of," said the older of the two. "There'll never be another like this."

"What do you mean?" exclaimed the younger, like a Yankees fan who'd heard his team disparaged. "Every week we'll have one like this."

Had their boss, Leslie Abraham Hyam, who is president of the galleries, overheard them, he might have judged that the ideal future course would lie somewhere between the Scylla and Charybdis of their forecasts. The house had won a momentous victory over its transatlantic rivals, Sotheby's and Christie's, in garnering the sale, but further triumphs of prestige, showmanship, and publicity would be necessary in the years ahead. The thought of tackling another sale of anything like the size without first taking a long spell for breath would have ruffled even Hyam, a tall man of massive composure.

As it was, he heard nothing of what the two men were saying. In a dark blue suit, with a celebratory carnation in the lapel, he was facing a perspiring audi-

59

ence of reporters in a mood of exultation, letting the evening's prices—they totaled $4,679,250—slide like ice cream over his tongue. "The final figures," he acknowledged benignly, "surprised everybody, including the buyers."

The Erickson auction was not so much a sale as a temporary way of life at Parke-Bernet. Each of the staff of 115, from the president to the rawest recruit to the mailroom, sweated out four months of waiting for the executors of Mrs. Erickson's estate to make up their minds which auction house should be given the prize.

"We simply had to have the sale," Hyam said later. "This was a prime battle, a prime test. If our competitors had taken the Erickson, they'd have taken the cream from the top of everything for the next five years. The publicity which we enjoyed would have gone overseas for the benefit of the other side. But the results, I think, justified our position that in the United States, the wealthiest country in the world, there are no limits to what people will pay, under competitive conditions, for the finest things."

Hyam goes into action in capturing sales contracts with the air of a D'Artagnan who has recovered from the initial surprise of finding that rival swordsmen will stoop to trickery to draw blood. He suspects that the opposition persistently spreads false rumors about the size of Parke-Bernet commissions. He is likewise convinced that rival houses pretend that their charges are considerably lower than they really add up to by the time bills have been paid for crating, shipping, handling, and other somewhat oracular services with which the consignor is unacquainted before the sale takes place.

He has said, almost persuasively, of his business opposition, "I have no personal animus against them. I know all of them to talk to, a few of them reasonably well. In the very nature of industrial competition, you can no longer complain if you resent a rival's methods. You simply do what you can to get business for your stockholders." Heavy odds are nothing new to either Hyam or the house. At one hectic point of their joint past, the odds included a suicide and an attempted murder.

In the precise manner which is characteristic of him, he currently lays six charges of plagiarism against his competitors, making it clear that he expects little better of them, though nothing which they may have originated has proved worthy of copying by his side. They have imitated Parke-Bernet, he says, in producing impressively detailed catalogues to help prospective customers; in staging evening sales; in abandoning the archaic method of selling silverware by the ounce instead of by the piece; in modernizing the spelling and dating of Chinese items; in adding scholarly footnotes to catalogue pages; and in the general application of salesmanship and showmanship to what used to be a fuddy-duddy business at best, at worst a catch-as-catch-can effort where a customer had to step warily.

If the entire contemporary process may be called glamorizing—a word shunned by everybody in the house—then glamor was introduced into American auctioneering by a predecessor of Hyam, Thomas E. Kirby, who in 1885 opened a salon under the name of The American Art Association, which after considerable tribulation eventually became Parke-Bernet. Kirby arrived in New York from Philadelphia,

The man with the million-dollar voice,
Thomas E. Kirby at 75

where he'd had a successful career with a gavel, bent on establishing an auction house where only the finest and most reputable objects of art and furniture would be sold in a setting luxurious enough to lure the richest clients.

Besides having wealthy backers for his venture, Kirby had the invisible but audible asset of "the million-dollar voice," which could reputedly charm birds from trees or bids from the tightest wallets of\Wall Street. The magnetic little fellow set up shop first at Broadway and Twenty-third Street, then at 30 East 57th Street, on the corner of Madison Avenue, a building specially designed for his purpose, with vaults, offices, storerooms, eleven separate galleries, and an Assembly Room for art sales with accommodation for 500 people. The audience of upper-crust New Yorkers who attended the gala opening had to listen to the audible asset roll on for two hours, extolling the talents of its proud possessor.

He had plenty to crow about. One observer reported, "His large, high display rooms were hung with velvets; his corridors were mirrored and marbled; every pre-sale display was arranged by an artist in interiors; the auction room itself was hung in red velvet, was opulent in gilt plaster; his catalogues were beautifully printed authorities, to be saved as source books about antique furniture, paintings, rare books and objects of virtue."

The Kirbys—Thomas's son Gustavus had joined his father by this time—were as well equipped with personnel as with property. On his staff as leading auctioneer and appraiser he had Hiram H. Parke, whose talents had become evident in his youth when a skeptic tossed him a twenty-dollar gold piece as a challenge—he promptly succeeded in knocking it down for $100.

The much-traveled "Harvest Waggon"

The biggest single sale Parke had handled brought in a record $2,293,693, when the collection of paintings, Chinese porcelains, and other items owned by Judge Elbert H. Gary, chairman of the United States Steel Corporation, went on the block. The prize of the collection was a Gainsborough landscape variously identified as "The Harvest Waggon" and "The Market Cart," which "Prinny," the future George IV, commissioned in 1780 as a gift for his light of love, Mrs. Fitzherbert, when the painter was James Christie's neighbor.

The picture turned up in Christie's auction rooms in 1841 and was sold for £651. Half a century later, it arrived for sale again on the same premises and made £4,725. Gainsborough was skyrocketing in price on the new millionaire market, manipulated on both sides of the Atlantic by Joseph Duveen. It was Duveen who carried it off, for £20,160, the next time it appeared on Christie's easel, selling it later for a profit of 14,000 guineas to Judge Gary.

The much-traveled "Waggon" made its first public appearance in an American salesroom under Parke's gavel. Among the audience of elite in the velvet-hung gallery sat the great Duveen, elegant and impassive as usual. Bidding went up by leaps and bounds until there was a moment's pause. Parke's mild eyes turned to the art dealer, who had already been knighted but had not yet attained his ultimate rank of Lord Millbank.

"Are you all through, Sir Joseph?" Parke asked.

Duveen's head dropped a fraction of an inch. To the auctioneer, this signified that the bidder had increased his price by $25,000. Only Parke knew that the contest now devolved upon only three men, including the British dealer. Up went the bidding to $350,000. Again Parke asked, "Are you all through, Sir Joseph?" Again Sir Joseph was not. He added another $10,000 to regain "The Harvest Waggon," returning to the appreciative estate of Judge Gary more than twice as much as the collector had originally paid for it.

But a Duveen Gainsborough had always to be protected in this fashion. Unless the price leapt up every time a Gainsborough appeared on the market, Sir Joseph's clients might lose faith in him as fast as he himself lost face. "The Harvest Waggon" later rolled on out of his storeroom into the possession of Charles T. Fischer of Detroit. Then its wheels turned again, and it came to rest in the Canadian Art Gallery in Toronto.

Among the gallery staff there was also Otto Bernet, another auctioneer with an astute business brain, and Arthur Swann, an authority on rare books, who had first gone to work as a sixteen-year-old apprentice in Leeds, England. Working in the cataloguing department was a rather aloof young Englishman, Leslie Hyam, born in London on August 19, 1901, who had graduated from Cambridge with a degree in physics in 1922, then arrived out of the blue in New York to see where he could launch himself.

"There was a considerable depression at the time," he has recalled, "and there were no jobs in England except in the teaching field. I had no inclination to teach, but there was no particular reason for my coming to the United States." After ten months spent writing a novel, which he burned, he landed the cataloguing job at The American Art Association through a friend who was Duveen Brothers' librarian.

Knowing nothing about this new field, Hyam drew up for himself an impressive course of self-instruction, haunting the Metropolitan Museum for six weeks of intensive observation, reading, and note-making. The three leather-bound, indexed notebooks which he compiled are still on his desk and in use today, a minor monument to what a scientifically trained mind can do to stretch itself. They include, for instance, such ready reference as pages of thumb-nail sketches of Italian coats-of-arms, dynastic classifications of Chinese porcelain, hallmarks for gold and silver, and a gruesome but useful listing of martyred saints categorized by method of dispatch.

"One of the proofs that cataloguing was not taken seriously when I came into this thing was the fact that after less than two years of experience I was put in charge of that operation," he said. "I had to learn my job by doing it."

The considerable stir that the galleries were making caught the attention of Cortlandt Field Bishop, who had inherited both a banking fortune and an extensive collection of art. He was smitten with the ambition to own a business that would give Christie's a run for its money, and he bought The American Art Association from the Kirby family. Then Bishop kept on going and picked up his only important competitor, The Anderson Galleries on Park Avenue and 59th Street, which had started in 1900 by auctioning books and progressed to art and antiques. Without bothering to find a new name, he simply called the new union "American Art Association–Anderson Galleries." There was nothing to approach it in size or reputation by the time Bishop died, when something close to $10,000,000 of property was being auctioned each year.

His death in March, 1935, touched off an explosive struggle for power and profits worthy of the Borgias in their heyday, marked by embezzlement, suicide, and attempted murder. Parke-Bernet Inc. was born as a business in the midst of the melodrama, with the New York tabloids serving as *accoucheurs*.

Bishop's considerable real-estate holdings had included an apartment house whose superintendent, Milton Logan, was variously reported in earlier days to have operated a lunch wagon, worked as a janitor, and clerked in an hotel. Rising rapidly in his employer's favor, he had graduated to the management of many of Bishop's properties and had been given a hand in the galleries' business affairs. He was favored, too, by the widow, Mrs. Amy Bend Bishop, and his late boss's private secretary, Edith Nixon, two impressionable women who were Bishop's principal beneficiaries. Late in 1937, when Logan offered them $175,000 for the galleries, there were no questions raised about further bidding. They were ready to sell without a moment's hesitation.

Logan, admittedly a tyro as an art expert who considered himself a financial wizard, was embarrassed by something close to a complete lack of cash. He resorted to a well-heeled insurance salesman, John T. Geery, who had been a school friend of his in Brooklyn thirty-five years earlier and was familiar with the value of the galleries, since he had written its policies. Geery was the actual purchaser of the company, agreeing to pay $75,000 in cash and $100,000 in notes. In fact, for a business which on "The Harvest Waggon" sale alone had earned $36,000 in three minutes, Geery put up only $10,000 in cash and borrowed the remaining $65,000 from the inheritance of the flexible Mrs. Bishop and Miss Nixon. With the title of president, Logan was put on salary, while Geery, as secretary-treasurer, held control along with the purse strings.

A year later, they were both arrested on charges of grand larceny. They had been stealing from art collectors by withholding payment for pictures and art objects they had auctioned. One halfway important painting involved was "The Madonna of the Pinks," attributed to Raphael, though more likely to be the work of a pupil, based on the Panshanger Madonna for which P. A. B. Widener had forked out more than $500,000 in 1913.

"The Madonna of the Pinks," jointly owned by Baron Feliz Lachovski and Captain Daniel Sickles, had been sold by the Logan-Geery axis to Mrs. Drury Cooper in 1939 for $60,000. The galleries collected the sale price from her but passed on only half that sum, minus commission naturally, to the two luckless former owners.

Parke, Bernet, Arthur Swann, Leslie Hyam, and Edward Keyes, who served later as secretary-treasurer to Parke-Bernet Inc., knew nothing whatever of the frauds, and what they knew of the series of disasters that followed for Logan and Geery, they only read about in the newspapers. Virtually the entire trained staff, forty strong, led by Parke and Bernet, pulled out of the American Art Association–Anderson Galleries a matter of weeks before the new owners took over. The date of their exodus had an upside-down appropriateness: it was Armistice Day, 1937.

In their closing days of control, Mrs. Bishop and Miss Nixon, demanding ever more out of the business, had ignored the advice of their lawyers and bankers and voted to put in as working head Mitchell Kennelly, who subsequently came to an unrelated but violent end. The executive staff of the galleries knew him of old, dating back to the time he had worked there before Bishop bought the place, and they flatly refused to serve under him. But the two women, who clung to the notion that the business could more or less run itself, refused to sell out to a consortium of the staff, who actually offered them more than Logan and Geery even theoretically promised to come up with.

Hyam, the last survivor of the five cofounders of Parke-Bernet, recently recalled some of the harassments of the beginnings. "We left behind the only building in New York suitable for auction sales, the only first-class gallery name in the country, and $1,000,000 worth of sales contracts still to be worked out there. We went out without a name, without a home, and with no sales to look forward to. But in a year and a half, our competition destroyed them."

The first task was to get a roof over the head of the new baby, of which Parke was president, with Bernet, Swann, and Hyam as vice-presidents. They were provided with temporary shelter by French & Company, the fine-arts dealers. "Forty-five of us sat in one of the outlying areas of a furniture depository among some choir stalls, trying to organize something. The Depression was under way. None of us was rich. Even with some capital subscribed from outside, our financial resources can best be described as modest."

They were saved by the fact that the landlords of the handsome home they had abandoned, the Mutual Life Assurance Company, were convinced that Parke-Bernet would survive while its progenitors were bound to fail, that it was only a matter of time before the new firm could move back as the most desirable and, in fact, only possible tenants of the highly specialized building at 30 East 57th Street. Meantime, Mutual rented them the Dobbs Building, close by on the corner of 57th Street and Fifth Avenue, now occupied by the store known as The Tailored Woman.

"We had to set up a business organization and a library," Hyam related, "and we kept staff on at their previous salaries. We had to meet stiff competition on rates to beat the other people. For eighteen months, we slugged each other. We had eaten up our working capital and had to start over again by the time we moved back, after the American Art Association–Anderson Galleries had gone bankrupt."

Residual goodwill and records of the bankrupts were bought for $12,500. But before that happened, Logan and Geery were up to their necks in trouble. With neither experience in the auction field nor trained staff to support them, they were doomed. As their financial difficulties piled up, Geery discovered in the files a life-insurance policy for $100,000, which the business had taken out some years earlier on the life of Dr. A. W. Rosenbach, the veteran book collector, when the gallery had sent him to Europe on its behalf. Geery examined the policy with a practiced eye and, a few days later, told Logan that he was going to take out similar insurance on his partner's life.

The pretext Geery gave was that, through an intermediary, he was trying to engineer a deal with Generalissimo Chiang Kai-Shek for $30,000,000 worth of Chinese art to be shipped to the galleries in order to raise money for China's prosecution of the then current war against Japan. The intermediary, Gerold Echelmann, was supposed to have commanded the U-boat *Deutschland* during the First World War, and later to have become a code expert for Chiang. Investigation showed later that the *Deutschland's* commander was somebody else entirely. Nevertheless, Echelmann collected expense money from Geery, went overseas, and was not heard from again. The Chinese treasure trove, if it existed, never did arrive at the galleries.

But Geery had taken out two three-month policies, for $100,000 and $50,000, with Lloyd's of London on Logan's life, paying a premium of $1,228.85. "If anything should happen to you," he told his unsuspecting partner, "we'd lose the commissions on this tremendous deal."

When the promised boat load of Chiang's art proved to be nonexistent, Geery cabled a further $3,686.51 in premiums to Lloyd's to keep the insurance active. Then the firm went bankrupt and was dispossessed from 30 East 57th Street, into which premises Parke-Bernet Inc. promptly returned. Logan and Geery, arrested on grand-larceny charges, were let out on bail, and the stage was set for the blood-bathed finale.

One evening in February, 1940, Geery took Logan for an automobile ride along the East River Drive. In the back seat of the car sat an accomplice he had hired, John Poggi, who at other times ran a downtown newsstand outside the Equitable Building on Broadway, where Geery had his insurance office. With a thirteen-and-a-half-inch length of lead-filled pipe, Poggi cracked the skull of Logan, who was dumped out and left for dead on the Drive near Sixth Street. But the victim managed to stagger to his feet and flag down a police car.

Geery had gone on by taxi to the Waldorf to meet his wife and celebrate their twenty-first wedding anniversary there when he first got the news that Logan was alive in Bellevue Hospital, though in no condition as yet to tell a coherent story. Three hours later, when he and his wife returned to their home in Garden City, Long Island, Geery went down to the cellar and fired a bullet into his brain.

Poggi was subsequently convicted of assaulting Logan with intent to kill. Logan, with a cigar-sized scar on the back of his neck, was tried for the original fraud, found guilty, then freed on suspended sentence. "Strong punishment," said the sympathetic judge, "has already been meted out."

There is a line from Richard Brinsley Sheridan, with which Leslie Hyam is well acquainted, to the effect that "sheer necessity is the proper parent of an art." Sheer necessity, matched with luck and day-and-night work, got the newly incorporated galleries off to a flying start in their first twelve months of business, though a letter-writing campaign to patrons left in the clutch of American Art Association–Anderson backfired.

"We told them we were pulling out, expecting that some sales would be canceled to our benefit," Hyam reported, "but the management there threatened legal proceedings, which kept all the sales in line for them. Nobody had the courage to cancel."

But within two months of starting, a sale came along which was to set a record for all auction houses that season. Jay F. Carlisle, with a socially prominent name which was pure gravy to Parke-Bernet, had over 1,000 items for disposal—English and French furniture, English and American sporting paintings, Flemish tapestries, decorations, and books. Working against a deadline and anxious to keep overheads to a minimum, Hyam and a crew of five assistants turned out the entire detailed catalogue in five days of perspiration and black coffee, a feat he still regards as a phenomenon above all others in the galleries' history. In half-a-dozen sessions, the sale realized $159,073. The continuing newspaper stories of trouble at the old homestead, together with the prestige of the sale, got the new business off and running.

If anything, the tawdry affairs of Logan and Geery served only to emphasize the impeccable rectitude of the new firm and the blue blood of its patronage. Lists were studded the first season with the names of such social luminaries as Mrs. Robert Patterson, Mrs. Paul Warburg, Mrs. James P. Donahue, and Ogden Mills, who had been Hoover's Treasury Secretary. As one season succeeded another, the elite names continued coming in—William Randolph Hearst, Frank Crowninshield, Harry Payne Whitney, Grace Rainey Rogers, the estate of the late J. P. Morgan.

The start of the Second World War in 1939 did not drive prices down. That December, the collection of Mrs. Cornelius J. Sullivan came on the block. Louis Marion, who rose from mail clerk to chief auctioneer, remembers her as "one of the first and most sincere of modern collectors." A founder of the Museum of Modern Art in New York, she bought Cézanne and Van Gogh simply because she believed in them.

For the two evenings of sale, which saw Cézanne's portrait of Madame Cézanne fetch $27,500 and Van Gogh's portrait of Mademoiselle Ravoux bring $19,000, the audience was happy to sit on the floor when all chairs had been taken. "The auctioneer finally had to enter by way of the fire escape," Marion remembers.

Somewhere along the line, the galleries, which have been called "the most elegant auction block in the world," ran across another of the quotations to which Hyam is partial as a discreet combination of scholarship and soft sell. This one, from the will of Edmond de Goncourt, who with his brother Jules set himself up as an international arbiter of nineteenth-century taste, began turning up in Parke-Bernet promotional material in the Forties and still makes an occasional appearance. It was spared a page to itself in a notable bulletin announcing the Erickson sale.

"My wish," declared Edmond, almost with prescience of Hyam's commercial philosophy, "is that . . . these things of art which have been the joy of my life shall not be consigned to the cold tomb of a museum, and subjected to the stupid glances of the careless passer-by; I desire that they shall be dispersed under the Auctioneer's hammer, so that the pleasure which the acquisition of each one has given me shall be given again, in each case, to some inheritor of my own tastes."

From any salesroom's point of view, the sentiment is admirable, though the Goncourts have their critics nowadays who insist that the precious brothers so intimidated many art lovers with their hauteur that collectors were scared to choose worthwhile works of art which failed to meet with Goncourt approval and settled instead for flotsam and jetsam because Edmond and Jules rather cared for it. Hyam displayed a not unusual degree of sardonic humor in giving the quotation prominent display on an occasion when some museum would almost inevitably finish up as the buyer of "Aristotle" and the paintings could, therefore, not escape being subjected to the "stupid glances of the careless passer-by."

In the war years, Parke and his colleagues saw that a respectable, medium-priced business would have to be developed alongside the more spectacular sales which capture headlines. This presented obvious problems. The sheer plushiness of the galleries' background, which was unblemished, and décor, which ran then as now to velvet on the walls and thick pile on the floors, were obstacles to attracting wider audiences. The difficulty has not yet been entirely overcome.

"Let's face it, there's a certain amount of resistance to coming in here," Hyam said recently in his own austere quarters on the second floor of the present building. "We have a reputation for being rather elegant and expensive. Many smaller people are afraid that things will cost too much, just as they might hesitate about going into Cartier's to buy a piece of smaller jewelry."

Much of the solution proved to be found in the catalogues themselves, Hyam's first and abiding love. After thirty-seven years, he still reads every galley proof of every catalogue, and they are produced at the rate of two a week during the selling season, often running to a hundred pages and more of text and illustrations.

The cataloguing teams, usually working under deadline pressure, strive to be ninety-five per cent accurate in their descriptions of period and subject, including a careful noting of any defects or repair work in the object destined for auction. Hyam's self-imposed task is to give an added turn of the screw and get the figure to ninety-seven per cent, if that is possible. The prose must be alluring as well as imposing and meet reasonable standards of English composition. Outside scholars are called in as consultants to help on obscure attributions.

In the summer of 1962, for example, a "Madonna and Child" by Joos van Cleve ("Flemish: c. 1485–1541") was described as follows:

> The youthful Virgin, her blonde hair covered by a white headcloth and wearing fur-trimmed turquoise blue and rose crimson robes, is seated on an open terrace with an illuminated Book of Psalms on her lap, her finger pointing to the *De Profundis*; her right arm supports the sleeping nude figure of the Child, who

nestles His head against His mother's breast and holds an apple in His hand, a coral bead chain about His neck; before the group on a green-covered table is a glass of wine, a compote of grapes and other fruit, and a cut pomegranate. In the distance is a rocky landscape with tiny figures engaged in agriculture, others walking on village streets, distant travelers near a castle, and a harbor with shipping; partially clouded blue summer sky above. Cradled Panel: 29 x 21½ inches.

Note: This was formerly known as a work of Jan Gossaert (Mabuse), but has been definitely assigned by Friedlander to Joos van Cleve; other compositions by this master illustrated by him show the characteristic arrangements of still life, including the knife and cut pomegranate, found in the present picture. Painted about 1525. . . .

Had the work fallen short of the perfection which Hyam sets for himself, his staff, and anything that goes under the gavel, the catalogue would have said so in a selection of tactful phrases: "some repairs and imperfections" or "has age cracks" or "some discoloration and small chips." In this Madonna's case, no such aspersions could be cast, and a New York dealer, Frederick P. Victoria, was content to pay $40,000 for her.

The degree of accuracy is more than the house's pride and joy. It has made it possible to build up what amounts to a mail-order business, which accounts for between fifteen and twenty per cent of each year's income. Every important dealer and collector in the United States, as well as the cream of the crop overseas, is on the master list, undoubtedly the world's most exclusive compilation of mail-order enthusiasts. For an extra dollar or so, marked up catalogues may be bought, carrying expert estimates of the selling price of each article.

Using one of these as a tool, a collector can write, wire, or telephone in his bid in advance, and the galleries will do the rest. Typically, one California bidder set his price at $1,500 for a Queen Anne sofa consigned by Mrs. Harrison Williams. Bidding at the actual sale halted at $1,050, so the sofa, together with $350 in change, went out to California.

While the catalogues created a mail-order business, Parke-Bernet expanded its curriculum for educating and attracting an ever bigger audience. A vice-presidency in public relations was set up in the person of Miss Mary Vandegrift, who with Carmen Gronau at Sotheby's is the only woman in a similarly exalted spot in the auction-house business. She now sits with Hyam and Louis Marion on the executive committee, which steers the destinies of the firm.

Before a sale, a week-long exhibition is held in the galleries, with staff decorators setting up the rooms as if expecting a joint visit from Mrs. John F. Kennedy and Queen Elizabeth with Emily Post in tow. In advance, every item on display is cleaned, polished, and, if necessary, repaired. The combination of factors—publicity, catalogues, and a free show—brings a couple of thousand sightseers into the galleries on an ordinary Saturday afternoon. For the Erickson display, the total reached a literally overwhelming 7,000, with lines stretching on to the street.

There was no chance of providing extra accommodation for crowds because, to the best of the house's financial ability, that had been done when Parke-Bernet rather sorrowfully departed from 57th Street in 1949. The normal Manhattan urge toward architectural self-destruction sent a 110-foot demolition crane to flatten the old home to make room for a new building. The gallery pulled in its financial belt to construct the world's fanciest auction house at 980 Madison Avenue. The trim four-story white limestone building, whose glass-doored entrance is set appropriately enough between the showrooms of Parke-Bernet's old benefactors, French & Company, and offices of the City Investing Company, would have been even more lavish if the building funds hadn't run dry.

These comparatively new quarters, occupying a whole block front, put every other auction house to shame. Included are a main salesroom, with theatrical lighting effects, air-conditioning, a tiered balcony, and accommodation to seat 600 bidders. Over the outside doors hangs the largest work of sculpture ever to be cast in aluminum, a fourteen-foot-long twosome entitled "Venus and Manhattan"; it was composed by Wheeler Williams, who has explained that the goddess is depicted floating in from across the sea to awaken the sleeping city to "the beauty of art and culture."

Parke-Bernet crews are always ready to desert the splendors of headquarters to conduct a "house sale" on the spot, to liquidate one of the handful of great estates remaining intact in this country. Such excursions afield are rare, partly because the hefty overheads of the business mean that it loses money unless the sale brings in a minimum of $80,000 to $100,000. One of the last turn-of-the-century mansions was gutted by gavel in the summer of 1962. "The Elms," a fifty-one-room "cottage" built in Newport, Rhode Island, in the golden era of the "Four Hundred," hadn't been occupied for two years by its owner, the ninety-five-year-old but apparently imperishable Miss Julia Berwind, before her death in 1961. Louis Marion went up in person with his assistants to knock down more than 600 lots of Gothic, Renaissance, and Chinese art, and Louis XV and XVI furniture. With the previously noted "Madonna and Child" by Joos van Cleve among them, the items fetched a satisfactory $415,292 in a two-day sale.

More usual grist to the mill is the contents of houses disposed of at the galleries themselves. Even there, the demon overhead makes the management try to avoid handling pictures valued at less than $100 apiece, simply because they lose money on them. They have a steady line in what are catalogued as "fine appointments," which London houses do not handle individually—table china, glass, and linens. "These are very lucrative," says Hyam, "and they attract a lot of women."

Unlike its English competitors, Parke-Bernet auctions furs, which are tagged on to jewelry catalogues, and the Madison Avenue house has something of a corner in selling cigar-store Indians; pre-Columbian art objects, made by Indians of a different stamp; and oddments like the canceled checks of Lieut. Colonel John Glenn, which sold in a bundle of the astronaut's correspondence for $425.

For all their efforts and steady gains in business, Leslie Hyam insists that "we are too honest ever to make any money." He likes to cite the stark impossibility of piling up fortunes from a concern whose fixed charges continue for twelve months but whose income-producing season is limited to eight months, from mid-September to mid-May. "We have prestige," he has observed, "but none of us has any wealth."

He has never pretended to "love" his work in the sense of dedication, which is what many collectors understand by the word. "My attitude toward the whole field of art," he said not long ago, "is one of interest rather than passion. I have no particular feelings for ownership. Everything passes through here in a continuous flux. We come into people's lives very often when a marriage is breaking up, or there's a loss of money, or the giving up of a house, or a separation. Perhaps a man is getting old and wants to put his affairs in order, so the property is disposed of for that cause. Here one gets no sense of any permanent ownership. Things pass from one set of hands to another all the time.

"There is no sense of dynastic feeling among most Americans, anyway. Children as a general rule don't want the things that their parents collect. So far as I'm concerned, I've no particular desire to own anything. I have the pleasure of seeing it, and that's enough."

It seems unlikely that the people who work for the house would stay on without some pleasure in their chores. "Nobody would endure what we go through," Hyam has judged, "unless they loved what they were doing, and you can use 'love' in any sense you want. We produce an average of two illustrated books a week, in five working days. Then there is advertising, publicity, exhibitions, cleaning, and everything else. When you produce under these conditions, work is very tough, and it involves a great strain on everybody." He claimed, with good reason, that he was working harder than ten years previously and could see no hope of let-up.

Once in a while, a customer is found whose emotional detachment toward the treasures of the house exceeds his own. One of those treasures was the blue-white diamond necklace, 213.10 carats of it, which established a record up to date in 1957 by bringing the highest price ever paid for a single item at Parke-Bernet: $385,000. It had been owned by Mrs. John E. Rovensky, a four-times married heiress who had inherited considerably more than $50,000,000 and once traded her Fifth Avenue home for two strings of Cartier's pearls.

Mae Caldwell Manwaring Plant Hayward Rovensky's collection of jewels, furniture, and paintings drew an auction audience of some 2,000 people, mostly women who seemed to regard the event as a substitute for a theater matinée. The crowd also craned to see Rocky Marciano, former world heavyweight champion, who carried off two pairs of platinum-and-diamond cuff links for $300, and Margaret Sullavan, the actress, who paid $200 for two gold pins.

It took thirteen separate sales to dispose of all the Rovensky property, for a breathless total of $2,438,980, though attendances dwindled after the big diamond necklace went under the hammer on the first afternoon. "In this business," Leslie Hyam said at the time, "it's easier to sell a $10,000 article for $15,000 than a $200

Mrs. Rovensky: 2,000 came to see the show

article for $200. An ordinary sale is something of a bargain sale. It doesn't matter to the rich that they pay $5,000 more or less for an object."

Bidding for the necklace was opened at $350,000 by a Mrs. B. H. Smith, of Westchester County. Harry Winston, the New York jewel dealer who had previously bought the Hope Diamond in a different venture, jumped in with an offer of $5,000 more. The two contestants saw one bid top another until Winston retired at $375,000 and Mrs. Smith at $380,000. The victorious final $5,000 was bid by a diamond dealer, on behalf of a certain shy businessman who wanted to give his wife a surprise present.

Hurrying home, he opened the velvet-lined box containing the necklace, a bauble some thirty inches in length with a solitaire as big as a pigeon's egg, which had originally cost Mrs. Rovensky's second husband $750,000 in 1917. His wife was overcome by all the dazzle; "staggered" is the word one recorder of the scene has employed. Her reaction surpassed even Leslie Hyam's disdain for ownership.

"I don't know what you mean to do with it," she said, in effect, to her crestfallen husband, "but I won't have that thing in my house."

V

IT DEPENDS WHOSE SIDE YOU'RE ON

RELATIONS between auction galleries and their customers are marked by a loving-hating ambivalence, since a gallery's livelihood depends on turnover, while collectors, curators, and connoisseurs are commonly concerned with keeping the pick of the market out of circulation by hanging it in homes or museums. For the most part, the unavoidable clash of interests is concealed in a comedy of manners; at the tap of a gavel, auctioneers pretend they are art lovers and art lovers feign to be businessmen.

In their relations with each other, however, rival galleries make no pretence of love. They are engaged in a business where competition is as naked as between Clipper ships racing home from Cathay. The Clipper captains had one advantage in that a lot of tea grew in China, but auction-house commodores face the unhappy fact that, while the habit of buying paintings spreads, the availability of first-quality pictures gets scantier all the time.

The tea trade was a transpacific contest; the art trade is a transatlantic affair. Some of the biggest prizes are the paintings which the galleries endeavor to pry from United States collections assembled in the earlier days of the century, when the Duveen brothers had established a mighty American market, with the Mellons, Wideners, Kresses, Huntingtons, Altmans, Fricks, and their emulators pushing up prices. Together, they gathered up billions of dollars' worth of Europe's choicest works because they had the most money to spend. Now that the salesrooms on both sides of the ocean compete to get the treasures out in the open for sale again, the bumping that goes on between them in the race would curl a yachtsman's hair.

Since many of the trophies likely to become available are to be found in the United States, Parke-Bernet finds itself engaged in a defensive action against the incursions of Christie's and, more notably, Sotheby's, which is the wilier, more aggressive invader. "Money" is the battle cry on both sides.

The American house's argument runs, "It is Americans who buy the important paintings and set the prices. Where's the sense in shipping pictures to London when they only have to be shipped home again?"

Both Peter Wilson and I. O. Chance have set up field headquarters in New York to carry their campaigns deep into Hyam's territory. Wilson appointed Mr. Peregrine Pollen as his commander-in-chief in the North American theater of operations "for the greater convenience of our increasing number of American clients." Pollen and his staff are stationed in a building on Fifth Avenue at 56th Street, primed at the ring of the telephone or doorbell to give "advice to intending buyers or sellers, specimen catalogues, information on forthcoming sales, and assistance to consigners with arrangements for shipping and insurance." The overall impression is that they will, in fact, do anything but paint the pictures, though they would certainly be happy to take care of the framing, or travel anywhere between Cape Cod and Carmel to "advise executors or owners of important property."

Chance's American strategist is Robert M. Leylan, who, all bustle and business, has established his command post in the heart of art-dealer country on East 57th Street. Like Pollen, he too mails out catalogues all over the American continent, handles the transmission of any bids to London, and roams the country, smelling out material for auction.

"This is a slugging, highly competitive business," he has reported. "There's an increasing scarcity of first-rate works." In one eight-month period, he visited twenty-five American and Canadian cities looking at collections and single objects that just might be put up on the block.

Leslie Hyam, confronting his foes on several sectors, long ago concluded that the only defense was attack, and attack with audacity. In many cases, he is ready to acknowledge that Parke-Bernet commissions are higher than its competitors', but he refuses to interpret the size of the commission as the all-important factor. What matters far more, he insists, is the size of the selling price, the final bid, the net return to the owner.

"Parke-Bernet," he has explained, "has never advertised a standard rate for its services for the simple reason that its charges are, and always have been, flexible, and are based on the value and character of the property offered, and the type of presentation required to reach the maximum buying power. As an example, sales running into seven figures and paintings and works of art of top importance have been taken here as low as twelve per cent."

Christie's brand of salesmanship is more generalized, gentlemanly, and historical by comparison with Parke-Bernet's coolly arithmetical arguments and Sotheby's neon-lit hucksstering. The "oldest fine-art auctioneers in the world" attempt to coax works of art out of America by depicting the attractions of London as a whole, rather like the British Travel Association, apparently resigned to the fact that Sotheby's in 1962 was leading the field but confident that Christie's would get its more modest share of any business that could be lured across the Atlantic.

John Herbert, who is a son of Sir Alan Herbert, M.P., and a former newspaper and public-relations man, is Christie's press officer. He has claimed unequivocally, "London is the undisputed centre of the international art market." And citing a bit of the past to support his point, he added, "Although it is only recently that London has again dominated the art market, many people forget that it has been an important center for over 150 years—ever since, in fact, the French Revolution. Up till 1789, Paris was the centre of this market, but with the fall of the monarchy, it shifted to London."

Herbert considers that two lesser reasons and a major one brought about this turn of good fortune. One minor reason is London's geographical closeness to Europe and convenience as a take-off point for transatlantic travel. The second is "the knowledge which its auction-house experts have acquired during the past 150 years." But the real persuader is acknowledged by Herbert and everybody else in the business to be London's low commission rate, amounting to "approximately half what is demanded in America and France," in Herbert's calculations.

The British rate, nominally a standardized one, used to be seven and one-half per cent, but it is up to ten on all sales other than coins and medals (twelve and one-half per cent) and a fifteen per cent category which includes books, manuscripts, autograph letters, engravings and etchings, Japanese works of art and prints, and Oriental miniatures. French charges are on a sliding scale, from sixteen per cent to twenty-one per cent. In America, according to Christie's publicity, the basic rate is fifteen per cent, though the report is spread in the battle for business that New York rates run as high as twenty-three and one-half. "It pays to sell in London" is a kind of war chant, if "chant" is a word applicable to the soft-spoken seductions of Christie's staff.

Sotheby's technique is to let their more gentlemanly British rivals stick to this institutional line of sales talk, while Peter Wilson does his best to spread the image of his establishment as the one real topdrawer, upper-crust place on earth for anybody with anything worth selling. "In recent years," he used to claim repeatedly before the Erickson sale, "all the most important sales of paintings have been at Sotheby's."

Both companies of invaders push hard for dollars, spelling out in simple prose what in less rarified circles would be termed the "sales pitch." London, claims a Christie brochure, is "the best place both to buy and sell works of art. So much so that it pays collectors to fly their treasures here from all over the world. Every year, works of art worth approximately £5,000,000 are imported into Britain specially to be sold on the London market and later exported. This is a measure of its dominance of the international art market."

Taking careful aim at Parke-Bernet, John Herbert has pointed out, "There is a three per cent sales tax in New York and a ten per cent Federal sales tax on certain kinds of goods."

Peter Wilson's battalions wage much the same kind of campaign, pointing out with artful pomposity in promotional literature that the firm "may" receive the raw material for auction sales "from any country, including the U.S.A."; that Sotheby's directors more or less commute across the intervening ocean "both to advise clients and to keep in touch with the trends of collecting." With Parke-Bernet as the clear target once again, the London house "begs leave to remind all overseas clients who wish to take advantage of the high and stable prices, the low commission rates, and the expert presentation of fine material" about a few facts of competitive life.

"There is," runs the Sotheby chorus, "NO import duty on works of art of any kind over 100 years old coming into Britain (only a certificate of antiquity is required); nor on pictures or books of any date. There is NO government or any other tax (as in some Continental countries) on sales by auction. There is NO export duty out of the United States."

Since the auctioning of everything, no matter what sentiments are stirred in buyer or seller, is essentially a hard-cash business, Wilson's copywriters state specifically, "Payments of the proceeds of sale in London can be made, without formalities or delay, in any currency (including U.S. dollars), or in sterling, as desired."

A marked difference in sale prices achieved in the two countries could obviously bring the seller much more than the difference between the two countries' commission rates, if Parke-Bernet arguments are valid. The results of sales, says Hyam, show that the highest market is in New York. "The idea that sellers get higher prices in London is British propaganda. With relatively few exceptions, the outstanding works offered here have gone to American buyers."

The British invasion started on a big scale in December, 1953. For the previous fourteen years, war conditions and continuing peacetime austerity had seen the flow of money into and out of Britain tightly controlled by the government. Dollars could be spent overseas only for essential merchandise, like guns and then butter, not for works of art. During that somber era, virtually no American property reached the London houses, since the sellers could not receive dollars, no matter what they consigned.

Then the London salesrooms, through connections within the British Treasury, succeeded in getting currency restrictions eased. Imported works of art and antiques could again be paid for in dollars if they arrived from the United States, or in the currency of whatever was their country origin. The Treasury later took a further step and provided for sellers to be paid in the coin of any country they chose, so long as they obtained Bank of England permission in advance. The bank discovered, incidentally, that Swiss francs were as much desired by some art lovers as by some Hollywood motion-picture stars, and for precisely the same reason.

The government's help for the London auction houses was scarcely an act of artistic altruism. The sales bring into the country a considerable amount of foreign exchange every year. Any overseas seller who consigns works for sale in London is sure to leave behind him at least ten per cent of the total price. The present phenomenon of constantly rising prices has brought prosperity not only to the auction houses over there, but also to the tax collectors, who take a big bite out of the profits.

The British internal revenue authorities indirectly render an enormous service by ensuring a steady supply of material to go under the hammer. Death and taxes have always been the invisible partners of the auctioneers, but never to such an extent as in this generation and never more effectively than among the British nobility and landed gentry. The cost of fighting two world wars increased British income taxes and death duties almost to the confiscatory level under a succession of governments, left-wing, right and center. Simply to raise money to pay the government, great estates and collections have been broken up, and the situation continues. From the Duke of Buckingham's sale in 1848 to the Duke of Westminster's sale in 1959, Sotheby's and Christie's witnessed the slightly mournful but profitable spectacle of aristocratic sales of necessity, the scattering of works of art which more prosperous ancestors began commissioning and accumulating three and four centuries ago.

A compilation which Christie's made not long ago of its achievements in the years following the end of the Second World War reads like Debrett's *Guide to the Peerage* in its listing of customers. Without implying that they were anywhere close to the poorhouse, the names of consignors included the Duke of Devonshire, the Earl of Guildford, Lord Swaythling, the Earl of Lonsdale, the Earl of Cadogan, the Earl of Wemyss and March, Earl Fitzwilliam, the Earl of Southesk, Kathleen, Duchess of Newcastle, the Earl of Shaftesbury, and even some items forwarded to the block by the Princess Royal and her husband, the Earl of Harewood.

A single season at Sotheby's—October, 1960, to July, 1961—provided much the same story, with names running from Lady Anne Rhys to the Duke of Leeds, the Viscountess Hudson, Lord Fairfax of Cameron, Lady Hague, the Earl of Shrewsbury, the Earl of Powis, and the Duke of Wellington.

Since even dukes are dazzled by the prices which the London *Times* faithfully reports, the noblemen and their executors would far rather consign their stuff to the block than to a dealer. One probable reason is that it is a dealer's business to know exactly what he is buying, whereas the consignor is not nearly as knowledgeable about what he has to sell. The auction process puts buyer and seller on much more level terms.

When a British estate is being broken up for whatever reason, the things almost inevitably gravitate toward Christie, Manson & Woods, or Sotheby & Company. Parke-Bernet's chances of picking up in Britain any of these fabulous crumbs from formerly rich men's tables are close to zero. "There is not much attraction for people to send their things from Britain to us," Hyam, a realist to the fingertips,

The National Gallery, Trafalgar Square, London

has noted. "We charge higher commission rates, generally speaking. We have only a limited reserves system. Added to that the cost of transportation and the disadvantages of having your things sold three thousand miles away. There is no reason why we should get this business."

The American gallery, steadfastly refusing to ape its British rivals except where economics force it to, has no London representative. It does, however, maintain a man in Zurich, Switzerland, and advertises its services widely in Continental publications, with the effect of producing "hundreds of inquiries" each year.

It is, perhaps, just as well that Hyam keeps no operative stationed in London. The fellow's presence might serve only to inflame chauvinistic sentiments among some already critical sections of the population. Ignoring the fact that the British salesroom business is a $60,000,000 market weighted in their countrymen's favor, they cling to the belief that art sales are really legalized robbery of the nation's inheritance, a one-way export which travels only westward over the Atlantic.

Victorian England gave very little thought to the question of its inheritance being depleted until some of the big agricultural estates began to feel the financial strain in the Eighties and the Duke of Marlborough found he was compelled to sell off paintings from his Blenheim Palace collection. The American millionaires hadn't entered the market place *en masse* in those days, so the Rothschilds, the Metropolitan Museum of New York, and the Kaiser Friedrich Museum in Berlin could be blamed for mopping up much of the treasure that slowly began to trickle out of the palaces, castles, and manor houses.

The German government of the day planked down some $45,000 for one bit of loot which had been identified by their experts as a hollow wax bust, "Flora," by Leonardo. She proved to have a recorded history dating back to an English retail shop in Southampton, where she was bought for $12.50 at today's prices. Within her bosom was further evidence of her origins—"the quilted early Victorian waistcoat of her maker, Richard Cockle Lucas."

The dismay with which English connoisseurs saw American collectors carry off millions of dollars' worth of "British" paintings in the Twenties is reflected today in the existence of a governmental watchdog committee commissioned to supervise the export of works of art whose loss would, in the official word, be a "misfortune" to the nation. Any collector or dealer from the United States or elsewhere overseas needs permission to take out of the country any important paintings which he has bought whether privately or at auction. This may be considered as an intangible asset in Parke-Bernet's favor; it sometimes has the effect of interfering with the free flow of trade in the arts, letting the finest work find its way to where the most money is, which is something the American gallery does its best to foster.

The committee has the power to turn down the overseas purchaser's application and to make a special government grant to enable, say, the National Gallery in London to buy back the picture at whatever the new owner paid for it. The watchdog attitude to guarding Britain's treasures cost Sotheby's a chance in the summer of 1962 to surpass Parke-Bernet's record for getting the world's highest single auction price for a painting.

The trustees of the Royal Academy of Arts selected Peter Wilson and his men to sell a preliminary charcoal drawing—a "cartoon" in the experts' vocabulary— by Leonardo da Vinci of "The Virgin and Child with St. John the Baptist and St. Anne." It is a full-scale study, 55 by 40 inches, for the painting now in the Louvre, believed by British experts to be the only remaining sketch of the many which Leonardo prepared for his major works. It was, according to the perhaps biased Academicians, "the most famous work of art ever to be offered at auction," though one ironic Laborite Member of Parliament, who got into the squabble later, pointed out that the Academy had rarely bothered to show it to the public for nearly two hundred years, and "neither the art world nor the public had taken the slightest interest in the work."

Nevertheless, Wilson leapt at the chance to put it under his gavel, and a national guessing game immediately got under way to estimate just how much the cartoon would fetch. The sky appeared to be the limit. The only Leonardo painting which the British National Gallery owns was picked up at almost fire-sale rates in 1897, when the Earl of Suffolk let his "Virgin of the Rocks" go for £9,000. But as long ago as 1913, Tsar Nicholas of Russia had come up with $1,500,000 for Leonardo's "Madonna."

Some hopefuls guessed that the cartoon would make at least as much as the

"The Virgin and Child, with St. John the Baptist and St. Anne"

"Madonna," taking into account the inflated market. Sir Charles Wheeler, president of the Academy and decidedly opposed to the whole contemplated procedure, reported that "much more" than $2,800,000 would be bid by several galleries "from one continent alone," which could mean only the United States.

The Academy made it clear that the cartoon was on sale not for want of patriotism but for lack of ready money to keep the place going. "It is our intention never to seek government aid," said Sir Charles, in the manner of a poor but proud relation of a *nouveau riche* tycoon. Within hours of the announcement of the impending sale, a money-raising appeal was in the making to keep the cartoon off Sotheby's block and safe in its adoptive homeland. It was led by the National Art Collections Fund, a voluntary organization which has been buying works of art for the nation since 1903, when the transatlantic trade was warming up. The Academy set a healthy figure of $2,240,000 as the price it wanted and hung the cartoon for all to see in an effort to stimulate public contributions. A date four months ahead was set as the deadline for the cash to be deposited in the collection boxes placed conveniently about. Otherwise, Sotheby's would get the Leonardo after all.

Members of the Fund voted to contribute the first $140,000 and later promised another donation of equal size. The Bank of England, showing itself concerned with retaining the drawing but not unduly so, forked out $2,800, while the collecting boxes pulled in $62,000.

The slow progress made toward the needed total got Sir Charles's dander up again. Britain, he declared in an after-dinner speech, probably did not deserve to keep the sketch. "If it does not, then let it go to America, or where it will, if there is a livelier care for beauty and a less unpolished pride in things of the mind."

The deadline was reached with only a little more than half the Academy's reserve price in the till when Prime Minister Harold Macmillan stepped into the scene to praise "one of the most beautiful things in the world" and to promise to make up the balance to keep the "Virgin" out of American hands. Sir Charles allowed that an auction would have brought in more money but expressed himself pleased, anyway. Parke-Bernet could breathe a sigh of relief that their archcompetitors would have to await another day before they could hope to catch up in the selling race.

While the British government in almost every case but this has proved to be on the side of the London salesrooms, the American gallery is not so well served by Washington. There are times when Leslie Hyam feels that his greatest competitor is Uncle Sam, who has always been a fickle ally at best. The London trade, for example, received immeasurable assistance in 1909, when the U. S. Government repealed a twenty per cent tariff on imported works of art, making a probably vital concession to the American millionaire market and starting a gigantic boom in the prices of all kinds of paintings which captured a tycoon's fancy, especially the English eighteenth-century school.

But Parke-Bernet in the business sense is concerned about the present, not the past. The sharpest thorn in its flank is a Federal tax regulation which paradoxically allows people to give things away and yet keep them. The Revenue Code of 1954 is the cause of the pain. It decrees that gifts to museums and galleries may be deducted from the donor's tax liabilities up to thirty per cent of his income. It allows the taxpayer to retain what is called a "life interest" in the deductible gift, meaning that he can hand over to a museum a picture which he may nonetheless keep hanging in his home until his death.

The result is that, consciously or not, Washington applies constant pressure upon the wealthy to endow museums with their most valuable works, and a picture donated to a museum is as good as lost to an auction house. The flow of the very essence of the art auctioneer's profession is siphoned off from the market. Worse than that—from the auctioneer's point of view—present tax laws not infrequently create a situation where it pays a man to give away works of art rather than sell them.

The senior partner of a firm whose business was the importing and selling of Persian and Chinese works came to Parke-Bernet a few years ago. He explained that now he had reached retirement age and the company had been dissolved, he had received a large portion of its stock, mostly Persian miniatures, rugs, and pottery. Would the gallery auction it for him?

Examination showed it to be a good, small collection, big enough to comprise a sale of its own. The house replied that it would be delighted to handle such a consignment, and the old gentleman, whose income put him in the eighty-five percent tax bracket, went off happily to have his accountant make the necessary arrangements. When he returned two weeks later, he brought the dire news that the tax expert had advised him to give the things away. An Eastern university was surprised to find itself in possession of the lot.

Exactly how in this topsy-turvy situation it can pay anyone to donate instead of sell was spelled out recently in *The New York Times,* which used as a hypothetical example a painting bought for $10,000 in the Thirties which had now acquired a market value of $145,000. Should the owner sell at that price, he would be charged a capital-gains tax of twenty-five per cent on his $135,000 profit. This payment to the Income Tax Bureau of $33,750 would leave him with a net gain of $101,250.

On the contrary, assume that he gave the painting to a museum, which established the fair market price at $145,000. If he were in the maximum bracket, the "averaging-out" provisions of tax law would set his peak payment rate at 87 per cent. The tax saving on $145,000 at eighty-seven per cent would be $126,150. Reducing this, the owner (or more probably his accountants) would have to subtract the original purchase price of $10,000, leaving him with a gain on paper of $116,150 on the transaction, which would leave him the lifetime enjoyment of his picture, even though he no longer owned title to it.

"Thus," *The Times* summed up patly, "the difference between giving the painting away ($116,150) and selling it ($101,250) would represent an advantage to the seller of $14,900."

Hyam, charitable to a degree, has never assumed that there is a conscious Federal effort to make life difficult for his calling. "The philosophy of the government is hard to determine," he has said, "but you can't have confiscatory tax rates and hope to survive. When you put those rates up to ninety-one per cent for political reasons to appease the proletarians, then you have to establish some loopholes to make the system workable. You have to provide a capital-gains tax of twenty-five per cent, expense allowances, and donation allowances so that the rich can continue to live and support all those industries which are dependent upon them including, if you like, ourselves."

Other taxes, Federal and state and city, impose a further burden on an American operation, increasing the total price of an object without benefit to the seller. For example, Federal excise tax is imposed upon clocks and such items of interior decoration as fall within the legal definitions of jewelry. Sales taxes imposed by numerous cities, including New York, and states add more percentage points to the bill the purchaser is compelled to foot. The British houses, naturally, do not restrain themselves when it comes to spreading the word of the surcharges.

Hyam's beloved catalogues are the artillery with which he counters the invasion of what he regards professionally as his native territory. The detail which he packs into their pages comprises a kind of do-it-yourself kit for would-be collectors. With these documents to guide them, it is possible—theoretically, at least—for any reasonably perceptive individual to bid intelligently in person or by mail for any object which interests him. It is a calculated policy on the American side to convert auctioneering into something approaching a democracy, with the word employed here in the sense of sovereign rights residing in the customers.

The European tradition, on the other hand, is to maintain the business as an oligarchy, serving the dealers primarily rather than the buying public. London methods put maximum power in the hands of what is called "the trade"—the middlemen. A newcomer to the British salesrooms is apt to be as much intimidated as impressed by the jumble of dusty merchandise which passes for an exhibition. It is harder for him to form intelligent judgments about, say, a needlepoint rug when it's rolled up like a discard from grandmother's attic, or to decide whether a grimy parquetry table is worth ten guineas or a thousand.

The tyro may well distrust his own eyes and turn to an expert for advice, and that will probably be a dealer. The well-scrubbed Parke-Bernet look is ostensibly designed to show the objects at their best and allow a potential customer to see, clean and clear, whatever it is he hopes to buy.

The "warts and all" approach to cataloguing, listing defects as carefully as the blood lines of a piece, is calculated to instill a customer's confidence in his own judgment. The British catalogues, which pay less attention to anything but obvious flaws, work to the advantage of the dealers, whose advice is likely to be sought by the cautious customer, much as you might take along a knowledgeable mechanic before investing in a secondhand car.

There is one long-established practice in British cataloguing which may be regarded either as a charming bit of tradition or a cabalistic code for experts, depending on which side of the Atlantic is being heard from. It works like this: If a painting is considered beyond question to be by, for example, Reynolds, then it is listed as by "Sir Joshua Reynolds RA (Royal Academy)." Should it be judged a near-Reynolds, or a Reynolds within reasonable probability, the catalogues trim their description of its creator to Sir Joshua Reynolds. When the odds increase further against it, then the cataloguers call whoever painted it simply and brusquely "Reynolds."

The practice irks Hyam both as a man of science and as a champion, for good commercial reasons, of the apprentice collector. Precision in attribution is something of a fetish with him. "If you go back to the Greek vases of the fifth century," he observed icily of his overseas competitors, "they will tell you that a particular vase was made in 480 B.C. In the case of a piece of Italian majolica, they will say it can be dated to the early sixteenth century. But take a piece of Worcester porcelain, which can be accurately dated within five years, and their catalogues will contain no date at all on it."

He made this particular point not so long ago to Peter Wilson in one notable face-to-face encounter. "Why do you persist in a procedure for which there's no logic?" Hyam asked. Wilson shrugged his shoulders.

"Everybody knows when this Worcester was made," he replied loftily. "We don't date it for that reason."

The American team regards Wilson and Sotheby's if not with approbation then with a certain fatalistic respect. The British operate with a mixture of cool dash and blazing determination that makes them dangerous opponents. They take advantage of their lower overheads—an English salesroom porter earns roughly $30 a week, his New York counterpart close to three times as much; printing, rents, and similar costs are proportionately higher in the United States, too. They undercut their advertised ten per cent if necessary to clinch a consignment. They have been accused by some disgruntled customers of underestimating their supplementary charges and overestimating their valuations of property in order to snag it for sale in London.

These accusations are made by the Americans in a spirit of forbearance, as though nothing more than is to be expected under cut-throat competition. What does rankle with the American team is the fact that in 1957 Sotheby's got off to a flying start in its postwar race to riches with a sale of paintings, the Wilhelm Weinberg collection, which Parke-Bernet had counted on as its own. This event, which put the Sotheby name on the front pages of newspaper on both sides of the ocean, must be credited to a prominent New York insurance broker, John Goldschmidt, who persuaded the executors to send the collection to London. "The sale got away from us, much to our astonishment and chagrin," Hyam acknowledged later.

Goldschmidt administered a second dose of the same unpalatable medicine the following year. He was instrumental again in steering across to Sotheby's the seven paintings from the estate of his father, Jakob, which brought $2,186,800 under Peter Wilson's gavel. Parke-Bernet was as chagrined as before, but this time not surprised.

In the tense, ultra-nationalistic world of the auction houses, such acts are regarded as flagrant disloyalty. Professional pride, prestige, and profits suffer in about equal measure. Neither side in the continuing transatlantic struggle enjoys brooding over its defeats. So, while Wilson likes to talk about Weinberg and Goldschmidt, Hyam prefers to mention "Aristotle." And Wilson undoubtedly hopes that someday the Royal Academicians will decide to unload something else along the lines of the Leonardo cartoon, and Hyam fervently trusts that they will not.

Like buccaneers after galleon gold, the unquenchable British made two important raids across the Atlantic in 1963 to singe the beards of U.S. auctioneers, once to gather a collection of rare manuscripts, the second to carry off booty comprising porcelain, paintings, and furniture.

Seemingly won over by Peter Wilson's reputation, the American Academy of Arts and Letters handed over for Sotheby's auction a load of material that had been sitting in the Library of Congress for twelve years, amounting to what the Library termed "a discriminating assemblage of letters penned by most of the major nineteenth-century American and British authors." No American house got a chance even to make an offer on this lot, though sixty per cent of it was Americana, which nobody in Britain or Europe collects seriously. There were letters involving Edgar Allan Poe, Washington Irving, Nathaniel Hawthorne; there was other correspondence signed by Presidents of the United States, including a note by George Washington.

The American auctioneers did not have to cry "foul!" in this case. The outcry was raised by collectors and dealers in New York, who wondered what was the point in shipping to London material that would inevitably be bought by Americans and returned to its native land.

The second British victory brought Sotheby's a $2,000,000 cargo, delivered by air freight, of treasure formerly owned by Réne Fribourg, a Belgian-born grain merchant who stuffed his town house on 84th Street in Manhattan with an incredible amount of stuff, ranging from the marriage bed custom-made for Napoleon at the time he took Marie Louise as his wife in 1810, down to seventy gold snuffboxes, which Fribourg treated more like matchboxes, spotting them casually through the five floors of his home.

Peter Wilson kept close tabs on the millionaire merchant before he died at the age of 82 in January, 1963. "I'd visited Mr. Fribourg perhaps a half dozen times," Wilson explained magnanimously after he had picked up the assignment. "He adored talking about his collection, not to people who were simply interested in how much each piece cost, but to those who liked the items for their own sake."

To the auctioneer who was at least partially interested in what the items had originally been bought for, Fribourg confided that one of his regrets about dying would be that it would effectively prevent him from seeing his pieces go under the hammer. "He liked to discuss the sale, though," Wilson told a reporter. "He said he thought it would be a notable one."

The invader from London joined in the customary scramble that followed the collector's death. Wilson comfortably beat out Parke-Bernet, Christie's and Maurice Rheims, from France. The booty was flown off to London, to await the sale in storage down in the already crowded Sotheby cellars, and Wilson came as close to rubbing his hands with glee as ever before in his well-disciplined life.

Had his house won the job by cutting its rates? Wilson denied it. "If you went to one doctor who said his fee was $100, another who said it was $50, and a third who said it was $10, you wouldn't necessarily go to the $10 man," he declared. "You'd go to the one you thought would cure you."

VI

THE OTHER END OF THE SEESAW

I^{T} is possible to make out the general shape of the art market and the growth of auctioneering over the last fifty years simply by using as survey points the three highest-priced painting sales recorded during that period. The comparative real costs of the three are open to debate, but the chronological sequence amounts to an abbreviated history of relations between dealers, buyers, and auctioneers.

It starts with what may be the most expensive picture of all time, the Leonardo "Madonna," sometimes called "The Blue Madonna," of the Benois family, which was found in Astrakhan in 1824. The king of all dealers, Joseph Duveen, had it ready and waiting in Paris for sale to Henry Clay Frick when Tsar Nicholas II stepped in to seize it as a Russian art treasure under a code of proprietorship which in one form or another has been exercised since Roman days. The Leonardo cost him $1,500,000, which would have to be increased to something like $5,000,000 in terms of today's money, and it provided one of the few defeats that Duveen ever suffered. Fifteen years later a syndicate of New York practitioners of his craft had an opportunity to lay hold of the "Madonna" again, this time from its Bolshevik proprietors, but they muffed it, as will be seen.

The second crucial painting was Raphael's "Alba Madonna," which was acquired from the Soviets on behalf of Andrew Mellon, though he breathed not a word for nearly four years after paying $1,166,400 for it—about $2,303,847 in present-day funds. It was a dealers' triumph, specifically for M. Knoedler & Company, whose representatives went to Leningrad for the affair.

By the time "Aristotle" was sold, it was not a firm of dealers but an auction house which reaped the glory. Times had changed in the marts of art, and the dealers were having a spell on the "down" end of the seesaw, sneering at the auctioneers on the "up" end and occasionally shaking a fist at them.

Dealers, though temporarily in second place in publicized victories, continue in business more or less as usual, a colorful band which ranges in dependability from outright sharks to distinguished scholars. To look at, they are astonishingly alike, running to slim moustaches, waisted jackets, well-shined shoes, and boutonnières for gala occasions.

As always, a few of them victimize and a lot of them subsidize their artists. Some pursue their affairs on the borderline between sharp practice and larceny; others regard price manipulating, extortion, and the promotion of junk as commercial necessities. A few of them are shabby peddlers, but many are merchants who conduct themselves with the air of princes, set up in elegant galleries where strangers tread with awe, even rich ones. For all their decline in popular prestige, none of them has apparently felt hardships such as were suffered by Jean François Millet, for instance, who starved for days on end; or Jean Louis Géricault, who was forced to trade his "Cuirassier" for nothing more than a fresh canvas on which to paint; or Alfred Sisley, who died in poverty in 1899, sixty-two years before his "Spring Near Moret" sold in Paris for $53,686; or Modigliani, who on a bitter winter morning exchanged an armful of new pictures for a dealer's tweed coat.

Dealers have helped to stock most of the public museums and private collections in the world today, and it would be unimaginable to believe that their day is over. Their sun came up in the late nineteenth and early twentieth centuries just as it dawned on the Impressionist and Post-Impressionist schools, and they made fortunes. There was young Ambroise Vollard, who at his little shop on the Rue Lafitte, Paris, would take in only paintings by the new generation, Gauguin, Redon, Guillaumin—and Sisley. Vollard's instinct for the future prompted him to trail Cézanne to Provence and gather his pictures for a handful of francs.

Some other merchants in art had equal influence but less one-sided luck. The father and son, Jean-Marie and Paul Durand-Ruel, have to be reckoned among the founders of modern art collecting. They drove themselves to the brink of bankruptcy to finance unknown artists when the public, the press, and fellow dealers were joined in a common effort to put them out of business. Paul, in the phrase of a fellow Frenchman, the auctioneer Maurice Rheims, was "in turn a father confessor, banker, and adviser to his painters." Those painters comprised the best of the Impressionist school—Corot, Manet, Monet, Pissarro, Renoir, Degas. Rheims had access to the firm's records, which show that emergent artists were encouraged with cash as well as kind words. In 1872, for instance, Monet received 10,800,000 francs, Pissarro 4,800,000, Renoir 400,000.

Payments continued fairly steadily until 1884, when the lean years set in.

Paul Durand-Ruel owed over 1,000,000 francs, and fellow dealers, demonstrating an instinctive reaching for the jugular, threatened to break him by throwing into the Hôtel Drouot every Impressionist painting they could scrape up for sale, without frames, at knock-down prices. But the firm survived to fight again, to start a New York gallery two years after and, spasmodically, to prosper when the boom in the Impressionists got under way at the turn of the century.

Renoir, whose portrait of Paul Durand-Ruel's daughters sold in Manhattan for $195,000 a year or so ago as befitting his rank as a salesroom status symbol, grew worried by his new success. He could never believe that any painting was worth more than $1,400, and he wrote to his dealer friend, "Inevitably there is a slump coming . . . At present there is too much worthless stuff being produced." That was in 1908. When Durand-Ruel died in 1921, he left little money but a legacy of 1,500 pictures.

The millionaire market in the United States was discovered and then excavated by European dealers who behaved like Forty-niners hurrying toward the Klondike. Durand-Ruel organized a traveling show of his Renoirs and Pissarros before he opened his New York quarters. Michel Knoedler, a dandy from Paris, got in three years ahead of the excitement at Sutter's Mill and founded the Manhattan business which still bears his name at the time when President Polk was deciding to wage war on Mexico. A few years later, Michel had managed to sell one picture for $300, which seemed such an astronomical price that he wrote home to say he doubted whether he could ever do as well again. A grandson of his, Charles Henschel, as head of the firm, played one of the leads in the drama which climaxed the golden era of the dealers, the purchase of the Raphael "Madonna" and thirty-six other Hermitage paintings from the Soviet Government for $12,000,000, the greatest coup that a dealer ever knew.

In the decade before the First World War, New York became a paradise of rich customers with insatiable desire, limited knowledge, and bottomless bank accounts. Following the lead of Knoedler and Durand-Ruel, Duveen Brothers hurried down from their original scene of operations in Boston. Nathan Wildenstein, with an Alsatian-German accent as impenetrable as sauerkraut, who launched himself in Paris by buying a Boucher for 200 francs and selling it for 20,000, opened a Manhattan branch. In 1905, gimlet-eyed Jacques Seligmann made up his mind to visit New York after he had exchanged some hot words with J. P. Morgan in his Paris hotel suite. His son, Germain, who continues the business after dropping the final "n" from the spelling of the family name, tells the story.

The monolithic Mr. Morgan stopped by Seligmann's gallery and decided to buy a fine eighteenth-century German porcelain called "Sylvie," representing a shepherd boy creeping up on an unsuspecting nymph. Morgan gave instructions for the piece to be delivered to him at the Hotel Bristol, where his check was also to be collected, since he was on the point of sailing home. Seligmann, who had met Morgan for the first time that afternoon, took the package himself, curious for a second look at the mighty American. He was nonplussed to find the foyer of the suite crowded with competitive dealers, several of them carrying packages like his under their arms. After a long wait, he was ushered into the presence.

Seligmann's pride, already bruised, suffered another drubbing when Morgan announced his decision that "Sylvie" was "not what he had supposed it to be and he no longer wanted it." The dealer agreed to cancel the sale on one condition—he must know whether there was any doubt about the porcelain's authenticity or merely a change of heart on Morgan's part. A look of thunder came on the tycoon's face. Pounding a table, he roared that it was none of Seligmann's business. But the dealer was not to be silenced. Morgan would never succeed as a collector, he said, if he consulted half a dozen people about every purchase; that only encouraged dealers to conspire against him and arrange commissions between themselves. The billionaire heard him out, but he would not change his mind.

"Mr. Morgan," said Seligmann, as quoted by his son, "I will see you shortly in New York and prove to you that you have been misled, but not by me." Before he carried out his promise and caught a boat, he visited a succession of experts, to obtain their written confirmation of the piece's authenticity and merit. Soon after he landed in New York, he made a present of "Sylvie" to the Metropolitan, whose recently elected president was John Pierpont Morgan himself. The great man liked the courage of Seligmann, who found he had landed a whale-sized American client; he subsequently became the consultant upon whom Morgan leaned most heavily in his advancing years.

From a dealer's point of view, Andrew Mellon was a tougher nut to crack. His blood ran cooler, his suspicions of everything and everybody lasted longer, and his opinions of dealers were even more critical. Asked once how he had acquired the paintings that stir the souls of men, he replied with unusual loquacity: "I was buying my pictures from a little dealer (I think his name was Duveen, but it may have been Knoedler or somebody else) and I discovered that the little dealer was borrowing money from a bank to secure pictures to sell to me, so I bought the bank. Most of the paintings from Russian sources were obtained by telephone. I ordered my broker to buy when the exchange was favorable."

It took the efforts of a number of "little dealers" to pull off the Hermitage purchase. The door may have been opened by a firm, Armand and Victor Hammer, which had nothing to do with the ultimate victory. Their original purpose in the chaotic U.S.S.R. had to do with medical relief, not art.

Armand, a doctor, was already there in 1922 when his brother Victor left Princeton to join him. Victor, a muscular, energetic little man who nowadays conducts an elegant East 57th Street gallery which, among its other enticements, is wired for the lulling sounds of Muzak, was reminiscing recently about those distant days. The brothers concluded that post-revolutionary Russia needed food more than medicine, and, by Victor's account, Armand closed a deal with Lenin. In return for one million bushels of wheat, the Hammers were given control of an asbestos mine in the Ural Mountains. With this as a mainstay, they started an import-export business, including among their customers the Ford Motor Company and United States Rubber.

The Hermitage, Leningrad, a treasure house of Bolshevik Baroque

Within a year or so, the Soviet government concluded that the Hammers' affairs were prospering too well to be left in private hands. The brothers found themselves squeezed out, and under new Party management, their business was transformed into Amtorg, the Russian trading commission. Lenin had a suggestion for the dispossessed proprietors: why not turn to manufacturing pencils, which were a sure-fire item in Moscow's attack on illiteracy?

Victor and Armand recognized a strong hint when they heard one. The rubles flowed in again for them, but any other currency was in exceedingly short supply. "We lived like kings," Victor remembered, "in a twenty-four-room house with eight servants." To do something with their money, they invested in objects of art, of which there was an abundance as the usual consequence of war and disruption. They were officially warned, however, that because they had paid for everything in rubles, nothing in their growing collection would be allowed out of the country.

Fortunately for the Hammers, Lenin and his colleagues made their first major compromise with their political faith at this time, and the New Economic Policy was born, which condoned the coexistence of private enterprise to help relieve starvation, though it entailed the forced sale to the government of some fifty foreign trading concessions, including that of the brothers. Victor and Armand pleaded that they had been operating for almost ten years and had accumulated many personal possessions. They managed to strike a bargain by which they agreed to sell, provided they were permitted to hold on to their collections.

In January, 1929, Victor had taken part in what, if it had been consummated, would have dwarfed Mellon's subsequent coup. A syndicate of New York dealers and collectors had approached Armand about the possibility of buying the entire collection in the Hermitage Museum, whose 322 galleries sprawl over fifteen acres of Leningrad. The ambitious purchasers undoubtedly had some idea of what those Baroque halls and storerooms contained—forty-two Rubens, twenty-seven Van

One hall of the Hermitage—there are over 300 more

Dykes, more than two dozen Rembrandts, and the rest—but it is unlikely that they realized the staggering extent of the stock; it totaled at least 2,000,000 items.

The Russians' answer to Armand was an immediate *Nyet,* but they might be willing, they said, to consider specific items if bids were submitted. The syndicate drew up a list of forty paintings. "They were of staggering importance," Victor Hammer has recalled, "but the prices New York came up with would be like offering $200 for Rembrandt's 'Aristotle' today." The functionaries at the Hermitage, all of them former capitalist art dealers now compelled to eke out a living in the only way they knew, replied to the Hammers, "If your principals are really interested, let them be more serious."

The syndicate reluctantly abandoned any hopes of taking advantage of a bunch of ignorant Bolsheviks. The next important offer was submitted by Max Steur, an agent acting for Duveen, who bid $2,500,000 cash for the "Blue Madonna." The offer was interesting, said the Russians, but it would have to be doubled to succeed. At $5,000,000, though, they would be prepared to make a small concession; they would arrange to waive the customary export duty.

Hammer remembers a session with Anastas Mikoyan, the Armenian deputy to Khrushchev who was then Trade Commissar. "You can have the pictures now," said Mikoyan, "that's all right. We don't mind if you take them for a while. But

Mikoyan wanted twice as much

we will make a revolution in your country and take them back." The year, it must be stressed, was 1929, but Black Monday, October 29, had not yet darkened the world of free enterprise.

Max Steur bowed out, but negotiations on behalf of the other members of the syndicate lasted for two months more. To no avail; nothing was sold to anybody. One member of the group was Knoedler & Company, who suddenly took off on its own and triumphed individually where the syndicate had failed.

According to Carman H. Messmore, who at the age of eighty-one stands a ramrod-straight 6 feet 4 inches and is the last representative of the age of the Knoedler moguls, the firm received an independent tip that the Russians were still interested in selling. They had little choice, since the communal farms and factories were desperate for heavy machinery and the Soviet people were hungry for food. The tip reached New York from the old London firm of P. & D. Colnaghi, whose representatives had been contacted by Russian commercial agents.

When the news reached Charles Henschel, the reticent, tidy-minded president of Knoedler, he offered Mellon first crack at whatever could be extricated from the Hermitage, and Mellon took an informal first option on everything that might be obtainable. The next step was to discover precisely what fell within that category, and Henschel sent five Knoedler negotiators to Leningrad to examine the paintings. "They had the whole run of the Hermitage," Messmore has said, "while Duveen (who had not given up all hope) was virtually confined to his hotel."

Messmore stayed on the home team, charged specifically with delivering photographs of the Hermitage collection as they arrived in New York, and then went on to Pittsburgh, where the lean-cheeked Secretary of the Treasury took them over.

"I sold Mr. Mellon all those pictures from photographs," the old man recalled proudly. "Calouste S. Gulbenkian was bidding against him; he got four pictures, one of them a Rubens portrait of the portraitist's second wife that was magnificent. But of the thirty-three Rembrandts in the Hermitage, we got six." He acknowledges that Knoedler missed the "Blue Madonna," asserting that "we were afraid of it because there was some question about its authenticity."

"Then Mr. Mellon regretted another picture—a Giorgione that they were asking $1,500,000 for. There was also some question about *its* authenticity. But he said later that he should have had that, too."

A team from the selling side arrived at the Hotel Biltmore on Madison Avenue. "They would set a price on a picture and we would bargain hard," Messmore said. "They would cable to Moscow for instructions, and then we would decide if it was the right price." Negotiations with the commissars took a full year with a continual turnover of Soviet representatives on the New York end, for all the world like a forerunner of "Ninotchka," though no beautiful lady commissar ever turned up as Garbo did. "The Russians wanted tractors," Messmore continued, "and I understand that they bought them, then let them run down without repairing them for three years."

Russian arrivals on the scene had evidently been indoctrinated with the Party line as expressed by Mikoyan. The stock market had crumbled and Depression stalked the world, but the Soviets didn't regard international revolt as being quite so imminent now, in Messmore's recollection. "I asked one of them if they didn't feel badly about selling the masterpieces," he said, "but he answered, 'Oh, no, we'll have them back in *ten* years when you have your revolution.'"

Knoedler was the nominal purchaser of thirty-six Hermitage paintings for a price of $12,000,000, twenty-three of them spoken for by Mellon, who paid $8,000,000 for them in 1931. They were squirreled away in a vault put at his disposal by the Corcoran Gallery in Washington, where he gloated in secret over his hoard.

The supreme masterpiece was the "Alba Madonna," a circular panel 37 inches in diameter, which hung over the altar of a Naples convent before it passed into the hands of a Belgian banker-dealer, W. G. Coesvelt, who bought it from the Duke of Alba's collection for £4,000 in 1801 and kept it in London for thirty-five years before he passed it on, at a £10,000 profit, to Tsar Nicholas I for the Hermitage.

Down in the Washington vault there also hung Botticelli's "Adoration of the Magi," painted in Rome in 1481 while the artist was working on the frescoes in the Sistine Chapel, bought by Tsar Alexander I in 1808 for an unknown sum, bought by Mellon for $838,350. There was Van Eyck's "Annunciation" ($503,-010), Perugino's "Crucifixion" ($195,615), and the $544,320 "Toilet of Venus," painted by Titian about 1565 and believed to be an idealized portrait of his daughter. At his death, it was found in his studio, then sold by his son to the Barbarigo family, who sold it to Nicholas I when they fell upon hard times. It is a blushingly nude portrait that Mellon, in the judgment of one observer, "never would have hung in his home."

His clandestine enjoyment of his haul continued unnoticed until August, 1934, when *The New York Times* ran a brief item carrying his denial that he had bought the "Alba Madonna." The newspaper returned to the theme in an editorial the following day, taking the former Treasury Secretary at his word, noting that it was no time to be spending dollars in such fashion, and judging that the U.S.S.R. would not demean itself by selling its art treasures to capitalists, anyway.

David Finley, personal assistant to Mellon, who was installed as director of the National Gallery of Art in Washington when his employer donated it to the nation in 1936, once endeavored to explain away the years of silence and the flat untruth by saying, "Mr. Mellon wanted to keep this a surprise until the right moment." Perhaps another explanation may be found in the fact that it would have been poor politics, to say the least, for a Cabinet member who was the third richest man in the country, after John D. Rockefeller and J. P. Morgan, to confess laying out millions for paintings when 11,000,000 Americans were unemployed.

It was not until February, 1935, that Mellon, who had meantime served a spell as President Hoover's Ambassador to London, finally admitted something of the truth. He had little choice in the matter. Most of the story had been brought to light, together with his plan for the National Gallery, in the investigation of his affairs which preceded his trial on charges that he owed $3,089,000 in income taxes for 1936, the year of his big buying. In its first report, *The New York Times* even then had him spending only $3,247,695 for only five Hermitage masterpieces. Though the newspaper failed to count them all, it had the taste to single out the true masterpieces. Only at that late date could Knoedler & Company edge an inch or two into the limelight with a formal, third-person statement, which the firm must have been yearning to make for five years, saying that it had been Mellon's agent.

The announcement has a certain elegiac quality. Art dealers, in concert or in competition with each other, have never been able to chalk up a similar triumph. The day of the titans among American collectors passed in the Thirties and with it went the old-style dealers who served them. Some of them retired on the fortunes they had made in commissions. Some of them died, like Duveen, who was taken with cancer, or Jean Seligmann, cousin of Germain, who was captured by the Nazis when France fell in 1940 and shot at Vincennes.

The gavel has become more fashionable than the series of discreet maneuvers which were the dealer's way of doing business. There are at least half a dozen cogent reasons for the change, the most important being a new attitude toward the price of a painting. When collecting on an important scale was the prerogative of the very rich—and Mellon could remark to an art critic, "Oh, yes, now and then I pick up something good"—prices were regarded as the concern of nobody except the principals and their agents. The amount of money that changed hands simply was not discussed, any more than a bridegroom would announce the size of his wife's dowry.

Reticence on the part of buyers and sellers suited dealers well enough. They could charge for a painting whatever they imagined a particular customer could or would afford. With comparatively few pictures reaching public auction, there was no yardstick for measuring market values, and when pictures did go on the block in London or Paris, the results were often so erratic that few collectors would be seriously influenced by them. Just how fantastic the variations in price were has been documented by Maurice Rheims. Rembrandt's "Two Philosophers" was sold three times within a comparatively short space of time for 2,400 livres, 15,000 and then 26,000 livres. Another Rembrandt was offered to a French collector for 60,000 livres and, when he turned it down, brought back to him a few days later marked down to 10,000 livres.

The current crop of collectors prefers prices to be set less arbitrarily. Some dealers recognize this sentiment to the extent of putting a plainly marked tag on everything they have on display. Most museums remain reluctant to disclose how much they pay for acquisitions unless they fall in the "Aristotle" category and are bought to a blare of publicity. Many private buyers nowadays seem to enjoy having the public know the dollars and cents value of their collections, since a continuing rise in prices bolsters a sense of self-esteem. An auction is the place where money talks loudest.

The dealers suffered along with many of their clients when the Thirties put a crimp in prosperity, the New Deal boosted income taxes, and Hitler waged war. The merchants had been busily buying up whole collections of the kind of paintings that the tycoons preferred, notably the eighteenth-century English school, but suddenly the calls for such works vanished, and in the storerooms they gathered dust. The extent of a leading dealer's stock is seldom divulged, but according to one knowing account, the New York vaults of Wildenstein have held as many as 2,000 paintings at a time. When the biggest collectors turned to counting their money instead of spending it, every dealer's inventory went into a decline, though Wildenstein went on buying right through the slump.

The auctioneer works at an advantage. He can take on a collection with no irreparable financial commitment, using estimates, not cash, while a dealer's desire for it must often be on a cash-down basis. These days, when overheads increase as fast as sale prices, there are very few dealers willing to buy an important collection outright. They prefer instead to act as selling agents for only some of the paintings or better works of art, trying to persuade the owner to let an auction house handle the rest.

Among dealers in general, a whispering campaign, which sometimes gets into a shouting match, is waged against the auction houses. One of the charges they level is that the auctioneers are becoming dealers themselves by trying to arrange the sale of anything of major importance before it reaches the block. One of the London tricks is to pay two per cent of the proceeds of any sale to a dealer who will send in a picture which the house knows it can sell to a particular collector. As a similar inducement, a fee will be paid to a dealer who passes the word along when he has a client interested in something which has been announced for future sale. The effect in both instances is the same; it inflates the selling price.

Victor Hammer, who has a reputation for believing in plain speaking as well as in plain price tags, has claimed that auction houses buy in much more material than is generally realized because it fails to make a reserve price, using a selection of stock names which are announced as purchasers. "It's a sort of code to their people," he elaborated recently, "to let them know something wasn't actually sold. They use all kinds of names, from Brown to Worthington. In the summer of 1961, one London house happened to hit on an Armenian name. The next thing they knew, the FBI was questioning them, because the G-men were looking for someone with the same name." Hammer regards attendance at an auction room as a kind of game for rich businessmen. "It's the new race track or the different Las Vegas."

He cited as an example a Degas pastel which he had bought some five years earlier. "The only thing is, it was done on two pieces of paper pasted together, and this was a flaw. The first year I marked it at a fair price, but I couldn't sell it. Over a period of four years, I raised the price four times, but I still couldn't find a client for it. Finally at auction it brought more than 150 per cent of what I was asking for it. I've never before been in a business where, if you can't sell something, you mark it up, not down."

Other gallery owners have not hesitated joining the critics of auctioneers, and some of their comments are vehement. Most feel that the auction room used to be a clearing house for the disposal of large estates. Today the situation is such that many auctioneers have come close to operating also as dealers. Many of their sales are made-up affairs—they purchase from many disparate sources, buy quantities and assemble them in a single sale, thus invading the dealer's field. Naturally this kind of invasion has caused grave consternation among the important dealers. Auction houses' popularity is due largely to their high-pressure publicity methods. In many minds the auction house is the place to get rid of second-rate paintings, because through them the prices go up.

A former certified public accountant who turned his hand to running the New York office of one international dealer has another complaint to make against some salesrooms—that they very often put up pictures and drawings as window dressing, solely to attract an audience, not for legitimate sale at all. As seen by his analytical eye, the big auctioneers enjoy a few major sales each year where the paintings fetch impressive prices and provide the opportunity for representatives of the auction houses to go scouting on both sides of the Atlantic, promising the earth to people with things to sell. He has judged that most of the furniture and many of the paintings which are consigned from the United States for auction in London come back to the consignors after being bought in by the house—for a commission—and only going through the motions of being sold.

To believe the dealers, there are scarcely any limits to the deceptions practiced by salesrooms. They have been accused of buying pictures outright, then putting them on the block, pretending that they form part of some anonymous collection. It has been said that they allow furniture of insignificant European origin to be palmed off on unsuspecting buyers as prestigious heirlooms from the collections of non-existent French noblemen, the fanciful titles adding a spurious glamour to the pieces and thousands of dollars to the prices. The annual turnover figures announced by some houses, dealers say, are inflated by about twenty-five per cent, representing the stuff that is never actually sold.

Suppression of known fact is the least of the sins implied in one incident related by a New York dealer not long ago. It involves a typical pretty painting allegedly by Eugène Boudin, a minor master of the nineteenth century, whose work caught on in the 1950's to the point where one of his somewhat monotonous Trouville landscapes sold for nearly $40,000 at the Galerie Charpentier in Paris. The dealer spotted that a similar painting which an American family owned was a fake but kept his silence when it was consigned to an auction house, which had no hesitation about identifying the painting in the sale catalogue as an authentic Boudin. It was sold as such, according to the dealer, and though the house subsequently discovered the truth of the matter, nothing was done to let the new owner in on the secret.

Louis Goldenberg, vice-president of Wildenstein, in New York, has developed a theory, not entirely disinterested, about the contemporary development of auctioneering in art. "In the beginning," he said, "the auction room served as a means of moving large groups of pictures from an owner to dealers and collectors. What has happened is that increased means of communication nowadays have projected the auction house into a retail establishment. There is confusion now about the difference between a gallery and an auction room. It makes a new kind of competition."

He makes the point that the auctioneers can work with very little capital in contrast with a dealer. "The only stock they need is promises. But eventually laws may be needed to regulate the auction rooms if everything continues in its present direction. If the Federal Trade Commission were advised of the practices of some of the auction rooms, it would probably promulgate regulations to control them. There would have to be a greater clarification of responsibilities. Today, a French auction is the most respectable, and if it weren't for the tax there, France would probably be doing the most business."

The auctioneers, being vocal by nature, have not listened in silence to the accusations coming from the other side of the fence. It is not difficult to establish that dealers in one generation after another have not always been overburdened with scruples. In earlier days, particularly in Paris, they used to rip down the posters announcing forthcoming sales so that the public would stay away. They used to connive with owners of large collections for permission to slip inferior stock items into auction sales so that a bit of prestige would rub off on them and they could fetch inflated prices.

There are not enough dealers in America for them to be the main support of the big auction houses as they continue to be in Europe, which explains the solicitude which a house like Parke-Bernet feels toward the private customers, and the antagonism many dealers have for Parke-Bernet. As late as the 1930's, dealers' rings were actively manipulating prices and rather successfully fending off private collectors when they attempted to buy anything. "In the bad old days," Leslie Hyam has noted, "the rings would bid a private person off the map. He couldn't get in to buy. We had to make it possible for him to come in and feel he knew enough to bid for himself."

The purpose of the rings was to hold prices artificially low or force them unreasonably high, depending on how the members' interest would best be served. The reserve-price system now operated by all major auction houses arose as a defense against the syndicates' maneuvers to depress values. It simply entails the owner's setting a minimum figure below which the item may not be sold. If bidding does not reach the required level, then the object is withdrawn and the salesroom audience can expect to be told as much. If the reserve had been imposed in secret, then a house pseudonym may be used as the apparent buyer.

The reserve system interferes with the functioning of a free market, and Hyam, an articulate spokesman for private enterprise, introduced it with some reluctance into his business. Its effect is clearly inflationary. If the reserve on a painting, for instance, is $75,000, no auctioneer will start by taking bids of $30,000. Not too many years ago, Parke-Bernet could announce with pride as a sort of credo, "The objects of art and literary property, stamps and jewelry sold by these Galleries have been offered under conditions of free and open competition, without reserves, to a public which, appreciating this feature of the New York market, has included an increasingly large proportion of private buyers, whose active participation in the proceedings of the auction room has effectively stifled the restrictive system which obtained in normal times among buyers in the auction houses of Europe." That statement, to Hyam's regret, is no longer entirely accurate, and he has pinned responsibility for the change on the dealers.

There was no discernible effort being made in 1962 to deter anyone from bidding prices up instead of down, though the out-and-out rigging of auctions is rarer these days than in the lurid past, when the French government moved in and offered a reward of ten gold louis to anyone who could prove that prices had been boosted fraudulently. The much-admired French guarantees of authenticity date back to another cleanup campaign directed against dishonest dealers in 1861.

The profession they follow compels them to regard art as a negotiable commodity, and their profits are tied to a rising market. Where two or more of them hold a stock of a particular artist's paintings, they may endeavor to increase its value by bidding up his work when it is offered in auction. They may make a market in an unknown painter by the same means, using the salesroom to establish first an artificial price and then a continually inflated one. From a buyer's standpoint, this is not altogether a disadvantage, so long as the dealers' stock holds out, since by protecting their own inventories they increase the value of the individual owner's property.

Smaller dealers try to eliminate competition by clubbing together to make a purchase of what are elegantly known as "joint account paintings," after which they divvy up the lot between themselves. This reduces the amount of capital each of them has to invest and minimizes the risk of tying up funds in a few objects. Victor Hammer, one of the least reticent of his kind, has said, "I buy paintings in masses and also in partnership with other dealers. That way, you share your judgments, and increase the circulation of paintings. You can buy where you might otherwise hesitate. If I'm in doubt about a picture, I might ask the opinion of another dealer. Then if it's a good work, he might say he'd like a half share. He backs up his opinion with money. That's good insurance. My clients wouldn't like me to name any pictures I've bought this way, but I bought two masterpieces on half shares in London last summer (1962)."

When four or five of the trade band together to buy, sell, and split the proceeds, they call themselves a combine. Dealers have been known to be paid by a combine to refrain from bidding, putting a further crimp in the auctioneers' argument that the salesroom is the place that can be relied on to create accurate market values. Furthermore, a combine, instead of disposing of its purchases through one or other of its member's gallery, may hold a clandestine auction after the public auction ends. This is the notorious knockout, which auctioneers point to as a typical dealer trick. If the traders want to elaborate the procedure, they stage a "French knockout," calling for all bids to be sealed. The highest bidder gets the goods, and the other members of the combine are paid off. It is easiest to follow this devious maneuver by imagining four dealers buying a painting for $1,000, or $250 apiece, which in the French knockout is resold for $2,000. The successful dealer pays his three colleagues the difference of $1,000, which is shared between them in accordance with the size of each one's unsuccessful bid. A man who bid $1,200 would receive his original $250 back plus a $200 "bonus."

A dealer's bids in the salesroom are governed by the fact that he must act as a businessman, loathe to sell for less than he has to pay. Victor Hammer recalled rather sadly having been squeezed out by a private buyer in a duel at Sotheby's Korda sale for a big blue Monet, one of the best paintings there, depicting the artist's wife and daughter in a rowboat. "I was in up to $170,000," the dapper dealer said, fingering a customary carnation boutonnière, "then the bids started jumping. The timing was amateurish, so we knew it was a collector. Finally we said to hell with it—it was getting too unreasonable."

Hammer has said, "Today a private collector will usually go higher than the dealers, who provide a 'floor' for an auction. Sometimes a dealer will overpay because he has other work by the same artist. Then the minute a work by a certain painter goes for a decent price at auction, all the other works by that painter come on to the market like worms coming out in the rain."

The "worms coming out in the rain" are one of the things that make the harangues between auctioneers and dealers of little more significance sometimes than the hasslings of Tweedledum and Tweedledee. Each group is essential to the other, and in private they occasionally admit it. The salesrooms need the dealers as suppliers and purchasers, for themselves or as customer's agents, of material for the block. The dealers, for all their jealousy to keep their clients away from the auction-house doors, know how high-priced auctioneering stimulates the public enthusiasm and lifts the whole art market up. After the Erickson sale, a lot of dealers went home and rewrote their price tags. When Joos van Cleve's "Madonna and Child" made $40,000 at the Berwind sale in Newport instead of the anticipated $15,000 or so which was the market valuation of the painter up to then, there are at least two known instances in New York of men with Van Cleves in their possession who doubled their prices.

A New York auction house once gave a cocktail party expressly for dealers as an armistice gesture. The dealers drank the martinis and nibbled the canapés and said they had a very nice time, but that was the end of it. There was then, and is now, no danger of peace breaking out. Both sides prefer to go on talking out of both sides of their mouths in public, while they privately work toward the commonly advantageous end of seeing that the boom goes on booming.

VII

BETWEEN SAVINGS BANK AND SACRISTY

O N November 18, 1961, seventy-two hours or so after it had passed into the possession of its new institutional owners, Accession Number 61.198 made its debut at the Metropolitan Museum of Art, hung against a rather crumpled panel of red velvet in the Great Hall, flanked by potted palms in assorted sizes. On the first day of exhibition, 61.198—the numerals signify that it was the 198th work acquired during the year—was seen by 42,000 people, who were kept by a guard rope a respectful twenty-five feet away after they had taken the necessary eighteen paces in from the main entrance doors, unanimously ignoring the painting's nearest neighbor, the Sphinx of Queen Hat-Shepsut, dating back to 1490 B.C., which was put together from bits of stone excavated at the site of her sarcophagus at Thebes.

The crowd's response to "Aristotle," Number 61.198, ranged from prolonged, worshipful stares to casual glances. Some admirers felt it proper to remove their hats. One stout matron munched steadily but not quite silently on a pretzel. A young man studied the brushwork through binoculars. A teen-age girl whispered, "You sort of feel like you're in the presence of greatness." Two suburban house-wives concentrated their attention on the condition of the velvet, which they de-cided should have been steamed to remove the creases, concluding that, "We could have done it much better in New Rochelle."

In his office, James J. Rorimer, the urbane director of the Met, winced at the

103

memory of the difficulties encountered in transporting the Rembrandt over the eight blocks from the auction house to its new home, a trip for which it had been covered with quilts and corrugated plastic covers and roped to the side of a moving van. For the ten-minute journey, an armed guard, a curator, and the driver occupied the cab, while a curatorial aide, three moving men, and another armed guard rode inside. The bill for the job, including carriage of another painting, an anonymous fifteenth-century "Scenes from the Life of St. Augustine," bought for the Cloisters at the same auction, ran to $63, but the big problem had been insurance. "We had difficulty," said Rorimer, who forecast that "Aristotle," the most expensive painting ever to come within his charge, would never be let out on loan from the confines of the museum so long as he was in command there, since the risk was "too great." He had insisted on extra insurance coverage being provided overnight at the auction gallery until his acquisition was picked up the next morning.

He bridled at an editorial comment of *The New York Times,* which spoke of "a persistent feeling of discomfort, even of distaste" with the price of $2,300,000 and wondered whether the money might have been better spent. A museum's public duty, Rorimer said, was to "make every effort to acquire great examples of the world's artistic heritage" and exhibit them. "Money is only a medium of exchange. Quite a few of us feel that this is the most important property that has been on the art market in modern times—say, since World War II. Time appears to be running out on American museums, and paintings which are not already in European museums are being kept at home by stringent export laws."

Over the next few days, the crowds continued to set attendance records as impressive as the purchase price, crushing in sometimes at the rate of more than 21,000 an hour. "He's done it again," said one tall, tweedy man; "once more he's done it with his lights and shadows. The golden glow of his mantle *illuminates* the blackness." Another middle-aged patron was overheard asking, "How can you put a price tag on a thing like that?" A chic young woman volunteered, "If you ask me, there are just as great Rembrandts upstairs. This place is *loaded* with Rembrandts."

By far the most significant statement from any auctioneer's point of view was, of course, that of Rorimer, who implied that the Met would be an enthusiastic bidder for any worthwhile work that came up for sale; he has declared on more than one occasion that he was never paid too much for *any* of his purchases. Museums, which were once happily defined as the churches of collectors, had now been formally identified as the allies of the auctioneers and perhaps the single most influential group of buyers in elbowing prices higher and higher.

Three days after the Rembrandt demonstrated its power as a crowd gatherer at the Met, the second most expensive picture from the Erickson sale was unveiled at the National Gallery of Art in Washington, and it proved to exercise the same attractions. "La Liseuse" by Jean Honoré Fragonard, a great favorite of the salesroom audience, was uncrated and hung in solitary state in a small, marble-walled lobby which is reserved for new acquisitions arriving at Mellon's museum. During

Fragonard's "La Liseuse"

the first week's showing of this radiant young woman in a yellow dress, which Louis Marion of Parke-Bernet considered to be the finest Fragonard that he had ever seen, attendance of the gallery was almost twice the normal figure.

The gallery already owned nine other works by this most rococo of all rococo artists in its eighteenth-century French collection, most of them featuring his usual gilded youths and maidens in the graceful pursuit of pleasure. A museum booklet, published before "La Liseuse" brightened the scene, took a patronizing view of the poor painter. "He depicted the primrose path which French aristocracy trod," it stated, "unaware that it led to the guillotine. The French Revolution scattered Fragonard's friends and ruined his patrons." The artist escaped alive, but he died in poverty of a stroke at the age of seventy-four, utterly unable to adapt to radically changed times, finding no market whatever for his work. A century later, in 1915, the ten scintillating panels which make up his "Roman d'amour de la jeunesse" were bought by Henry Clay Frick from Duveen for more than $1,000,000, and the Erickson "La Liseuse" fetched $875,000 under the hammer.

The actual bidding was done by the late Chester Dale, a rugged, red-haired individualist whose collection of Modern French painters ranks as one of the world's best. He divided his allegiance between the National Gallery, of which he was president at the time, and the Metropolitan, where he was a trustee, but his labors for "La Liseuse" were performed on behalf of Ailsa Mellon Bruce, daughter of the former Treasury Secretary. She wanted the delightful Fragonard only to donate it to the gallery which her father built.

Whether they win their pictures by direct purchase or by someone else's generosity, the museums of the world mop up a staggering number of paintings. Virtually all the best Old Masters which trickle on to the market at the rate of three or four a year find their way immediately on to museum walls or, by instruction of private purchasers, are destined to end there. The same holds true for hundreds of paintings of every school, except the Moderns, in which only a handful of museums are consistently interested.

Since 1870, when the Met was founded, more than 2,000 museums of various kinds—art, science, and history—have been established in the United States, a four-billion-dollar investment of real estate, endowments, and collections. Over the thirty years beginning in 1931, the number of museums in New York State alone more than doubled, for a total of over four hundred. In every corner of the earth, among old nations and new, collections are being formed for public inspection. Brazil, for instance, which had nothing worth talking about up to 1950, suddenly found itself with an art museum in São Paulo that boasted something like $7,000,000 worth of stock as the result of a fund-raising blitz waged by Assis Chateaubriand, the country's publishing and television tycoon.

In a $50,000,000 splurge ending in 1961, the Samuel H. Kress Foundation bought a total of 3,414 paintings, sculpture, drawings, tapestries, and porcelains. Included in the list of this biggest collection in the United States were 1,424 Old Masters that were bought only to be given away. The man who started it was a

Samuel H. Kress:
beauty for half a billion dimes

self-made millionaire who had launched a chain of dime stores before a friend thought he would "get Sam interested in beautiful things" and delivered him into the hands of Duveen. Kress had so many beautiful things by the mid-Thirties, notably Italian Primitives, that he planned to build his own museum for them. Instead, he presented the National Gallery with 380 pictures. The Foundation named for him went on to share the wealth among ninety-one other institutions.

One art commentator, Richard Rush, has tabulated the buying carried out by a number of museums. He counted twenty-one paintings that went by direct purchase to the National Gallery of Victoria in Melbourne, Australia, in one twelve-month period, including "Calvary" by Jan, the Elder or "Velvet," Brueghel, while five other works were donated. In 1959, the Montreal Museum of Fine Arts added seven paintings and drawings of the eighteenth century or earlier to its stocks. The Los Angeles County Museum in 1957–1958 was picking up important paintings at a rate of better than one a month. The Tate Gallery of London one year later gathered a total of sixty works, among them two each by Picasso, Renoir, and Modigliani.

Many of the fanciest-priced auction-room items go straight on to museum walls. Picasso's "La Belle Hollandaise," which a previous owner had bought for less than $30,000 in the years following the Second World War, left Sotheby's for the Brisbane Gallery, Australia, at a price of $155,100; it remains the record fee paid at auction for a single work by a living painter, remembering that the $244,000 Picasso of the Somerset Maugham sale was a double-sided canvas.

From the same auction house, Rubens' "Meeting of Abraham and Melchizedek" journeyed to the Mellon gallery, Georges Braque's "Nature Morte" to the Municipal Museum in The Hague, Gainsborough's "Portrait of Mr. and Mrs. Robert Andrews" to the British National Gallery (at $364,000), and Henri Rousseau's "The Football Players" to the Guggenheim Museum (at $103,600).

"The Football Players" by Henri Rousseau

Turning to Christie's, Rush has traced twenty-one of the most important paintings sold in the early postwar years to museums from Denmark to New Zealand, Glasgow to Detroit. One of the pictures, incidentally, was another Gainsborough which has been subject to tidal fluctuations in bidding over the centuries—"The Harvest Waggon" sold for some $15,000 when it came up in 1867; it leapt to $360,000 in 1928 when Hiram Parke hammered it down to Duveen; and in 1946, another version of it was on its way to its present home, the Barber Institute of Birmingham, for a much more modest $82,514.

Museums of one kind or another have been accumulating art objects almost without interruption ever since the pharoahs stuffed their tombs with treasures to duplicate those that they enjoyed in life. Works of art—crowns, sceptres, jewelry—were originally currency, a medium of exchange sought as plunder in war or tribute in times of peace. The collections of the Egyptian kings lay "halfway between the savings bank and the sacristy," in the phrase of Francis Henry Taylor, the late director of the Met. Tutankhamen gathered together the art of all kinds of periods and nations. In the annex of his tomb at Luxor, when Lord Carnarvon and Howard Carter discovered it in 1922, there was a collection of walking sticks, along with statues of the boy-king and the protective gods, the chariots and the gold-sheeted burial furniture.

The temples of ancient Greece were storehouses of art, haphazardly filled with gold plate, furniture, captured weapons, precious stones, votive statues, and pictures. These collections were the property of the community, and their contents were formally listed in annual inventories. The treasure houses also served as branch banks, where the spoils of battle were deposited. Statues by the sculptor Phidias formed one of the sought-after items—they were worth any curator's attention. To make his statue of Athene Parthenos, which used to stand on the Acropolis at Athens, he had at his disposal approximately a ton of gold, worth well over $1,000,000 at current values. When the statue was finished, Phidias was accused of theft, of enriching himself by using cheaper metals to adulterate the gold of its ornamentation. He could not establish his innocence by chipping samples out of the Athene, but he had anticipated the problem. He asked his accusers to weigh the cloak, which he had made as a separate piece, a removable cover for her stone shoulders. It proved to be gold as specified.

Phidias was an exception in having a personal reputation. In general, it was the work of art and not the artist that was admired. Socrates began as a sculptor but gave up the profession because it was "low and ignoble." Plato rated artists as common laborers and decorators. Much of the work was done by slaves, the rest by artisans paid at the same wage scale as bricklayers and bakers. In the reign of Alexander the Great, a statue could be made to order for $600 in stone, $200 in bronze. Then prices slumped to about a third of those figures after the Romans occupied Greece. The marble friezes of Athens, which by today's standards were among the noblest creations of man, were chiseled out at the rate of $24 for a man on horseback, $12 for a man on foot. The wonder is that any survived; the Greeks thought so little of statuary that when the citadel of Athens was destroyed in 480 B.C., they broke up the fallen statues and used them as fill on which they rebuilt the temple.

The Romans matched a taste for conquest with a taste for sending home anything removable from the lands they invaded. Collecting became everybody's hobby; every new temple had its annex where works of art were on show. Julius Caesar deposited his collection of carved gemstones in one hall of Venus, and he allotted something like $2,000,000 to buying two works by the painter Timomachus. Art dealers and galleries filled an entire quarter of Rome. Citizens thronged the national exhibitions and seized the opportunity to examine private treasures when proud collectors opened their houses to the public on certain days of the week. Stone masons grew so busy that they produced headless statues by the dozen, adding the head when they found the customer.

The Prado in Madrid: suddenly all the doors were opened

When barbarians ravaged Rome, its treasures were scattered halfway around the world. For the next five centuries, the monasteries were the only museums in Europe. Some of the prelates developed into connoisseurs who would put contemporary curators to shame. Others, looking to impose a stamp of Christianity onto a heathen inheritance, tinkered with their stock. Frank Arnau, the German student of art forgery, cites a Greek carving in which monkish hands transformed a struggle between Athene and Poseidon into a contest between God and Satan, with an Hebraic inscription added for good measure to identify it as a Christian work.

There were monastic collections which had a flavor of Barnum and Bailey. Cologne Cathedral used to harbor a child's skull which a visitor known as Mark Twain noted was labeled "Head of Saint John the Baptist at the age of twelve years." The chalice so lovingly preserved in a hundred sacristies was invariably the one and only original used by Jesus at Cana, the splinter was a fragment of the True Cross, and the scrap of cloth came from a martyr's shroud.

Museums remained private showcases for the collection of emperors, popes, and the elite of society. The Medici, from Cosimo to his grandson, Lorenzo the Magnificent, befriended artists like Bertoldo and Botticelli, while they piled up the biggest accumulation of art treasures the world has ever known—Lorenzo was accustomed to spending between $3,250,000 and $3,750,000 a year on books alone. The family palace on the Via Larga in Florence, "the hotel of the princes,"

Inside the Prado, after the doors were opened

was in effect the principal museum of Europe, crammed to the doors with paintings, sculpture, tapestries, furniture, mosaics, and jewels, with medallions by Donatello in the arches of the *cortile*.

The Vatican collections were rapidly being built up, too, and not always with cash. Pope Julius II, the patron of Michelangelo and Raphael, was fascinated by antiquities even before his election in 1503. That year, the Laocoön group of entangled men and serpents, which had been sculptured in Rhodes by Agesander and his two sons, was found buried in a Roman vineyard. One of Julius's aides immediately offered the farmer $3,000 for it, but Julius wanted it, too. So he appropriated the statue and paid off the farmer by awarding him a job in the Rome city government.

The idea of the museum as a public institution was reborn with the French Revolution, owing something perhaps to the temporary showings of art which had been held in Rome from the days of Pope Leo X, who had once appointed Raphael as his superintendent of Antiquities and who lived to the hilt his philosophy of "Since God has given us the Papacy, let us enjoy it." The Napoleonic concept of a permanently public exhibition of art caught on around the world. The Prado in Madrid, the Vatican, and the Louvre all opened their doors; the National Gallery was formed in London. As the nineteenth century grew older, there was scarcely a city of any size in Europe and the United States that couldn't boast of a museum of some sort until at last the mighty Metropolitan came into being, dedicated to giving "our whole people free and ample means for innocent and refined enjoyment, and also supplying the best facilities for practical instruction and for the cultivation of pure taste in all matters connected with the arts."

The foundation had been laid for the phenomenon of the twentieth-century art market—the almost continuous rise in prices, which is the basis of the auctioneers' prosperity, produced by competition for important works between private and public buyers. Throughout the previous era, starting with the breakup of the Duke of Orleans collection and its sale at Christie's and elsewhere, shiploads of stuff were unloaded in New York, Boston, and Philadelphia, for sale to the new American rich. In 1897, the most spectacular collector of all, J. P. Morgan, made his first outright gift of a work of art to the Metropolitan, but the bulk of his treasure remained in his ownership and in Europe. He intended to keep it there until there was a change in the law of his homeland, which levied duty at the rate of twenty per cent on imported works of art.

But he wanted to bring his collection home and bequeath it to a museum. That was an open secret in the salesrooms and galleries of London, Paris, and Rome. "Napoleon the First plundered Europe for art treasures to make the Louvre," wrote one commentator of the day. "Why should not Morgan do likewise? The Seligmanns of Paris, the Agnews of London, and the Imberts of Rome hold that he can and will."

They were absolutely right. As a result of his persuasions, matched by those of Senator Elihu Root, a bill was passed by Congress in 1909 repealing all duty on imported works more than 100 years old. The courtesy was extended to living artists four years later. In London and Paris, the crating of the Morgan collection began, for delivery to the Met. Between February 15, 1912, and January 29, 1913, 351 packing cases arrived at the museum. One of them contained the Raphael "Madonna," others the Fragonard panels, now in the Frick collection. There were nine crates filled with Sèvres porcelain, seven with Dresden. Eventually, more than 4,000 objects were counted, worth probably $60,000,000 gold dollars, of which 3,000 were presented to the Met in memory of Morgan, who was never to see the cases unpacked and his gifts displayed in all their splendor. He died in Rome two months after the last of the crates was shipped to New York.

Not all his buying has withstood the tests of time and changed taste. One estimate of the collection in today's terms values it at $600,000,000, but this is inflated currency, worth only a fraction of the dollar's power in the twenty-year period when Morgan was amassing his paintings, porcelains, and the rest. Some items were assuredly fakes, as they must be in an aggregation of this size, though none so demonstrably spurious as a pair of lapis lazuli columns in Renaissance style which the banker stood in his New York drawing room, flanking an impressive stove with embossed tiles bought in France. The first time the stove was lit, the columns came apart. An Italian forger, Augusto Valenzi, had used gilded bronze instead of gold and cheap stone with a lapis lazuli veneer instead of the genuine article. The stove's heat melted the glue.

The cancellation of United States import duty was one milestone in the development of American museums by way of gifts from collectors. Another of at least equal importance must be credited to Duveen. As a result of playing off one tycoon against another and whipping millionaires into a frenzy of purchasing, Duveen prices soared into the stratosphere. He spent millions at the business of buying back his masterpieces whenever they turned up at auction in the effort to support those prices. But there was an end to what he could do in this respect, and he had to devise some means of permanently protecting his market. He found the answer in persuading his clients to remove their precious, but possibly overpriced, possessions from circulation forever by presenting them to museums, where they would never be exposed to the chill of falling valuations.

A contributory factor was the United States Revenue Act of 1917, which introduced income tax deductions for charitable purposes. Then came the Revenue Code of 1954, when much of the world's art had already been earmarked by museums, and increasing prices were draining their purchasing budgets. To stimulate fresh bequests to institutions, the Internal Revenue Service ruled that such gifts of art could be set against the donor's taxes up to thirty per cent of his total tax liabilities. "The amount of the deduction," says the pertinent Section 1,170–1 (c) of the tax regulations, "is determined by the fair market value at the time of the contribution."

Duveen's most enthusiastic convert was Andrew Mellon. The United States Government came in for $50,000,000 of his money as a direct result of the dealer's scheming: $15,000,000 to build the National Gallery, $5,000,000 as an endowment toward its operating expenses, and $30,000,000 worth of paintings and sculpture. This was the very peak of any man's generosity, but the donation of contents—126 paintings and twenty-four sculptures—did not begin to match the capacities of the pink-marble building itself, with its ninety-three exhibition rooms on the main floor. Someone noted after Mellon died in 1934 that here was a museum six blocks long with "enough paintings to decorate a good-sized duplex apartment."

The donor's hand-picked director, David Finley, was an enthusiastic apostle of the Duveen principle of having rich men hand over their prizes for public viewing. One of his colleagues in the profession has been quoted as saying, "In this day of a dying plutocracy, the chief task of a museum director is making sweet music to people who have pictures to give away. David is the consummate performer in our line."

Among his early post-Mellon contacts was Samuel H. Kress, who was persuaded to let the museum staff choose some of his paintings to hang in the echoing new halls. "I remember the time we told Mr. Kress what pictures we wanted to take," Finley recalled later. "He gave us a look like a father saying, 'I am trusting you with my daughter, but I hope she doesn't come to any harm.'" The first consignment numbered 375 pictures and sixteen sculptures. Others arrived at regular intervals, until an astronomical total of 552 paintings and fifty-five sculptures had been delivered, making up more than half the museum's inventory.

Joseph E. Widener, the crusty proprietor of the Hialeah race track and one of

Duveen and Mellon: the super salesman with his best customer

the four greatest collectors of his era along with Frick, Benjamin Altman, and H. E. Huntington, was the next name on Finley's calling list. In Widener's keeping on his Pennsylvania estate were hundreds of magnificent works. There was a Giovanni Bellini, "The Feast of the Gods," that had changed hands and homelands half a dozen times before it reached Pennsylvania. There was Raphael's "Cowper Madonna," Rembrandt's "The Mill," Titian's Althrop "Venus and Adonis."

Widener had long been associated with the Philadelphia Museum of Art, but he'd been slighted, so he thought, over a gift he made to the institution of Cézanne's "Bathers," which he went specially to Paris to buy at a price of $110,000. Unfortunately, there was a smaller, later version of the same subject by the same hand in existence; it had been bought more than twenty years earlier by the vitriolic Dr. Albert C. Barnes, who looked like a dentist, cussed like a bargee and made millions from the antiseptic Argyrol. Barnes organized picket lines of students to march in protest against "The Bathers," denounced Widener as "a boob" and the museum as "a house of artistic prostitution."

The race-track connoisseur never forgot the slight. When he had listened to Finley's siren song, he made up his mind to hand over his whole $50,000,000

Titian's "Venus and Adonis"

collection, lock, stock and stretchers, to the National Gallery, not to the Museum of Art, which had confidently been expecting it. There was only one condition: the will of Joseph's father, P. A. B. Widener, who started his working life as a butcher in a South Philadelphia slaughterhouse, forbade his son to pay the Pennsylvania gift tax which was involved, amounting to $2,500,000. If Washington wanted the collection, Washington would have to pick up the tab.

The art of diplomatic persuasion is a talent as essential in a museum director as an acquaintance with most of the other crafts of mankind. Finley, with friends in the right places, set himself the task of getting Widener's donation devalued for tax purposes, while President Franklin Delano Roosevelt considerately addressed a letter asking the Congress of the United States to accept the paintings now and pay later whatever tax was involved. The appraisers went to work with a will, but they could come up with a figure no lower than $7,141,000—tax of $357,050— which nevertheless could be regarded as a worthwhile bargain.

The third success which Finley scored for his Washington establishment locked him in a silent but painful contest with the Metropolitan Museum for the favors of Chester Dale, who started buying modern French artists when he picked a single painting by Toulouse-Lautrec, plunged heavily when the pictures from the fabulous Mrs. Henry O. Havemeyer collection were knocked down at the old

Chester Dale:
Toulouse-Lautrec got him started

American Art Association salesrooms (for a ten-day total of $374,506), and spent millions in the course of the following years. Officers of the Met had their eyes on Mr. Dale, just as they courted Mrs. Erickson.

Now Mr. and Mrs. Dale both had their portraits done by George Bellows, that vigorous depicter of barrooms and prize fighters who was a proud latter-day member of what was called the Ash-Can School. Bellows was a friend of theirs, and when the Met was arranging an exhibition of his work, Mrs. Dale offered to lend her portrait for the show. The selection jury, possibly less versed in the finesse of the business than museum directors are, turned her offer down. That was the end of the Met's hopes so far as the Dale collection went. A fine choice of Dale paintings was hung in the National Gallery at a somewhat later date, along with Bellows' portrait of Mrs. Dale. The portrait of Mr. Dale could be seen in the Founder's Room.

Very few museum directors come within a mile of Finley's talents. As a group, they are looked down upon by many art critics and most art dealers. "Weaklings incubated in the Fogg factory" is one of the milder descriptions which has been applied to them, in reference to the origins of many of them in Harvard's Fogg Museum. One prominent New York dealer was recently offered the directorship of a well-endowed institution, but he refused with all courtesy, knowing in his heart that life as a functionary would be too tame for him.

One of the dealers' complaints is that a museum director too often agonizes by the week when he comes to them as a customer, while in the heated atmosphere of an auction room the same man will snap up within minutes a painting which he has examined only briefly beforehand. They find that directors, with big endowments to draw on and eager to impress museum benefactors, play into the hands

of skillful auctioneers. It is noticeable that the auctioneers are much more restrained in their criticism of museum men, though it may have been appreciated
by this time that a certain amount of back-biting all around is endemic in the art
markets.

Inheritance and gift taxes, which remain at an almost confiscatory height in
the United States and Britain, tend to make life simple for a museum's chief. A
millionaire has no real choice between donating a valuable collection of pictures
to a museum and bequeathing a crushing tax bill to his heirs. So long as a director
is a social lion over teacup or martini, he is reasonably certain of receiving more
than crumbs from a rich man's table. The inevitable result continues to be the
slow extinction of private ownership of fine painting, the drying up of the supply
of everything but Contemporary pictures.

Federal provisions concerning donations to museums contain two jokers. The
first is that a taxpayer may keep a life interest in a deductible gift, meaning that he
can donate a painting to a museum but keep it at home so long as he lives. The
second is that the value of the gift may be assessed by the museum which, in theory
or practice, is to receive it, or by the dealer who sells the picture to the donor.
Whether a particular museum is presented with a painting may depend on whether
its assessment is high enough to satisfy the owner, or the owner's accountants.

The Internal Revenue Service suddenly became acutely interested in the situation soon after the auctioning of "Aristotle," though there were no questions raised
about the propriety of the sale itself. In Washington, Tax Commissioner Mortimer
Caplin promised that, as a check against abuses of the law, "all claims for deductions for such contributions would be scrutinized closely."

The Internal Revenue Service cited some examples to show exactly what it
had in mind. A museum director who was also a painter had offered his pictures
for sale at prices ranging from $150 to $250 and never found a customer. But after
he donated three of his daubs to another institution, he claimed a deduction of
$75,000, citing an expert's appraisal. Tax examiners discovered later just who
the "expert" was—the caretaker at the director's museum.

One dealer had offered his customers a "package" made up of a painting
priced at $7,000 which was accompanied by an appraisal putting its value at
$24,000; for tax purposes, he said, the two figures need not tally, and, in fact, no
dealer can be held accountable for the accuracy of his valuations. In yet another
illustration of what the tax investigators were out to stop, they turned up an art
assessor who filed suit against a customer on the grounds that he had broken his
promise to share the money saved on a tax return as a result of a generous appraisal which the assessor had provided.

United States tax concessions have been blamed overseas—notably by the
British—for draining art treasures out of Europe into what are derided as "mush-
room museums" here. The chairman of London's Tate Gallery, Sir Colin Anderson, has criticized the Internal Revenue Service system for inflating the interna-

tional price of pictures. Gerald Reitlinger, the British painter turned art historian, considers that Washington is indirectly "the main source of the champagne and television-screen entertainments of the modern salesroom."

He may be right at that. American tax experts concerned with art questions regard May 14, 1952, as a red-letter day. The event was the sale at the Galerie Charpentier in Paris of the collection of M. Gabriel Cognacq, a chain-store proprietor who had turned to buying French Moderns late in life. Prices, which had held very steady after VE-Day, suddenly surged upward, most startlingly in the case of Cézanne, whose still life, "Apples and Biscuits," set a new record for a Post-Impressionist at auction by fetching $82,500, or, as someone pointed out, roughly $6,000 for each apple.

From then on, the inflation process spread fairly rapidly to the big Anglo-American auction houses: in the Rees-Jeffreys sale at Sotheby's, the Bradley Campbell sale in New York, the excellent Lurcy sale at Parke-Bernet, the Goldschmidt and Weinberg sales in London. The beneficences of the Revenue Code of 1954 were making a deep impression on some status-seeking businessmen who discovered that they could have money and win admiration simultaneously.

Along with the museums which benefit sooner or later from these dual impulses, the new collectors make up an important part of the auction-room audiences. Like almost everything else developing in the art market today, the Code of '54 helps the auctioneers. Though the museums will inherit most of the worthwhile things that come along, the stiff prices attract more and more paintings to the salesroom easels. And there is one "fair market value" that few tax investigators question: the price made under the gavel.

VIII

PATTERNS OF THE PASSION

WHAT compels a collector to collect is a riddle of the human heart which seems likely to remain permanently unanswerable except in general terms. Agnostics say the urge is essentially the same instinct that moves dogs to bury meatless bones, magpies to carry off wedding rings, and marmots to pile up in their burrows anything that they can drag down there. Cynics dismiss it as nothing more than an example of arrested development, the case of children who hoard stamps or dolls going on to more worldly items when they grow up.

Many people, some of them devotees of the salesrooms, have tried to pick their way through the maze of motives and reach a solution to the mystery. Joseph Herman Hirshhorn, the newest of the world's major collectors, explained his activities recently by saying, "I have a madman's rage for art." The sculptor Jacques Lipchitz, whose pioneering work now stands in most of the world's leading museums, has said, "Collecting is an illness with me," to answer how he amassed thousands of examples of primitive art, from African masks to Indian spears.

Francis Henry Taylor decided that the role of the collector was to hold the balance between the artist and the layman and to hand down the tangible remnant of the history of civilization. Maurice Rheims has detected in the purchasers traces of hunter, detective, and historian, mixed in with a horse trader's cunning. The ancient Greeks had a word or two for it: "The image of a collector is a donkey

119

in front of a lyre." Chester Dale was once asked how anyone became a collector; he replied, "One good way is first to go into the utilities business and make millions."

As a pastime that can grow into a passion as fast as Jack's beanstalk reached Giantland, collecting has come in for quite a few hacks of the ax. "Collectors thrive among the dead," says one old maxim. It has also been said that the third rarest treasure among collectors after the pictures of Michelangelo—he may never have painted any—and Medici porcelain, which vanished in the abyss of the past, is that simple virtue called goodwill.

Men and women have been driven to collect from the moment some shaman in a smoke-filled cave saved a broken hand ax because it had acquired some quality of magic or sentiment greater than immediate usefulness. As soon as members of a tribe dared to venture far away from familiar territory, they collected trophies to bring back home. The same strain of souvenir hunting showed up in a French collector who used to roam through Germany with a prepared glossary of questions saying, "Good morning, may I look at your showcases? Do you have any ancient weapons, collectors' pieces in Dresden or Sèvres, carved ivories, lace, stained glass, antique jewelry? . . . I am looking for pictures of the Flemish and Dutch schools . . . Do you have any manuscripts, or books from the Aldine or Elezevir presses?"

One of Leslie Hyam's auction-house "bulletins" for 1962 carried on the tradition in some detectably cynical lines entitled "Phrase Book for Foreigners." It read, in part:

Q. I come from Lille (Stuttgart, Issy-les-Moulineaux). I am a collector of paintings (paperweights, autographs of Balzac) and I wish to purchase one (some).

A. You may purchase it (them) at a reasonable price at public auction (public sale) . . . Let us go in. Here is the elevator. Take us, if you please, my friend, to the salesroom.

Q. Good afternoon. Have you a Rembrandt (paperweight, letter of Balzac) for sale?

A. Not at the moment, sir. We are selling today English furniture.

Q. I am (am not) very fond of English furniture. My uncle says that Hepplewhite (Sheraton) is more refined than Chippendale. I read somewhere that the English were forbidden to use anything but mahogany.

A. Mahogany lasts longer. Come, sir, here we are in the salesroom. That is the auctioneer, who is chanting loudly from the rostrum . . . Do you wish to bid on this night chair (stool, washstand)?

Q. I bid six hundred dollars.

A. The auctioneer is very excited. He sees your bid. Look, he has knocked the chair down to you. . . .

Q. How amusing it is here! See. The lady in the fur hat bought a large bed (sofa, settee).

A. She is smiling at you, and is standing up (beckoning, waving). The at-

Mazarin:
scruples were out of place

tendant courteously makes way for her. She is doubtlessly wealthy (very rich).
Let us follow.

Collectors, great or small, are caught in the personal dilemma of having to
decide whether the ends justify their means—is the painting they yearn for worth one
more bid; can they possibly afford what they are doing, in any event? When the
passion progresses into mania, which happens more often than a casual reader
might think, then the questions lose any significance. Kleptomania is an occupa-
tional hazard of the salesrooms, for which there are some distinguished precedents.
One of the most respected connoisseurs of all time, Queen Christina of Sweden,
suffered from a form of it.

When she ascended the throne, aged six, her palace in Stockholm contained
just one picture, and that by a Swedish artist. At her death fifty-seven years later
in Rome, where she had lived following her abdication and conversion to Catholi-
cism, the inventory at her palace there listed 122 sculptures, 6,000 coins and medals,
240 paintings, and thousands of drawings. In the twenty-two years of her reign,
she had piled up a royal collection worth 30,000,000 gold francs. Refusing to distinguish between what she personally owned and what belonged to the nation, she
took every stick with her when she left Sweden. The Spanish ambassador once
found that her servants had picked his coach clean of every ornament while he
called on her in her adopted city. Staying temporarily in the Duke of Parma's
magnificent villa, she had his priceless silver removed and plated copper substituted
for it. She had crews digging at every site in Rome where ancient treasures might
be buried.

When Cardinal Mazarin, who had few scruples as a collector himself, heard
that she was visiting Paris, he wrote to one of his staff, "I beg you to ensure that
this madwoman keeps away from my cabinets, because otherwise some of my

Anne of Austria,
an accomplice in the plot

miniatures might be taken." Mazarin, incidentally, was up to tricks that Christina never thought of. From a fellow cardinal, he once commandeered a Correggio painting he coveted by pretending that it was wanted by another queen, Anne of Austria. The outwitted owner could do nothing but present it to her personally and see it hung by a courtier in her bedroom. As soon as he had left, Anne, who was an accomplice in the plot, simply had it taken down and handed over to Mazarin.

A relic of Christina's, a writing desk covered with strips of silver studded with precious stones, has the distinction of being accorded the longest description to appear in any sales catalogue—sixty pages of it when this glittering piece of furniture came up for sale in Brussels in the eighteenth century. What its price was, who bought it, whether or not the turquoise, jasper, lapis lazuli, and other decorations were removed and sold elsewhere—nobody knows.

Christina claimed always to be "reasonable" in her love of fine things, but Catherine of Russia had no illusions. With the same collector's mania, she admitted, "I am not a nibbler but a glutton." The results of her gluttony fill room after room of the Hermitage in Leningrad, which she commissioned a Frenchman to build for her in 1765. She set to work to make her conspiratorial regime respectable from the day she was proclaimed empress; that day she was wearing a guard's uniform but had got up in too great a hurry to wash her face. Her agents started combing Europe for pictures.

Andrew Mellon is the only collector who approached her in the power and speed of her buying, though he was manipulated by Duveen and had to buy at astronomical figures, while she had the market pretty much to herself. When she was buying, prices temporarily rose; then there would be lulls in her gluttony, when she was complaining that prices were "horribly expensive" and swearing "not to buy anything more, not a picture, nothing," and the market would slump again.

The first collection she bought, from a German merchant, included three Rembrandts. One of them, "Joseph and Potiphar's Wife," was picked up by Mellon

Catherine:
"not a nibbler but a glutton"

from the Hermitage for about $250,000 and now hangs in Washington, D.C. During the next fifteen years, she acquired five other collections for a total in today's values of some $5,000,000. Pictures arrived at the Hermitage by the hundreds, though in one consignment there was only one canvas, all that was saved from a ship that was wrecked off the coast of Finland on its way from the Netherlands.

She grumbled that she was "poor as a church mouse" but admitted that she had "picture fever," along with the richest purse in Europe. She probably loved pictures more than power or the ministers who shared her bed. Sir Joshua Reynolds was commissioned by her to paint anything he liked and charge any fee he fancied. He turned out "The Infant Hercules Strangling the Serpents," supposedly an allegory of Catherine's efforts to make her court the equal of any in Europe. She sent him a gold box studded with diamonds by way of thanks and had his bill, for 1,500 guineas, paid without a quibble.

The times were on her side in keeping most prices much more reasonable. Profligate aristocrats, running short of cash, were eager to unload their pictures on any willing customer, and Catherine was usually willing. She pulled the greatest bargain in art history in 1770 when her ambassador offered £40,000—about $1,400,000 today—for the 198 items of the collection that Sir Robert Walpole had gathered at Houghton Hall. His son, the Earl of Orford, needed the money to pay his debts. Vain attempts were made by some Englishmen to get their government to put up the cash for the British Museum's sake, but governments were less concerned about the flight of national treasures in those days.

More than half the collection was made up of Italian and French paintings, which were out of favor in the salesroom. In most cases, the pictures, which had been valued by Benjamin West, the expatriate portraitist from Philadelphia, had price tags on them that doubled the latest auction-room figures. West had not been unduly impressed, however, by a Diego Velázquez portrait of "Innocent X," which he put at £60. When Mellon acquired it from the Hermitage 161 years later, it cost a thousand times as much.

Catherine bought in a calculated frenzy, certain that some of her pictures' glory would rub off on her and deodorize the scent of her upstart reign. It is a motive for collecting which has never lost its power. It goes a long way toward explaining why Rothschilds in the nineteenth century surrounded themselves with enough works of art to cover their tracks as merchants and bankers and give them the style of Renaissance dukes. American billionaires who had started as miners or railroad section hands were putty to the art dealers for exactly the same reason. It would be ingenuous to believe that they were the last generation of the rich to start collecting for the sake of picking up new social identity and prestige along with the pictures.

Albert Barnes was born in the slums of South Philadelphia, son of a slaughter-house butcher who stuck to his butchering. Young Barnes worked his way through medical school, then at the age of thirty-five discovered Argyrol, a popular antiseptic which rapidly made him a millionaire. The young collector's first idea was to fork out some of his profits on the Barbizon School of painters, which were the peak of respectability in those Edwardian days. But an old schoolmate whose opinions he respected steered Barnes to the Impressionists and Post-Impressionists.

He was a man who said what he liked, much of it obscene, and did what he liked, with very little concern about price. The miracle is that he liked the best when he saw it, then usually tried to obtain it. He bought Matisse until he had the greatest collection of that painter's work in America. He picked up Soutines cheap and paid a record-breaking $185,000 for "Mussell Fishers at Berneval," a magnificent Renoir to add to the others he already owned.

The Argyrol millionaire showed one quality which is characteristic of the most influential American collectors—a fighting determination to lay hold of the very best, come what may. Not all of them have listened as carefully as he did to advice, but in a comparatively few years two generations of them, from the Morgan era to Barnes, transformed the United States from a cultural wilderness into a land overflowing with treasures.

Albert Barnes:
Argyrol held the secret

The pity of it was that Barnes, "a combination of Peck's Bad Boy and Donald Duck," did his damnedest to maintain his collection as a strictly private affair, to be seen only by himself and a few hand-picked, worshipful students, even after he had housed it at Merion, Pennsylvania, in a museum which he contrived to get recognized as a tax-free educational institution. He had a spike fence built around the place to intimidate public visitors, and the spiked prose of his letters taught most art experts to steer clear of him and not even ask to see the pictures. When the terror of Merion was killed in an automobile accident, his museum became a little more accessible, but it was still akin to crawling through the eye of a needle to gain admission.

Given a little time, however, and the distasteful memories of Dr. Barnes and his Argyrol fortune will be nothing more than a footnote to history. The world will remember him, as he intended it to, in the reflected glory of Matisse and Renoir and Cézanne.

The prodigious pleasures of a purely private collection are rare in the United States today. One of the last of its kind is housed at 7 West 54th Street in New York City in a five-story house of heavily-ornamented white stone, which is owned by the investment banker, Robert Lehman. To complete the magnificent display which hangs on the walls he had the Metropolitan return to him three roomfuls of his paintings—Italian primitives, works by Cézanne, Renoir, Holbein, Rembrandt, Goya, and El Greco—after they had been on loan for eight years.

Lehman was at Yale when his parents began to buy pictures during visits to Europe. Two years later, he had graduated; they had acquired an early Rembrandt, a Raeburn, and a Hoppner; and he joined them in deciding future purchases. Money was never a problem. Banking is a family business; his father, Philip, built the mansion which now houses a collection valued at something between $50,000,-000 and $75,000,000, comprising a thousand pictures and objects of art.

When Philip Lehman died in 1947, Robert and his wife had no immediate desire to move into the empty house, so they stayed in their eighteen-room Park Avenue apartment while they slowly assembled all the items of the collection behind the locked doors of 7 West 54th Street, which overlooks the fenced-in garden of the Museum of Modern Art. Armed guards mounted watch over the house around the clock, an alarm system protected every door and window, a caretaking couple lived in the servants' quarters, a member of the banker's personal staff checked the establishment every working day, and a young curator from the University of Toronto got to work on a new catalogue, to replace one that Lehman himself prepared some years ago.

There was plenty of cataloguing to be done in the dozen rooms and hallways where the collection hung and stood, the decor supervised by a French interior designer, the placement of the treasures worked out by the proprietor. According to Arthur Gelb of *The New York Times,* who was permitted to make a preliminary tour, a sixteenth-century tapestry of wool, gold, and silver threads dominated the dining room, where Mr. and Mrs. Lehman planned to entertain their guests, strictly limited in number at any sitting "in order not to create a hazard to the delicate objets d'art that are not protected by glass cases."

The ground-floor salon held a group of pictures of the Sienese School, an era that was "modern" before the Medicis flourished. The ground-floor drawing room contained more Sienese art, Renaissance furniture, and majolica from as far away and long ago as Persia in the thirteenth century. In another drawing room one floor higher were Giovanni di Paolo's "Expulsion from the Garden of Eden," Bellini's "Madonna and Child," and Sassetta's "Saint Anthony in the Wilderness."

It would be difficult for the wisest salesroom experts to evaluate these paintings, for lack of anything but scattered sales and fragmentary price records of the Schools and artists concerned. Two hundred years ago, only English dilettantes like Horace Walpole gave much thought to early Italian work, which was often brought back as souvenirs by young men on the Grand Tour and later exchanged at three or four guineas apiece. Nowadays, few examples of it, in spite of doubtful attributions, sell for less than $5,000 or $6,000. A Bellini "Madonna and Child" was bought by another art-collecting banker, Jules Bache, for $150,000, but it made only $5,500 on resale because questions had come up about its pedigree. As for Stefano Sassetta, the National Gallery in London paid $30,000 each for seven panels in 1937—they were owned by Duveen, who was a trustee of the gallery, and he had to resign in the uproar that arose over this conflict of interest. Bernard Berenson once came across three other Sassetta panels in a junk shop in Florence. At $500, they were his, to hang in his villa nearby, and he was quoted as saying he wouldn't dispose of them for half a million dollars.

The Lehmans' second floor has another sitting room, holding Velázquez's "Infanta Maria Theresa," two Rembrandts, two El Grecos, and a Goya; there is also a butler's pantry. Up one flight, the visitor finds a room given over largely to the Flemish School and another to the nineteenth-century Frenchmen. The fourth floor is reserved for drawings, two roomsful of the work of Rembrandt, Dürer, Leonardo, Goya, and others, and one of Lehman's most recent acquisitions— Canaletto's limpid view of the church of Santa Maria della Salute in Venice.

By the time his private pleasure dome was completed, Robert Lehman was seventy years old and the subject of acute interest on the part of museum directors and auction-house chiefs-of-staff. There was no museum in the world that could afford to buy a quarter of his collection at prevailing market prices, yet it was a true collection, a beautifully balanced accumulation that had been subtracted from and added to for maximum effect and importance over the course of half a century. It was divisible into separate parts—the French, the Flemish, the Italian Primitive, and so on—but it would suffer cataclysmically if it were ever broken down into individual components for donation or sale, as a symphony orchestra ceases to exist when all its musicians have left for separate jobs. In the autumn of 1962, Lehman was asked if he would ever earmark the collection as an institutional gift. He said he had reached no decision.

To find the like of the hurry and scurry that was going on at Lehmans' hide-

Bernard Berenson (left) with Paolo Lamanna, rector of the University of Florence

away, it would have been necessary to turn the clock back a couple of centuries, to Horace Walpole and his transformation of a commonplace villa in Twickenham, just outside London, into a mock-Gothic castle with a cloister, tower, turrets, and battlements added according to his fancy. He named it Strawberry Hill, and it still stands, a Catholic college for boys.

Strawberry Hill's gallery was the largest room in the place, its windows gleaming with stained glass gathered from abbeys and churches all over England. The furniture was covered with the same crimson damask as the walls, and the walls were loaded with pictures—landscapes, portraits, works by Rubens, Reynolds, Lely, and lesser artists whose names are scarcely remembered except by scholars. Porcelains, marble, and bronzes stood everywhere on the floor or in canopied recesses. The chapel of the extraordinary house was crowded with shelves and showcases chock full of silver, jewels, enamels and illuminated manuscripts, miniatures, a bust of Caligula, a Cellini silver bell, a dagger owned by Henry VIII, a ring of Charles I. Among the statues occupying more niches stood reproductions of the Medici Venus and the "Apollo Belvedere" and a bust of Walpole's mother—he was a bachelor. "The entire room," according to his biographer, Captain W. R. Ketton-Cremer, "was an indescribable display of pictures, bronzes, carvings, ivories, enamels, faïence, *potpourri* jars, snuffboxes, kettles, teapots, cups and saucers, seals and rings."

Getty spelled out the reasons once

Besides being the most enlightened art critic of his day, the pale, gangling amateur Walpole was nobody's fool when it came to judging the value of what his friends could buy. But his enthusiasm for painters he admired sometimes led him astray. In one of the thousands of letters on which his present modest reputation rests, Walpole reported the arrival in London of a new Correggio, "Venus, Cupid and Satyr." He wrote: "It is divine, and so is the price; for nothing but a demi-god or a demi-devil, that is a Nabob, can purchase it. What do you think of three thousand pounds?" That was too much for anybody; a dealer acquired it for half that sum, and when it proved to be something less than a genuine Correggio, it went at Christie's for about one-fifth of Walpole's ecstatic valuation.

In many ways he was the archetype of the eighteenth-century English collector, not overlooking the title he inherited from his nephew five years before the sage of Strawberry Hill died, the fifth Earl of Orford, at the age of eighty.

A new-rich collector today is often the target for sales talk from auctioneers and dealers to the effect that nothing will do for him except a picture if he wants to spend $100,000 without incurring big overheads for upkeep. It was a favorite argument of Duveen's, and its effectiveness has never worn out. In every generation, it has produced a fresh crop of believers.

Jean Paul Getty, the oil billionaire, who began collecting in 1931, is customarily described as the world's richest private citizen, and he assuredly has enough money to make him a strong candidate for the title. He is one of the very few collectors in anything like his tax bracket who have taken the time and trouble to spell out, in some detail, the reasons for their passion. They are complex in his case, which is not surprising in a complex man.

He has bought things, he has explained, because he liked them and also because they appeared to be first-rate investments. A deep personal interest in history has been a factor, too, and his reading there told him that intelligent buying brings immediate pleasure as well as long-term profit. He has gone to dealers to

William Randolph Hearst, not exactly an epicurean

enjoy bargaining with them and for the sake of their expertise, and to auctions where salesrooms provide a better opportunity to pick up spectacular new items. While the pace of his operations in Tidewater Oil, the principal source of his wealth, was swift, his growth as a collector was agonizingly slow, with his purchasing dawdling along at an annual average of less than $200,000 for years, to the dealers' despair.

He has behaved as an epicure, rather than a glutton like Catherine II or her male equivalent, William Randolph Hearst. The lord of San Simeon would happily buy a roomful of stuff at a sitting, or a complete Spanish cloister for $500,000, only to let it gather dust in a warehouse—and then sally forth and buy another, like the Cistercian monastery of Santa Maria de Ovila, which had to be dismantled stone by stone, carried by mule team, ox cart, and railroad to Madrid, then loaded into the holds of twelve cargo ships before it reached San Francisco.

When Hearst had to sell, toward the end of the Depression, Getty began to buy. He has told the story of his first venture into unmapped territory. "The room was packed—but times were not good, and it became evident that the public was there to see rather than to bid . . . I did my own bidding. The dealers, sensing my determination to secure certain objects, had little interest in bidding prices up in

Sixteenth-century Flemish tapestry in the refectory at Hearst's San Simeon

vain, so resigned themselves to the inevitable. I acquired some wonderful pieces for a proverbial song . . . The dealers left almost empty-handed."

It is doubtful whether he has spent as much as $10,000,000 of his fortune on this special pleasure, a considerably smaller proportion of his resources than Lehman or even Morgan devoted from theirs. He has bought Greek statues and Louis XV furniture; a Savonnerie carpet and Rubens' "Diana and her Nymphs"; the Sienese School as well as Gainsborough's "Lady Chesterfield." The price of anything has always been vastly important to him—he once moved out of his London hotel and bought a house because he said it would be a cheaper way of living—but he has seldom been deterred by the tag put on a painting. "Lady Chesterfield" cost him $95,200 in 1959, but she was a bargain, since she had sold thirty-four years earlier for almost exactly the same figure.

Getty has managed to be vocal about his pleasure in a book he wrote about it,

San Simeon: the morning room

Collector's Choice, in which he enthused, "To me my works of art are all vividly alive. They're the embodiment of whoever created them—a mirror of their creator's hopes, dreams and, yes, frustrations, too. They've led eventful lives—pampered by aristocracy and pillaged by revolution, courted with ardor and cold-bloodedly abandoned. They've been honored by drawing rooms and humbled by attacks. So many worlds in their life span, yet all were transitory."

But the tight-lipped tradition among his fellows dies hard. Parke-Bernet has told a story against itself concerning the sale of items from the collection of Irwin Untermyer, the former justice of the New York Supreme Court who specializes in seventeenth- and eighteenth-century English furniture. He describes himself as an "accumulator" in the belief that "collector" sounds too pretentious. The auction house printed 3,000 copies of the catalogue it had prepared, with the imposing title of "Judge Irwin Untermyer" on cover and title page. Most of the copies had already

The place, Saks Fifth Avenue: the occasion, a sale of some Hearst possessions (including a Van Dyke lady, stage center)

been distributed when he objected forcefully that this use of his title smacked of publicity in poor taste. So the gallery rushed out a correction, for immediate mailing: "Due to a misunderstanding . . . the cover and title page . . . should read 'Hon. Irwin Untermyer.' "

The entry of industrial corporations and banks into the business of art buying has produced a spate of public-relations prose but nothing as yet with the ring of Getty's analysis of the joys of possession. Robert Lehman had some of his pictures on view in his office. United States Rubber, Seagram's, and the National Cash Register Company have been actively buying antiques. The Music Corporation of America, completely up to date, rented works of art and furniture from its board chairman, Jules Stein, at the rate of tens of thousands of dollars a year, making every branch office of the show-business empire an oasis of eighteenth-century furniture, in originals or reproductions, and young men in charcoal gray suits.

The Chase Manhattan Bank has a president in David Rockefeller who insists that he is no collector of art, buying Impressionists and Post-Impressionists only "for the walls" of his homes in New York and Pocantico Hills, which are also adorned with English porcelains and furniture, Queen Anne chandeliers, and eighteenth-century Chinese wallpapers in successful, eclectic taste. His father, John D., Jr., had a private passion for porcelain; he spent $60,000,000 on the reconstruction of Williamsburg; and he donated the Cloisters as an uptown, medieval annex to the Metropolitan. But David has nothing like his brother Nelson's one thousand and more of Modern and Contemporary paintings and sculpture; David's real collecting runs to beetles, of which he has 40,000.

John Davison Rockefeller: nothing
was prettier than a dollar

Yet the Chase Manhattan set up an art committee, under Chairman David
Rockefeller, with a budget of $500,000 and advice from the Museum of Modern
Art, the Metropolitan, the Guggenheim Museum, and the Boston Museum of Fine
Arts, to buy some far-out Contemporaries for the bank's new Manhattan headquarters. The committee's choice, of dozens of items, could by no stretch of imagination be called conservative. It ran to the supersonic abstraction of Georges
Mathieu, the abstract, introverted cross-hatching of Pierre Soulages, and adhesive
concoctions of collage. There was no better evidence that the chairman, a conservative in taste and profession, considered that Contemporaries were here to stay and
multiply as an investment.

Some people in the art business believe that the typical twentieth-century
American collector of the jet age is an immigrant Jewish boy, raised in a Brooklyn
tenement, who hustled his way up by way of the New York Curb Exchange to make
a fortune out of Canadian uranium. "You're talking to a sixty-three-year-old kid,"
said Joseph H. Hirshhorn one day in 1962 when 444 sculptures from his collection
of more than a thousand went on exhibition at the Guggenheim Museum in New
York. He also possesses more than 4,500 paintings and drawings—the precise
total has not been counted, since his buying never stops.

Traveling steerage from Liverpool to Ellis Island, he arrived in Brooklyn to join his mother and the rest of her thirteen children after his father died. Joe, born in a village in Latvia, was six years old. "I stayed alive on garbage," he has said. "Poverty has a bitter taste. I swore I would never know it again." He started a kind of collecting soon after that, cutting out the lush landscapes and doleful dogs that decorated calendars and pinning them on the wall next to his bed.

Twenty years or so later, after a fast run up from $12-a-week office boy to broker's broker with the instinct to pull out of the stock market with $4,000,000 two months before the Crash, he began buying pictures. The first looked pretty much like those he had cut from calendars—a Landseer dog, a Bouguereau Madonna. He had no advisers then and has none now. "This is my money and my taste," he has said. "I've operated that way all of my life—in my life and in my business. I like to test my own judgment. I don't care if my grandfather or my friends like it."

His judgment in the Thirties, as his fortune continued growing, carried him straight from syrup on canvas to the American Realists, who were painting the Depression in terms of hungry children, bloated bosses, and well-muscled construction gangs. They remain in his collection; unlike virtually all of his fellow collectors, he has never sold any American painting he has bought in thirty years, though their prices in some cases have multiplied ten and a hundredfold. He did get rid of the Landseer and the Bouguereau.

"Art stays with you," he believes. "Some people love horses, yachts, or cars. I just love art. I've never exchanged anything, and I usually have more than one piece by everyone. I don't exchange things because I figure this was my choice at the time."

He bought the quiet mysteries of Louis Michel Eilshemius, the statuesque Walt Kuhns, delicate Kuniyoshis, the irony of George Grosz, the pungency of Ben Shahn. "In 1946, I bought a Jackson Pollack water color. I didn't see the 'drip' painting of his then, but now I own four or five. I don't buy paintings or anything else when they get out of range. I wouldn't pay what they charge for Pollack now (sometimes more than $100,000), and I wouldn't pay $60,000 to $70,000 for Andy Wyeth."

The bouncy little man with the big cigar, who abdicated as the "uranium king" when he sold his Rio Tinto mining interests in 1960, became the terror of 57th Street, where art dealers congregate. In between business deals, he would dart out of his office at 100 Park Avenue, where pictures stand stacked against the walls and furniture, and bustle off to buying more, as often as not several new items at a crack. He enjoyed battering prices down, and he usually succeeded. Most dealers got so jumpy when he walked in that they tended to lose their heads. At least one of them has reported that she showed him the door when his bargaining became too intense. Others quickly calculated that it was better to reduce prices for Hirshhorn and sell a lot of pictures within minutes than to dispose of each canvas separately and laboriously to other buyers at better individual fees.

He liked to bargain, but he did not boggle over paying for what he wanted. He added sculpture—Etruscan to Henry Moore and pre-Colombian to Marino Marini—to his "rage for art," and he set his mind on Auguste Rodin's monumental six figures comprising "Burghers of Calais," the men who sacrificed themselves to save their town and its people during the Franco-Prussian War. Rating it the greatest thing the sculptor ever did, he paid $250,000 for it—"but I don't buy Abstract or Expressionist works for prices like that," he is quick to explain.

He has always been an enthusiastic maverick, disinterested in buying for speculation or for social prestige. He owns more works than most museums and lends far more, too, on both sides of the 49th Parallel, with a special affection for Canada, where the biggest part of his $130,000,000 had its origins. Instead of manipulating his income taxes by donating to museums, Joe had plans eventually to start one of his own, to be built somewhere on the Eastern seaboard of the United States and to be as busy as he is, "otherwise it's a mausoleum."

Museum curators, for their part, are inclined to question the sheer exuberance of his operations, just as some dealers half hope he will pass them by on his next sortie and auctioneers tend to write him off unless his habits change. Though there is no perfect way to form a collection, some curators regard Hirshhorn's purchasing as a prime example of how not to do it. He will buy a cast, for example, lose track of it in his memory, then see the sculpture again somewhere on his rounds and buy a second cast of it, stirred by the same spinal thrill he felt the first time around.

The tenacity with which he clings to every item disturbs other critics, who insist that any good collection must be worked over and pruned like a flower garden to get rid of the weeds that are bound to creep in and make room for more roses. But Joe Hirshhorn goes on buying. "If you see a piece that you really like," says Joe, "it hits you in the brain, and in my case, I've got to buy it."

But the typical American collector certainly is not Hirshhorn. Neither does Lehman qualify, nor Getty, nor any Rockefeller. The age of auctions and the contagion of works of art in many forms have produced a different people entirely from the rich men who spend millions in a lifetime of speculation or devotion. A survey (which is another phenomenon of the times) disclosed their composite identity, when it was made soon after the boom began. The collectors who by sheer numbers carry most weight in the world market are the newcomers to the scene, usually something less than forty-five years old, who live in American suburbia on the comfortable incomes of the upper middle class.

IX

VOICES ABOVE THE CROWD

AUCTIONEERING, the most exhilarating means of transferring property yet devised by man, is a trade which in the United States is actively followed by at least 20,000 people, and the figure would probably have to be doubled to include part-time practitioners. There is no recognized collective noun for them, along the lines of a pride of lions or a gaggle of geese, but if one may be suggested, this *outcry* of salesmen is responsible for the disposal of the country's $1,500,000,000 tobacco crop each year, used cars and surplus steamships, bloodstock and most livestock that changes hands, along with furniture, jewelry, paintings and many other items.

By a recent Washington count, they were employed in 1,872 wholesale auction houses grossing $3,400,000,000 a year and in 1,872 retail establishments which were earning $22,800,000 in commissions. Under conditions which add Monte Carlo excitement to dull commerce, they have been handed such diverse lots as King Farouk's collections of stamps and erotica, Hedy Lamarr's bathing suits and Hal Roach's motion-picture studios, as well as "Aristotle." Two Los Angeles members of what can fittingly be termed the calling, David Weisz and Milton Wershow, went so far as to buy the complete logging town of Westwood, California, for $780,-000 with the primary intention of auctioning it, though they afterward found it paid better to dispose of it privately piece by piece.

As a real-estate transaction it paled into insignificance by comparison with

137

the spectacular era 2,000 years ago, when a Roman frenzy of bidding put current performances to shame. One unknown auctioneer knocked down the entire Roman Empire on a spring day in A.D. 193 after the Praetorian Guard had put an abrupt end to the three-month reign of the emperor, Publius Helvius Pertinax, by murdering him in his palace and carrying his severed head through the streets. This occurred after he had stubbornly refused to flee, and the adjective *pertinacious* serves as his only monument. The Praetorians ordered the auction, at which Didius Julianus was the top bidder, though he held on to his far-flung properties for only two months before the Guard slew him, and the succession descended on Septimus Lycius Severus. The only kind of auction which comes anywhere near that ancient Praetorian knockdown for excitement these days is a big night at one of the art houses.

Auctioneers make up a special fraternity, having more in common with each other than with their audiences whether the day's business is sculpture or a bankrupt bottling plant. They wear the marks of their calling—conviviality, a glib tongue, a door-to-door salesman's unquenchable exuberance—like an Elk's tooth. The accents of the art auctioneer are usually smoother, but he is the same essential mixture of croupier and hypnotist as humbler members of the brotherhood. With a change of pace and a little less *hauteur,* Peter Wilson would be equally at home knocking down fresh fish as at coaxing bids for a Fragonard. I. O. Chance would probably warm instantly to one North Carolina veteran who boasts that he has sold more tobacco than any other man in his line of duty and gives warning that any bidder who so much as looks at him has to pay for it, because "I don't exhibit my beauty for nothing."

The trade knows no national boundaries. A New York auctioneer would take to it as a duck to water if he discovered himself in the grimy old Hôtel Drouot, the auction rooms of Paris, a city which has nothing comparable to the British or American houses. French law not only calls for an auctioneer to be licensed, but also gives him official status, since under some circumstances the estate of a dead Frenchman, rich or poor, must be sold at auction. The Drouot's daily hour, 10:00 to 11:00 A.M., sees everything from pots and pans disposed of in the minor rooms to great paintings in the major ones, a tide of human possessions flooding and ebbing under the hammer.

Wherever he operates, the auctioneer's task is the same—to increase prices by arousing competition in its most elemental form. The ground rules under which he works have been altered very little since the Romans enjoyed an *auctionem,* "a sale by increase of bids," but the nature of the audience changes, of course, depending on what is up on the block, and it is the audience, not the man with the gavel or the merchandise itself, that invariably sets the style.

The chief auctioneers at the major art salesrooms regard themselves as the elite of their calling, though they would find they had an argument on their hands if they put that point of view to their humbler, workaday colleagues who preside over sales of government surplus binoculars, lost property, and fittings from haberdashery stores. In New York City, whatever their specialty may be, all auctioneers need an official license, which costs $100 a year and is obtainable upon application, provided the applicant is of good character and can raise the necessary $2,000 bond. Applicants are invariably male. Within the memory of the Department of Licenses, there has been only one woman auctioneer; she was the widow of the owner of an uptown art gallery, who never used her accreditation after she obtained it, but she holds a certain place in the folklore of the trade. "It's a tough enough business already without having a lot of talkative women to compete with," one midtown auctioneer said, only half jokingly.

Only an iron-willed woman could stand up to the considerable tension of wielding the hammer at a star-spangled art sale. In London, New York, or Paris, it is the same nerve-racking job, and as he mounts the rostrum the auctioneer is likely to wear the forced smile and abstracted manner of an actor on opening night before curtain time. The art auctioneer, however, is buoyed by one thing the actor lacks—the salesroom audience is invariably even more nervous than the man who will wield the hammer.

Experienced patrons suffer the anxiety of wondering whether fortune will favor them and allow them to carry off a desired piece at the price they want to pay. They sit poring over their catalogues like professionals at a racetrack taking a last peek at the form before getting down a bet. The novices are more visibly perturbed, twisting restlessly to look for friends or familiar faces. They are subject to a salesroom *malaise* dating back to an incautious Roman named Apponius who went to a sale with the notorious Emperor Caligula and fell fast asleep when the emperor's property was on the block. The auctioneer took the nodding of Apponius's dazy head as signaling bid after bid for purchase after purchase, and Apponius discovered when he woke that he was the new owner of $5,000,000 worth of Caligula's property which he'd never set eyes on.

The unwitting bidder is a little more than a legend. Eric Rosen, the owner of a restaurant on East 79th Street, has related that he was once landed with a painting which he had no thought of buying when he waved a silent greeting to a friend. He hung up his unwanted picture to decorate his restaurant and was offered twice its purchase price a month or two later. An exuberant woman on her first visit to an important gallery made precisely the same mistake and was approached by an attendant who asked her name and address. Realizing then that she was landed with something or other, she decided to go through with it and went downstairs when the sale was over in the spirit of a child about to open a Christmas package. She discovered that she had bought an eighteenth-century embroidered silk portrayal of "Elijah and the Ravens" at a price she could comfortably afford. "I was so impressed," she reported later, "that I came to value that picture more than anything else I have bought with forethought."

Louis Marion, Parke-Bernet's chief auctioneer, recently felt constrained to issue a general warning that "women who use their catalogues to salute late-coming friends do so at their peril." He cautioned one sociable matron, "Madame, you

Louis Marion:
"wave your catalog at your peril"

are going to flick that program once too often and find yourself with ten thousand dollars' worth of furniture you didn't know you had."

The auctioneer is not worried about knocking down a lot to an unwary bidder principally because such accidents very seldom happen, and the "Conditions of Sale" (known archaically in Scotland as the Articles of Roup) are explicit on the subject of disputes. In law, a bid amounts to an offer on the part of the would-be purchaser. Being an offer and nothing more, it can be retracted at any time before the completion of the sale is announced by the fall of the hammer. The actual sales contract is not completed until the offer has been accepted by the seller's appointed representative, the auctioneer, and formally declared by a knock from his gavel. The "conditions of sale" are the terms on which the property is put up, and they form an integral part of the contract between seller and purchaser. The buyer is not bound by conditions of which he has not had "actual or constructive notice." Generally speaking, it is enough for the house to print these conditions in a catalogue or exhibit them in the auction room.

One typical stipulation has it that the highest bidder acknowledged by the auctioneer will be the purchaser, and in the event of any dispute his determination is final. "If any dispute arises after the sale, the galleries' sale record shall be conclusive. . . ." Some auction companies have installed tape recorders behind the rostrum to help settle any disputes, but this practice is unknown in the art houses, and the legal standing of such recordings, made in the flurry of bidding by a dozen unidentifiable voices, is uncertain.

At the moment of picking up his gavel, the art auctioneer has no mind for the legalisms of his job. His overriding concern is likely to be whether the valuations he or his colleagues have put on the property will be met. In any contest between houses to lay hold of an important collection, the tendency is to make an optimistic estimate of the prices the lots will bring. In deciding which house shall be given the job, the owners or executors are apt to be influenced by the value set on the goods, and the higher the better. Scrupulous appraisers will arrive at a figure and stick to it. Less scrupulous houses will inflate the valuation to capture the collection, then try to reduce it shortly before the sale, lest hard facts reveal the deception.

One New York auctioneer who is also his company's chief appraiser of jewelry was called on to put a price, for tax purposes, on a collection which had found its way, as most of them do, into the vaults of a bank, in this case those of J. P. Morgan & Company. On first examination, one particular stone seemed to be worthy of a tag of $18,000, but the appraiser was not quite satisfied. Color and number of carats are of equal importance in evaluating precious stones, and the light in a bank vault is often deceptive. So he asked permission to take the stone upstairs where the light would be better. There, its qualities became more obvious, and he increased his estimate to $25,000. To make a final check, he carried the diamond some floors higher, took another hard look at it, and his valuation went to $30,000. "In the salesroom," he recalled recently, "I had a little luck, and that stone sold for precisely $30,000. A vice-president of the bank, Bill Hobson, who was with me at the appraisal, still tells the story."

In these days, when a well-publicized auction makes a public sensation, the auctioneer at the start of a sale may be preoccupied with another problem, for which there is no apparent solution: have the tickets, often as hard to come by as seats to a Mary Martin first night, gone to the people most likely to be active buyers? Will a potential customer feel aggrieved by being placed beyond the pale in a secondary gallery with only a closed-circuit television screen to watch?

Until recently, when Sotheby's developed the evening gala technique, the London houses ran into no such problem. There, the front rows of the main room would be reserved for the international dealers, a few choice seats would be allotted to well-known private collectors, and the rest of the audience could sit where it pleased. The American dilemma is aggravated by the fact that, with the emphasis on private buyers rather than on dealers, the house never knows to whom it will sell an expensive work of art.

"A man may come up from Texas, and we don't even suspect that he's got a big collection," Marion has explained. "If he's given a seat in the main room, he may buy four or five of the most important paintings." If he is barred from a seat there, the implication is that he may decide to spend his evening elsewhere, with depressing results to the final gross.

Decisions about who shall be seated where must be taken some two weeks ahead of the event. "It's a terrific strain trying to turn down important people with good collections who we know are not interested in any paintings in this particular sale," Marion has said. "We have an awful lot of new buyers and bidders coming up now who we feel belong in the main room because they are active." Keeping in mind the essentially commercial nature of an auction house, it is not difficult to see that a strong bidder ranks very close in desirability to an active buyer, nor is it hard to understand why some staunch old customers are sometimes put out to find that, come what may, they can't lay their hands on a white ticket for the equivalent of the orchestra and have to content themselves with a pink ticket to the dress circle.

Invariably, an important if not conclusive bid comes in by way of closed-circuit television from the outer reaches of the emporium, which provides Marion with one of the standard bits of humor employed to loosen up tense spectators and keep the ball rolling. "Ladies and gentlemen," he will say, "can you imagine my embarrassment tomorrow when the successful bidder for this painting comes to me and says, 'I told you I was interested, but you wouldn't give me a ticket to the main room'?" It is some kind of testimony to his knowledge of collectors' quirks that this sally has not yet failed to draw a higher bid from the satisfied customers in the main room. The outstanding picture of a collection has never gone, so far as records show, to a bidder in the outposts of the salesroom's empire.

Between the appraisal and the exhibiting of the material in advance of the sale, the auctioneer enjoys a spell of more or less relaxed days, while the necessary work toward staging the affair is carried on by other hands. The Parke-Bernet approach to making friends and profits demands a carefully counted seventeen steps from the initial offering of property to its dispersal on the block, each being docketed and ticketed in a traffic-control system worthy of a Detroit assembly line.

Once a collection is evaluated and accepted, a date for the sale is set. It is comparatively rare for a single owner's pieces to make up a sale alone, much more usual for a dozen and more sources, with the total occasionally reaching up to sixty, to be combined for a single session. Again, the dossiers of ownership must be scrupulously maintained, for hell has no fury like a seller spurned. To attract a crowd and focus international attention on the house, advertising and publicity are planned, and the work of cataloguing begins.

To handle art objects and furniture, there are three teams of cataloguers, comprising a writer who is simultaneously an authority in his field, a porter to carry each piece to him, and a secretary. Some catalogues are compiled with help from outside specialists, possibly from the Metropolitan or other museums. The reliability of the catalogues is vouched for by the auction house, though envious dealers have been known to question their scholarship.

American galleries, oppressed by higher overheads, are much quicker to reject articles offered to them for sale. The fortunes of the human race being what they are, the little old lady who arrives with what proves to be a lost masterpiece unearthed in the attic is outnumbered, thousands to one, by the hapless heir who brings in an "Old Master" treasured by generations of his family which turns out to be no more than a poor copy, worth nobody's further time or attention. The American houses will reject it, as they will reject a more valuable article, unless it is rare and readily salable. An exception is made for an old customer who perhaps picked up a single chair for $100 at some bygone sale and feels strongly that the house should take it back and resell it for him. A transaction like that represents nothing but deficits all along the line, but shreds of sentiment and the desire not to alienate a good customer override commercial sense.

A forthright American auction house will often advise a would-be consignor to offer his goods to a smaller salesroom, to the advantage of everyone, since he will probably get a better price there and the bigger house will be spared from losing money on him. The British establishments, with lower running expenses, are much more likely to take on the smaller, chancier consignments.

An American auctioneer in London on a visit not long ago took the opportunity to drop in at one of his transatlantic rivals. His attention went to a higgledy-piggledy assortment of paintings, some of them without frames and at least one with a sizable hole in it. He asked ingenuously when they would be put into condition for exhibition.

"But they are on exhibition now, sir," said an assistant, "though I do admit they looked rather better than this upstairs when they were being catalogued."

The Manhattan method would have been to make a firm recommendation to the owner to have the paintings framed and repaired, with an estimate sent of how much the work would cost. Experience shows that an American buyer is hesitant to bid if anything under the hammer—painting, furniture, china, or whatever—is in obvious need of fixing. The British purchaser, a dealer in most cases, prefers to take home his trophy in its warts-and-all state. The major American gallery would feel remiss if it couldn't persuade the seller that the cost of fixing would be more than repaid on sale day.

It maintains a staff to cope with most of the work—a cabinetmaker, upholsterers, a crew that in the selling season does nothing but polish silver. The flow of material is so heavy that some of the chores of dressing up the goods are farmed out, and major repairs are usually done outside the house in any event. Special pieces, once they have been brought to prime condition, are taken to the house's own studios for photographing, in color or monochrome, as illustrations for the catalogue. Outside photoengravers and printers take over the job from that point on.

An auctioneer's jitters over a particular collection start up again a week or so before the sale, when the exhibition opens. If a big sale is in the making, his nervousness increases proportionately with the size of the figures he has estimated for newspaper and television interviewers. No matter how many years he has served at his trade, the self-questioning persists, though an auctioneer needs to be an extrovert by nature, or he could not stomach the job.

Shortly before the Stanton jewelry sale in November, 1962, Louis Marion was reminiscing about his early days, when he had worked his way up from the lower levels of the old American Art Association, where he enlisted. After serving as a record-keeper to Hiram Parke, Marion was in 1937 considered to be ready for his debut as an auctioneer, and he was broken in on selling some unimportant books.

"You never forget your first sale," he said. "Major Edward Bowes, who used to have the amateur show on radio in those days, was one of my biggest supporters; he had done an awful lot for me when I was coming up. He told me, 'I won't be able to come to the sale, but I'll wish you luck.' I walked into the salesroom and sat on the rostrum as nervous as a cat. Then I looked down, and who

Hiram Parke, the old master

was sitting there but Major Bowes. He looked up at me, and I tried to get started. It took me a while to reach Number One. It was a $20 book. I had other friends in the audience who wanted to buy the first item I'd tried my hand at, but they didn't have as much money as he did. The bidding went on up until he paid $380, then he gave it away to some library. He just wanted to encourage me."

Having survived his baptism under bidding, Marion had four or five more years of selling nothing but books, which in the normal order of things do not rate high in prestige or excitement, excepting windfalls like the enormous Robert Hoe library which earlier in this century brought in the staggering total of $2,536,663, taking seventy-nine sessions to dispose of it; even without multiplication to bring it up to today's equivalent prices, the figure still stands as an American record.

In 1942, Marion got his first art sale. "Major Parke decided to try me out on paintings. I don't know whether I was good, bad, or indifferent, but about two years later, I was allowed to handle a painting sale in the evening. Then I found out what auctioneering really was." He discovered that one way of calming his nerves was to remind himself that the customers were jumpier than he was. On both sides of the rostrum, there was a great difference between handling a $20 chair or a $100 sideboard and disposing of a $5,000 oil. "After I'd had a few painting sales, selling furniture was much easier. After you've done anything very difficult, it always makes everything else look easy."

By the time the twenty-nine paintings of Arnold Kirkeby, the hotel magnate, came into his company's hands, Marion had reached his fiftieth birthday and acquired the controlled calm of an old campaigner who can hear bullets fly without flinching. He spent two hours on the December afternoon of the sale going over final details with Kirkeby, whom he found in a state of tremor. "What are you so nervous about?" asked the auctioneer. "I'm the one who's going to do all the work tonight."

The prices might not be high enough, feared Kirkeby, who was left only partially assuaged by the assurances Marion gave him on that point as he departed.

From there, he went on to visit an important New York dealer, who had three bids in his pocket to make on behalf of clients. The dealer was in much the same state as Kirkeby. "What are *you* getting so upset about?" Marion asked. "All you have to do is bid."

"Well, this is a big thing, a big thing," the dealer replied.

On the rostrum, it took exactly sixty minutes to sell the twenty-nine pictures for $1,548,500, with $152,000 made by an early "Madonna and Child" of Picasso. "Even after that, Mr. Kirkeby was still nervous," Marion recalled. " 'Well, we lived through it,' he said. You'd have thought he'd been doing the auctioneer's job."

Since that time, the invisible pressures of a big night with the gavel have been measurably increased by electronics, not confined to the now-familiar giant television screens. In 1960, at a benefit sale for the Museum of Modern Art, Marion had to contend with the first art auction in which *intercity* television was employed, pitting bidders against each other in New York, Texas, and California.

"Who'll give me $80,000 for this painting?" asked Marion when "Composition: The Violin" by Georges Braque, the priciest of post-Cézanne masters, came up. A woman in his immediate audience raised her hand. Instantly, a man in Dallas went to $90,000. In Los Angeles, a motion-picture producer topped that, and within a minute or so David Rockefeller had gone to $140,000. Marion cast a final look at the crowd in front of him and at the television screens, and a bidder for the Alexander Iolas Gallery of Manhattan carried off the Braque for a record-breaking $145,000.

The tension increases as the sale day draws nearer. The chief auctioneer may very well take part in a telephone campaign to drum up bids for any important works that will be up for sale. "There is practically no limit to the people we can call on," Marion said in a recent conversation. "I could pick up the telephone now, with a painting from almost any school, and call people all over the United States, knowing very well they may not be the successful buyers, but also knowing they'll be the underbidders."

Any auctioneer working for the big houses is subjected to several different kinds of pressure, all of them disturbing to his blood pressure. The demands of the publicity campaign which heralds every major sale cast him as a spokesman for his company. He is called upon to forecast with an air of utter infallibility a fresh astronomical total as the potential take. He is compelled to cast caution aside and name another breathtaking sum as the price the star attraction of the sale will bring. He has to weigh the value of headlines against the loss of face occasioned to everyone concerned if his estimates prove to be vainglorious.

In his warm-up for the Erickson sale, Marion resolutely quoted a figure of $1,000,000 as the minimum price "Aristotle" would bring. As one day followed another and the sale drew closer, he waited in vain for the written advance bid to come in that would assure him that his reputation was intact. He envisioned himself standing on the rostrum unable to raise more than half the sum, and the prospect filled him with something less than joy. He had swallowed down an early dinner on the actual night of the sale before an opening bid of $1,000,000 was safe in his pocket. That afternoon, he had seen James Rorimer, who finally carried off "Aristotle," but the director of the Metropolitan said nothing about his intentions.

"You just don't know who the buyer's going to be," Marion said later. "You think that, say, the Carnegie Institute is sure to take a painting; then at the last moment the Metropolitan picks up some money from somebody and turns out to be the top bidder."

Part of the auctioneer's function is to work out with recognized collectors and dealers the prearranged system of signals which they often like to employ for major sales to preserve their anonymity as they bid, the collectors to avoid being badgered later by dealers anxious to sell other things to them, the dealers to keep their competitors from forcing the bidding up out of proportion. Salesroom novices have heard all about the mysterious significance of a wink, a nod, or a waved catalogue, and they may be seen peering suspiciously at anyone who tugs at his ear, taps his nose, flutters a handkerchief, opens his spectacle case, crosses his legs, straightens his tie, or even breathes a bit hard. It seems to be the working of a secret code which makes the gallery an intriguing place in which to spend an hour, and it very often is precisely that. An auction which has got up a good head of steam, with experienced bidders eager for the run, can move along at a fast clip, with only a handful of the audience aware of who's bidding what.

The auctioneer makes a point of stating the opening bid slowly and clearly, so that amateurs and professionals alike know exactly where they stand. The first increase usually sets the amount of each succeeding bid until a change in the size of the unit is signaled. For example, the next call after an opening bid of $10,000 will probably be $11,000; at least, this would be the auctioneer's ambition, to keep the pace lively and the essential excitement mounting.

One seemingly obvious bit of preliminary work can never be done, and that is for the auctioneer or anybody else to sit at a desk and decide at what prices to start the paintings. "At each sale, you have to feel your way, get the trend," Marion has explained. The divining process begins the moment the auctioneer enters the main gallery and picks his way through the sea of people, some familiar, but most of them unknown to him, to reach his rostrum. The big room, always quiet, grows even quieter, with sound deadened by the velvet-hung walls. Spectacles flash and catalogues rustle as the audience takes a last look at the programing for the show.

A sale is a play, and the gallery has most of the marks of a theater. Spotlights blaze, flooding with flattery everything that's brought up on to the platform. Backstage, a crew of green-uniformed porters, whose faces will soon shine with sweat, waits for the maestro's opening words, ready to manipulate the stage curtains, to hoist paintings and tapestries up on well-oiled pulleys for public view. Everything for sale has been assembled in a serpentine line, with the first item waiting to be carried through the curtains, the tail reaching out into a backstage corridor, the whole assemblage snaking forward as the sale progresses.

The auctioneer, his lips close to banked microphones, is flanked by assistants—his record-keeper and uniformed attendants who bell out the bids, each taking a small section of the audience as his domain and covering it like a bird dog. At one side of the room, another attendant announces bids submitted by mail, cablegram, or telephone by collectors *in absentia*. At European auctions, the heavy preponderance of dealers and highly-skilled professionals, who have already inspected and valued the lots, make a sale almost anticlimactic, the swiftest possible gallop through the agenda so that everybody can get home. The American pattern, with private buyers predominating, emphasizes the auction itself as the climax, the final act of the play which has already gone through its ritualistic scenes of appraisal, cataloguing, cleaning, and exhibition.

A tap of the gavel brings the meeting to order. The auctioneer's eyes rove ceaselessly around the room, looking to see whether the expected sure-fire bidders are in their customary places in the front rows; watching the doorways for some surprise arrival; trying to identify the strangers. The first items up arc invariably the more modest things in the collection, the intention being precisely that of a playwright who allows ten minutes after the curtain for his audience to swallow its coughs and settle down.

Already the auctioneer has calculated the mood of the house and is prepared to test its financial temper. "You have to find out your audience," Marion has said. "Certain people sit in front of me that I've known for as long as thirty years. I know what they collect. I've been in their homes, and I'm well aware of what they want, so I know where to look when the bidding begins. Then another example. Let's say I'd decided to start a Utrillo at $5,000, but in the middle of the sale I see Mr. X come in, who I know wants a Utrillo. I wouldn't start at $5,000 because the trend has changed. Mr. X has arrived, so you start higher."

The buyers and the sellers are eager for diametrically opposed results and quite different means of reaching them. Buyers, interested in keeping prices down as low as their blood temperature will permit, are out for what the trade knows as "a quick knock," a concluding rap of the gavel with no delay. They customarily inquire of the auctioneer after the evening is over, "What happened to your arm? Did it get paralyzed?" Sellers, wanting maximum returns, like to see bidding extended close to the point of boredom. Both groups are apt to find fault with the auctioneer. With the current rapid turnover in paintings, especially the Impressionists, one month's buyer may be next month's seller, and the luckless gaveler finds it impossible to keep any customer wholly satisfied.

London and Paris may be relied upon for a quicker knock than New York, where the Peter Wilson style would probably not sit too well with American audiences. They are given a final chance of a minute or so to make up their minds before the hammer falls. There is a moment of silence from the auctioneer, then a few words of deft salesmanship to squeeze out perhaps one last, winning offer.

Hiram Parke put it this way: "There seems to be an instinct that tells you when to hesitate and perhaps enter a word of encouragement. At certain times,

Billy Rose went to $30,000 to win

you must be stern and then again resort to joviality. An important point is to know when to pause and reassure your audience of value. Above all—know when to sell."

Billy Rose, the mercurial impresario, once found himself under Parke's discerning gaze when a Frans Hals came to the display easel. A Baltimore dealer was also in the audience, intent on the same painting. When the bidding had climbed to $15,000, Parke fixed his mild eyes on Rose, remarking, "Here's a painting worthy of any collection, especially *yours*." Rose responded by going $5,000 higher, hoping to knock out his contestant. It looked as if the strategy had worked, but still Parke's gavel remained raised while the dealer sat pondering. "I know

Billy Rose presented this Jacob Epstein sculpture to the National Museum of Israel

you came all the way from Baltimore to get this picture," Parke sympathized. That roused the out-of-town visitor to action, and he and Rose fought another round until Billy went to $30,000 to win.

"Until you made your little speech, I thought I'd get that painting for $20,000," he told Parke after the sale. The other partner, Otto Bernet, knew he had a weakness; he was too hasty with the hammer, so it was Parke who handled the big events.

Marion employs the same technique as his late chief, Parke. "This should be in your collection," he will say during the pause that refreshes. "This is specially for you" was the phrase that sold a Degas to a hesitating Arthur Murray. When Pierre Bonnard's "Open Window" was the star of the day, Marion launched into longer oratory. The bidding had reached $98,000, then faded out completely. "Now wouldn't it sound a whole lot better," he asked the audience at large, "if when your friends come into your house, you could say 'I paid $100,000 for this painting'?" Laughter broke the silence, and the price jumped up to $110,000.

"You talk to different people different ways," Marion explains. "You can't be a comedian, or the audience would lose respect for you, but to be an auctioneer in this country you have to be a sort of actor. You can't just get up there and say, 'I have sixty thousand pounds; any more?' then down with the hammer. If you did that over here, you'd never hear the end of it. The consignor would know there was more bidding left in the room. The underbidder would complain when he went home, 'Why, if I'd had a little more time, I'd probably have made another bid on that thing.' The underbidder always tries to explain to his friends how he lost it, trying to save some face."

So the drama builds toward the hammer's blow, the climax of the encounter, the almost cathartic moment. The pace has gradually slowed in readiness for it. A skilled auctioneer by this time has the audience in his hand, straining to follow the volley of bids like spectators at a tennis tournament. The man on the rostrum struggles to keep calm, to go slow and watch the underbidder like a hawk for the resigned sign-off signal, making sure he is completely finished.

"There's a lot of criticism to the effect that I wait too long," Marion says, "but I'm thick-skinned. Waiting is the hardest part. You're under high pressure when you're that close to the end, and you've always a tendency to be nervous. The average auctioneer feels the urge to forget everything, don't talk, bring the gavel down and get it over with. But anybody can do that. It's the waiting that calls for great auctioneering."

At the end of a big sale, the man on the rostrum is exhausted, physically depleted, no matter how many years he has spent at his trade. But if it's been a good sale, he feels something of the sense of triumph that a world heavyweight champion experiences when he's knocked another contender out of the ring.

Nobody has ever come up with an accepted slogan for the outcry of auctioneers, but there is an old one that might serve them well: *festina lente,* "hasten slowly."

X

ART IN HIDING

MAJOR William Mandeville Peareth Kincaid Lennox always regarded the daffodil as a prime example of the handicraft of God, infinitely superior to anything any artist could paint. "I'm not an artistic sort of chap," he used to say. "Don't understand pictures at all." His wife felt much the same as he did, though she rated dogs above flowers, particularly pedigree elkhounds, which she bred.

The major, a tweedy, portly old gentleman, had almost a passion for his flowers. "I don't know where you could find more beautiful daffodils than in our grounds," he said. "We can't stop planting them." When he spoke, he had 200 different varieties in the gardens which took up an appreciable share of his 14,000 acres at the remote Gothic castle on the banks of the River Teme, Shropshire, England. He even opened the gates one day each spring for the public to inspect the sea of yellow blossoms, but getting inside Downton Castle was a different story. It remained perpetually closed to stray visitors, and most people were refused if they asked to see another collection of the major's, the more than ninety paintings that were hung in helter-skelter assortment in the library and echoing halls.

They were gathered together by Richard Payne Knight, a Gothomane who designed the castle for himself and, in 1824, passed along a number of items to the British Museum, though he kept enough pictures to make the collection one of the most romantic—and least known—in the Western world by the time Major

Lennox acquired it by inheritance. It included a Nicolas Poussin and a Van Dyck—
"a lovely one of a galloping horse," in the major's words. He owned a portrait of
Grotius which was attributed to Rubens though it was probably another Van Dyck,
and a picture by the seventeenth-century Dutchman, Gerard Dou, entitled "Woman
Drinking Soup out of a Bowl," about which the major had one reservation: "Personally, I think she is drinking wine."

But towering in importance above all the rest were the Rembrandts, three of
them, possibly the last of real importance remaining in private hands. When the
major took over the castle from his mother in 1952, the place was lit only by
acetylene lamps, twenty-six of them, which he had to light every evening. But he
had the place wired for electricity, so that he could watch television on the big-
screen set which stood on the floor beneath Rembrandt's "Flight Into Egypt." On
another dark wall there hung "The Cradle," which could be seen only by carrying
a reading lamp over to it. "The Cradle" once fell off its hook and nearly hit the
budgerigar that lived in a cage below. Then there was the third Rembrandt, "St.
Bartholomew," the disciple who carried Christianity into India and met martyrdom
by the flail.

The day came when the major had to choose between his paintings and keeping up the acreage, on which he raised sheep and cattle along with his daffodils.
He plumped without hesitation for selling an Old Master, feeling that the market
for such things was ridiculously high and doubting whether it would continue. This
is the kind of decision which sets art auctioneers to shoving pajamas and toothbrush
into a briefcase and catching the next plane, train, or office car to the scene as soon
as they hear the news. The unhanging of Old Masters at comparatively short notice from the manorial walls of England is a process which currently puts financial
jam on Sotheby's bread and butter, thanks to the consistent publicity which the
house enjoys in British newspapers as lofty as *The Times* and as popular as the *Daily
Mirror*. In this case, as usual, Sotheby's got the word first, and Peter Wilson
snagged the prize.

The painting which was crated off to London was "St. Bartholomew"; Rembrandt completed it in 1661, eight years before he died. It formed part of a series
of Jesus and the disciples, and the quiet tip from the auctioneers was that it might
make about $840,000, since "Aristotle" had brought more than $2,000,000 a few
months earlier. This portrait of the apostle shows him in an oddly businesslike
posture: white shirt, gray doublet, buff cloak. He sits fingering his chin, holding
what looks uncommonly like a carving knife, though it is more accurately a flail,
symbol of Bartholomew. In the eighteenth century, it was known as "The Assassin,"
in the nineteenth simply as "Rembrandt's Cook," and then as "The Suicide."

At least one collector in England was not at all perturbed by the talk of steep
prices; he has money enough for almost anything. In a notable illustration of how
dealers can help to keep prices healthy and auctioneers amiable, Colin Agnew of the
London firm of Thomas Agnew & Sons pleaded with Paul Getty to bid for "St. Bartholomew," estimating that the price might reach as high as $980,000. The figure

"St. Bartholomew": first an assassin, then a cook . . .

seemed "realistic," in Getty's words later, "but I wasn't at all sure that I could go to that."

For the sale itself, Major Lennox made one of his rare excursions to London, a city which he visits mainly to see its annual daffodil show. Wearing one of his customary tweed suits, he sat in the main room of Sotheby's looking not unlike a bulkier version of the painting under the gavel. The only comment he passed was an audible "Phew!" when the bidding got to $280,000. His mild eyes blinked every time it jumped in $28,000 leaps beyond that. In ninety-one seconds, "St. Bartholomew" had been knocked down to Colin Agnew, who for four days managed to keep secret the identity of the man he was acting for. The major, who had never bought a picture in his life, drove home to the castle and the daffodils.

Getty was run to ground as the new owner of the Rembrandt, bought as a comparative bargain for $532,000. He was well pleased by the price. "You might say," he pondered, "that a year or two later it would be over the top." He had been prepared to go to the $980,000 which Agnew had suggested "after an expert I called in gave me a similar figure." The billionaire had done his best to keep his purchase quiet "because there is always so much houha when anybody buys a painting of value."

The new Rembrandt, apostle, cook, or would-be suicide, hangs in Getty's library in his Sutton Place mansion in London now, keeping company with "Diana and her Nymphs," over which there was an argument with the Cleveland Museum, and his other Rembrandt, an early portrait of Marten Looten painted when the artist was a youngster of twenty-eight.

The treasures of Downton Castle are only one of the previously inviolate sources of grist for the auction mills, and Major Lennox was only one of the previously indifferent owners who may be prompted to sell because current prices are irresistible. There isn't an auction house or dealer's gallery of any consequence that fails to keep tabs on where the treasure lies. Their files bulge with carefully maintained records of where the best paintings live and where they go after every known sale. They court the owners by letter, telephone, and personal call, endeavoring to bring fresh pictures into the open. The best of them have an instinct for the moment when their chances run most favorably, conditioned perhaps by a death in the owner's family or a decline in the family fortunes.

Probably the most thorough job of record-keeping anywhere is done by Georges Wildenstein, whose Paris establishment contains eighty indexed cabinets chockablock with photographs of paintings, their history, bibliography, and any articles published about them. In a matter of minutes, he can have in his hand a complete listing of the pictures in, say, the collection of an English nobleman who hasn't sold anything in a lifetime. The files will also provide a clue, accurate to a few thousand dollars, of what each painting might be worth at current market conditions.

It must be said that the glamor of the salesroom sometimes outweighs the expertise of the Wildenstein archives. A representative of his had his eyes on a collection in another castle, this one in Scotland, and came within an ace of persuading the owner to sell it, for cash, at an impressive figure. But at the eleventh hour, an auctioneer from London convinced the proprietress that her paintings should go on the block, where they ultimately sold for $20,000 less than the Wildenstein offer.

The big dealers, faced with ever stiffer competition, make cash advances to secure a collection against the day it is put on the market, relying on their educated estimates of what its contents can be resold for, if not this year then next or during the coming decade. One member of the profession in New York noted recently, "We dealers make our evaluations by consulting the auction records. We can't consult each other's because we're all so secretive. We don't want people to know what we've paid for what we sell. The one advantage of an auction is that it helps set values, whether they're founded on a fad of the moment or not. But the publicity given to the auction houses is dangerous and makes for inflated prices. Some people lose their logic completely. Some collectors pay two to three times the prices that they would pay at a dealer's. They like the publicity. In contrast, Edmond de Rothschild once told me that if I ever disclosed what he had bought from me, I should never see him again."

Auctioneers and dealers alike, for all their skepticism about each other, retain a trace of ingenuous hope that they may come across that standard item of daydreaming, the forgotten Old Master found in someone's closet and worth a fortune. Wildenstein's find of de La Tour's "The Fortune Teller" is etched on everyone's memory, and though discoveries of any consequence are rare, enough of them come along to keep everybody's hopes up. Sotheby's not so long ago sold for close to $9,000 a Rubens oil sketch, "The Suicide of Dido," that had been bought at a country auction twelve months earlier for seven dollars. The tuckshop of Canford, an English boarding school, proved to be something of an Aladdin's cave when seven Assyrian reliefs were discovered mounted in the walls under several layers of paint. The best guess was that they had come from the palace of Sennacherib, built by thousands of slaves at the peak of his glory seven centuries before the birth of Christ, which Sir Henry Layard excavated in 1849. The tuckshop had originally been the private museum of Sir Henry's father-in-law, and the school picked up $39,900 minus commission from the British Museum when the souvenirs of Nineveh were sold at auction.

As even a casual reader of history would expect, Europe has it all over the United States when it comes to treasure hunting. It was in Italy, in the sacristy of the cathedral at Udine, that a painting ignored for two hundred years proved to be the work of Giovanni Battista Tiepolo and hopefully assessed at $392,000. That may have been a wild overvaluation, since the best recorded sale price of this painter was the $70,000 made at the Galerie Charpentier in 1960 for the huge pagan portrayal of "Beauty Abducted by Time."

In Germany, an anonymous artist's portrait of Marie-Louise of Parma, the wife of King Charles IV, was finally identified as a Goya, but it was still not for

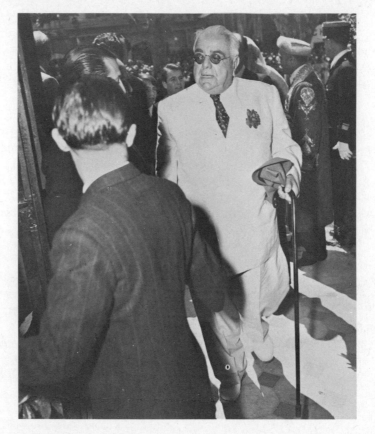

The late Aga Khan: some people have all the luck

sale. The Aga Khan, who had bought it for a few thousand francs, didn't need the money. In Dublin, five grimy canvases found in a garden shed were painstakingly cleaned and announced to have been painted by Francesco Guardi, with an estimated value of $1,400,000 set on them as a group. That was another unlikely price; a pair of paintings by the same artist was considered to have done well when it made $58,800 at Christie's in 1956.

The British Isles have a slightly uncanny reputation for providing discoveries in unlikely places. A garage proprietor in Hertfordshire was stripping wallpaper from the bedroom of the pre-Elizabethan cottage that he had bought next door to his gas station when he got the shock of his life. "It was as if those pictures were waiting to get out," he said after he had examined the five mural panels buried under six layers of paper and one of crumbling linen. Museum examiners judged that he had uncovered a virtually intact example of fifteenth-century religious wall paintings, their colors still bright, and that the tumble-down cottage must once have been a pilgrims' wayhouse on a road between shrines.

The lounge of a suburban hotel in North London provided almost as big a surprise. Guests used to gather in the dim light among the potted palms for their after-dinner coffee, few of them sparing a glance for the grimy picture painted on the low ceiling. Then the manager decided that the painting was worth cleaning. An art restorer uncovered, inch by inch, a canvas six feet by four feet that swam with gods and cherubs cavorting under a creamy gray sky. Weeks later, an architect who had lunched in the hotel took a look at the picture and was struck with the fantastic idea that it bore a striking resemblance to Tiepolo's "Olympus and the Four Continents" in the Bishop's Palace at Wurzburg, Germany.

Another expert was called in and confirmed the architect's judgment: this was the undoubted article, probably a preliminary study for the Wurzburg picture. It took art historians a while to decide how a Tiepolo arrived at the hotel, but they eventually came up with a solution. The building, originally erected in 1652, was bought as a home by the actor David Garrick, whose travels took him to Wurzburg; there, he probably visited the Bishop's Palace. He also traveled to Venice, where he could have bought the ceiling study from the painter himself— Tiepolo lived until 1770. That was enough for a London art dealer, who gladly paid $28,000 for the gilt-framed canvas after it had been gingerly peeled from the ceiling.

Experience has taught the high-quality auction houses to regard every bit of treasure trove with deep suspicion. The bonanza in grandmother's attic is a favorite theme for newspaper feature writers, whose readers may receive the impression that lost masterpieces turn up constantly and be led to imagine that every moldy canvas is a missing Rembrandt. The truth is that the odds against such near miracles are longer than for collecting on the winner of an Irish Sweep.

A favorite story in the business had to do with an American tourist in Italy just before the outbreak of the Second World War. In Florence, where the faking of art always was a factory business, he bought a Titian at the appropriate price of several thousand dollars. To beat the government ban on exporting Old Masters, the American engaged a restorer to varnish the painting liberally and, when it was dry, to daub a modern landscape over it as a disguise. The deception tricked the Italian Customs, and the canvas arrived safely in Paris. There, the gleeful collector had another restorer strip off the overpainting and bring the picture to its original glory. The first week's labor removed the landscape, but the restorer, a conscientious worker, felt that he could do better. At the end of the second week, he presented the tourist with his masterpiece: under the Titian he had uncovered an excellent portrait of Mussolini.

When lost works turn up in wholesale lots, auctioneers, dealers, and museums grow extremely nervous, though there seems to be no limit to collectors' optimism. In 1959, the late Jerry Giesler let it be announced from his Hollywood law offices that a TV repairman living in Pasadena had brought with him from his native Italy fourteen years earlier $10,000,000 worth of Old Masters. He had been keeping these family heirlooms under his bed and in a closet. A respectable art appraiser had examined them and pronounced them as sixteenth- or seventeenth-century work, in poor condition, and without particular value.

"Stones in the street," said the appraiser, Taylor Curtis, in a memorable admonition, "may be millions of years old, but you can't sell them as art."

But the repairman had an "agent," who owned an electrical-supply store, and that businessman called in an authenticator described as Professor Amadore Porcella, "a cataloguist for the Vatican Gallery of Art," who thoughtfully attributed three of the ten pictures as a Caravaggio, a Tintoretto, and a Lorenzo Lotto. Porcella urged an old associate of his, a Chicago restorer and sculptor named Alexander Zlatoff-Mirsky, to come and take a look. The two of them had consulted together before, in Chicago, when two local attorneys bought for $2,200 three paintings which Porcella identified as masterworks of Giorgione, Bellini, and Raphael Sanzio, whose worth he put at $1,600,000. An enthusiastic Chicago art dealer disclosed that Porcella had also authenticated a "Leonardo" for him in the past.

Zlatoff-Mirsky took on the painstaking task of restoring the Pasadena paintings. Under usual circumstances, it could take as long as twelve months for each. But in three weeks all the restoration work was announced as complete, the works were secure in a bank vault, and it was time for the conference in Hollywood, an area where art collectors abound, including Vincent Price, who went to work as a determined and discriminating mass buyer for Sears, Roebuck, and Edward G. Robinson, fifty-eight of whose Impressionists and Moderns sold to Stavros Niarchos for $3,250,000. The day after news of the TV repairman's treasure broke in the headlines, a Vatican official acknowledged that Porcella had indeed worked there, on a guidebook about a quarter of a century earlier. There was no immediate rush on the part of the auction houses to stake a claim on the Pasadena pictures.

Word of discoveries and the availability of paintings for sale reaches the auctioneers in any number of ways. Professional scouts have been scouring Europe since the Renaissance princes went bankrupt in sixteenth-century Italy after control of the world's finances was wrested from their fingers by the new merchant classes. The major auction houses have always been glad to pay, in cash or a share of commissions, for information leading to worthwhile finds. Some dealers have similar commercial ties with the auctioneers, tipping them off when they get word of a painting or a collection which the owner wants to sell.

The competitive facts of life compel the auction houses to search for top-notch material, where in the comfortable, less profitable past they could afford to wait for trade to come to them by way of letters, telephone, or inquiring visitor. Some European houses keep "runners" on their payrolls, though it is more customary for tipsters to operate as free-lances, shopping for themselves if they can afford it or if they see the chance to make a quick profit, otherwise selling only to the highest-paying auctioneer or dealer the information that works are available.

Occasionally a runner is blissfully ignorant of the value of what he is peddling, as in the case of one panel by Piero della Francesca, none of whose work has turned up in the marketplace for nearly twenty-five years and whose finest paintings would now command something in the region of $1,500,000 apiece. Dr. William F. Suida, the late curator of and adviser to the Kress Foundation, was once approached in Vienna by a runner who had been trying for weeks to find a buyer for a sizable panel which he toted through the streets by day and checked into hotel or restaurant cloakrooms every night.

The tout, possibly feeling that there must be something wrong with unsalable merchandise, asked Suida what the painting might be. The Viennese curator, who arrived in the United States as a result of the Second World War, had an amazing knowledge of Italian art, his first love. Examination convinced him that the panel was a Piero della Francesca, and he asked the runner's permission to announce the find. He never again heard from or saw the peddler. Some months later the panel reappeared—"St. John the Evangelist" was now one of the proudest possessions of the Frick Collection after passing from hand to hand in one of those unrecorded chapters which stud the lives of most Old Masters of such antiquity.

The first task which a dealer or reputable auction house undertakes when an unknown but interesting work comes along on offer is to try to check its credentials. No dealer has archives more extensive than Wildenstein and no salesroom leader has a handier ready reference than Leslie Hyam's homemade pocket-size notebooks, but every gallery, dealer's or auctioneer's, maintains some kind of library of photographs, catalogues, sales records, books, and magazine articles. Usually there is no need to resort to any scientific testing of pigments or canvas; a good pair of eyes can judge if the painting is worth close study or opinions from outside experts.

Valuations of genuine discoveries, no matter how well pedigreed, owe much more to guesswork than foreknowledge. They are susceptible to time, the tide of public opinion, and the popularity of the painter. To take an extreme example, "A Reading from Homer" by Sir Lawrence Alma-Tadema (1836–1913) made $33,000 in 1903 when it came up in the Henry Marquand sale in New York, but when "Roses of Elagabalus," which had originally been commissioned for $20,000, reappeared at Christie's in 1960, it received not a line of publicity anywhere and fetched just over $200. On the other hand, George Stubbs, whose uncompromising eighteenth-century horses and hounds could be bought for as little as $125 just before the First World War, regularly sells for $100,000 nowadays, when his reputation stands at its peak.

All too often the excitement over a new-found masterpiece develops into an altogether different discovery. A very large proportion of "treasures" are clumsy fakes, often nothing more than two clobbered-together halves copied from two separate originals to lend a spurious style to the forgery. French Impressionists are currently a favorite target for this form of handicraft. It was a dual forgery of this kind that helped set off an international scandal in the fall of 1962.

Walter Chrysler, Jr., the automobile manufacturer's son who is no longer connected with the family business, has been described as probably the "most active collector in the world today," with paintings and sculpture running beyond 3,000 in number, with an estimated value of $50,000,000. He has been exceptional among fellow enthusiasts in that he has sold almost as heavily as he has bought. Some of his disposals have commanded top-quality prices, such as the $613,256 earned when twenty-five Impressionist and Modern paintings and four drawings from his stock went under Sotheby's gavel in 1959.

By popular account, Chrysler bought his first painting, a little Renoir, when he was a fourteen-year-old schoolboy at Hotchkiss, where his proctor ripped it to bits because a small nude was included in the landscape. The incident left the young automobile heir undeterred. In 1956, some thirty-two years later, he had $5,600,000 worth of his massive collection packed into three moving vans for an eighteen-month tour of United States museums. In 1959, he opened his own museum in an old Methodist church in Provincetown, where he was often to be found during Cape Cod summers sitting at the door collecting the tax-free one-dollar admission charge levied on visitors to this educational display.

The range of his taste and the daring of some of his purchasing stirred comment from fellow collectors and art specialists, who talked of his "bizarre," and "eccentric" assemblage of works of art. Some of the titles alone supported their comments: "Samson Bringing Honey to his Parents"; "The Infant Savior Demanding the Cross from St. John"; "The Continence of Scipio." His explanation was that he consistently sought out buyers' markets. "When other collectors bought large canvases," he said, "I would buy small pictures. Later, when small paintings were more readily hung, I acquired large ones. When interest lagged in English, Dutch, and Flemish schools, I added them."

As early as 1939, thirteen years before the Cognacq sale in Paris set new levels for the painter, Chrysler established an auction record by paying $27,500 for Cézanne's portrait of Madame Cézanne, a picture which he resold at Sotheby's twenty years later for $112,000 to raise funds for his museum. Very few dealers had a kind word for Chrysler, and he in turn expressed poor opinions of most of them, questioning their ability to judge paintings and squabbling with some of them about prices. As a buyer, he has operated with the courage of his convictions. One of his supporters has said, "Mr. Chrysler is apparently a man who insists on his own judgment and makes his own decisions, based on his own information, education, and the extent of his knowledge of the art world, without the very expensive services of the so-called experts. Most collectors buy certificates. Mr. Chrysler buys paintings. He has done so honestly."

The first public questioning of the reliability of some of his possessions arose after 187 of them, part of a larger show which had hung in Provincetown, were exhibited in the National Gallery of Ottawa. He had offered them here on the understanding that he would choose what was lent and the Canadian museum would agree to display everything he sent up. There had been private gossip for some time previously about the authenticity of a considerable number of items in his collection, but the National Gallery plunged ahead with the show, lending its prestige to the borrowed paintings.

Georges Braque's "Woman with a Mandoline," owned by Walter Chrysler, Jr.

The ensuing scandal was explosive enough to blast holes in the confidence among buyer, seller, dealer, and auctioneer upon which the international market is founded. The trouble began when John Canaday, the art critic of *The New York Times,* was prompted to take a close look at the Ottawa display. What he saw prompted him to decide that "within this large and fine exhibition there is secreted a second and smaller one in which pedigrees are nonexistent or dubious, and attributions are arbitrary to such an extent that, the stylistic evidence being what it is, one must question them."

The catalogue of the exhibition also came in for some close study. It provided some strange prose. There was, for instance, attributed to Seurat, a "Seated Figure of a Man and Woman, oil on canvas, 8 x 6 inches, horizontal, 1885, not dated, not signed." Its list of credentials began by citing its sale at the Hôtel Drouot, Paris, in 1949. The word from Paris was that "there was said to be no record" of that sale. The painting was one of many which Chrysler bought from the Hartert Galleries, of Manhattan, conducted by Joly Hartert, who originally started his career like many other dealers by handling furniture and bric-a-brac before moving into pictures. His attorney described Hartert as one of the few who "have no pretensions. He guarantees nothing. He sells as is."

The straightforwardness of the bills of sale apparently appealed to Chrysler. They stated that any artist's name on a painting "is description only," that the gallery did not warrant any picture's authenticity. "Chrysler was fed up with the plush showrooms and the experts with their expensive certificates," said Hartert's legal spokesman.

The rest of the Ottawa catalogue listing for the "Seated Figure of a Man and Woman" simply noted that it had been shown in Dallas (as part of Chrysler's moving-van expedition) and recorded in a book published in connection with the Texas show. Certainly it was not listed in the definitive catalogue, "Seurat," prepared jointly by Dorra and John Rewald and published in Paris by Georges Wildenstein in 1960. One Paris expert ventured further and flatly declared that the painting seemed to have been copied from two authentic Seurat works, the upper half from one and the lower half from another.

The doubtful Seurat was only one of dozens of pictures—including some with pretensions of being by Cézanne, Renoir, Degas, Van Gogh, Matisse, and Bonnard—that came under critical fire. The target for questioning was their pedigree. A painting's authenticity, or "provenance," is supported by its record of previous ownership. Ideally, this can be traced back to its creator, a point which another dealer who had sold work to Chrysler was quick to emphasize. Harry B. Yotnakparian, with a gallery on Madison Avenue, said, "We guarantee the period but never the authenticity of a painting. We never sell anything 'by' any artist. How can I do that when I wasn't there when it was painted?"

Almost always there are chapters in the life of an Old Master when the record was interrupted, but in the case of Impressionists and later schools a continuous and foolproof pedigree is more usually obtainable. In the Ottawa show, something like half of the total had question marks in their background, for catalogue references to unknown French galleries or for the citing of experts and collectors unidentifiable by other art specialists.

Chrysler himself, who perhaps owed some mistakes to undue reliance on his own unsupported judgments, remained at his Provincetown museum at the height of the critical storm, selling copies of the catalogue of his collection at four dollars apiece. "So far as I know, the pictures are what they purport to be," he said at the time, "and I don't know what all the excitement is about. If there is any serious doubt about their authenticity, they will be withdrawn."

Behind the uproar stood the New York attorney and collector, Ralph F. Colin, who on earlier occasion had led a successful fight to close down a local gallery after its proprietors tried to sell him a fake Soutine. Colin's concern over the dubious ethics which are increasingly part and parcel of the boom in prices prompted him early in 1962 to act as godfather, administrative vice-president, and legal counsel of the new Art Dealers Association, established as a watchdog of the marketplace. With his wife, he stopped by the Chrysler museum one summer weekend before the show got on the road for Ottawa. "We were struck by the large percentage of fakes," he said later. "They weren't even good fakes."

Returning to New York, he went into conference with the association's president, Alexandre Rosenberg. With the approval of the group's forty-five members, it was decided to take "any necessary steps to bring the Chrysler situation to the attention of proper authorities and the public." That membership is made up exclusively of dealers. Colin happens to be counsel for and a director of Parke-Bernet. Leslie Hyam wanted to enroll Parke-Bernet in the organization, but because of potential conflict of interests between the trade and the auction houses, he has not at this writing been admitted.

The association lived up to the promise, made early in its life, that it would pull no punches in first investigating and then prosecuting abuses. The first move was to pass along the word to Ottawa that there were possibly fakes among the pictures. This was done through the services of an official of another Canadian museum, but the National Gallery put on the show, undeterred. Then the dealers' group notified the United States Customs, hoping that the doubtful paintings would be seized at the border on their return trip on the grounds that they were not what they purported to be and were therefore dutiable. Customs officials, as it happened, simply handed them over to Chrysler when they were shipped back to the U.S.

The Internal Revenue Service was alerted "because," as Colin explained, "we believe Chrysler operates his museum as a tax-exempt organization." The association also urged the tax men to investigate the returns of dealers who had sold the pictures to Chrysler. In Colin's words, "If they had sold real Impressionist works, the market price would have been something like $2,000,000, and they should have filed returns on that income."

Finally, in a flurry of alarms set off among art experts and dealers outside the bounds of the association, the group filed a formal complaint with the New York County District Attorney's office, asking it to determine whether fraud had been perpetrated. "The unwary public," said Colin, "assumes all the paintings are good when they see them shown with undoubted masterpieces."

That warning applies most particularly to what is loosely called Modern Art, the most important "discovery" of all, in that it keeps the gavels of the auction houses banging when the Old Master traffic dwindles closer to the vanishing point every year. Generally speaking, American painting can be divided into two eras, with the dividing point established as the night of February 17, 1913, when the Armory show opened in New York. In the following days, a record crowd of nearly 130,000 crowded into the maze of temporary galleries created in the headquarters of the Sixty-ninth Regiment, to jeer at their first glimpse of the primary colors of Matisse, the cubist shapes of the Picassos, the gleaming metals of Brancusi, and that epochal nude of Marcel Duchamp caught in midstride descending her transcendental staircase.

Yet these Moderns made the Traditionalists, whose work was hung in the show, too, look like pale ghosts. Within the next decade or so, the world of American art was shaken to its axis. The academic tradition among contemporary painters never recovered from the earthquake. The avant-garde schools of Futurists, Neo-Plasticists, Non-Objectivists, Abstract Expressionists, Tachists, and the rest flourished like a sprouting forest of green bay trees. Associative "meaning" in their pictures vanished. Recognizable objects of living, from bison to bathers, which had been depicted in murals and on canvas ever since cave-dwelling epochs made way for increasingly abstract harmonies or dissonances of color and form.

From the auction houses' point of view, it has meant money in the bank. There is an endless supply of Modern Art to be bought and sold in the salesrooms. Traffic is so steady that a scale of prices has been established, most of them rising steadily and some sensationally. Thomas Hart Benton, the great American muralist and one of the last of the Traditionalists, regards his former pupil, the late Jackson Pollack, as the one native genius among the Contemporary schools.

Pollack's "drip" paintings could be bought in the mid-Forties for $100 apiece; in 1960, one sold for $100,000. Georges Mathieu, a particularly abstract Frenchman, is reputed to be able to cover a fifteen-foot canvas in twenty minutes. A more modestly scaled picture of his sold in New York for nearly $4,000 in 1960, and some of his heroically sized works sell for four times as much.

They are by no means exceptional so far as price is concerned. The "Big Four" among the Moderns, who are now regarded as the Grand Old Men, can be listed as Picasso, Matisse, Braque, and Fernand Léger. The analyst Richard Rush, in a study of how their prices have surged, has noted that a good Matisse can scarcely be found today at less than $50,000. But in 1918 Gertrude Stein sold his ferocious "Woman with a Hat" for $500, and he once traded an important drawing for a samovar. In the span of twenty years, Braque went from $475 (for his "Vase of Anemones") to $145,000 (for "Violin Composition," owned by Nelson

Rockefeller and auctioned for the benefit of the Museum of Modern Art). Léger's poster-bright abstractions could be bought for $500 in 1944, but a purchaser had to come up with $82,500 for his semi-abstract "The Smoker" in 1960.

For auctiongoers outside the millionaire market, there is a constant supply of medium- and modest-priced Modern paintings. The demand for them keeps a lot of artists and their dealers happy, or at least well fed. It is not at all certain that every purchaser knows what he is buying, but the pictures have become what Thomas Benton has labeled a "prestige commodity." So long as the prices hold up and the turnover is swift, nobody complains.

Louis Marion's composure was once put to the test when the bidding for a small Contemporary by the German Abstractionist Hans Hartung had reached $10,500, and someone noticed that the picture had been hung upside down. "Upside down or downside up, will someone give me $11,000?" asked Marion without a pause.

Needless to say, someone did.

XI

LIFE BENEATH THE SURFACE

WHEN Sir Alexander Korda died in 1956, he left behind a reputation as the producer of some superior British motion pictures, a young widow who subsequently married again, and an art collection for which he had paid something like $140,000. It turned up in thirty-three lots, a handsome gathering of French paintings and magnificent small bronzes, at Sotheby's one June evening in 1962, as did the former Lady Korda, along with a sprinkling of actors and actresses whose careers he had helped to establish.

To the customary flourish of pink awnings, white ties, and imported evening gowns, they arrived with the crowd of two thousand lesser luminaries, including Graham Greene, Henry Moore, and the Maharani of Baroda in canary-colored silk, in the expectation of seeing fresh sales records made.

The Somerset Maugham dispersal of thirty-five pictures a few weeks earlier had brought $1,466,864, and the auctioneers had spread the word that the Korda event might well top that figure by quite a wide margin, perhaps making as much as $2,000,000 in those summer days when only Wall Street bears seemed to doubt that prices could go on climbing forever.

The widow, a Toronto truck farmer's daughter, had put the works up for sale to provide a trust fund for her four-year-old daughter and two-and-a-half-year-old son by her second marriage to David Metcalfe, an insurance broker. In the span

167

Soutine's "Confectioner"

of sixty minutes, Deborah Kerr, Jack Hawkins, and the rest of the throng watched Soutine's powerful, pathetic "Confectioner" fetch $68,400, a Degas nude go for $201,600, and the real star of the evening bring $224,000. This was a well-known Van Gogh still life, impeccably pedigreed in a letter of 1889 sent from Arles by the painter to his brother Theo: "I have just finished a new canvas which has almost what you would call *chic, a* wicker basket with lemons and oranges, a cypress branch, and a pair of blue gloves."

The two Metcalfe children, asleep in their parents' Chelsea home, grew richer at the rate of $270,000 a minute, but it was a somewhat disappointing evening, producing only $1,308,116 instead of a total to overshadow Maugham's. The explanation lay partly in the fact that the New York Stock Exchange was acting up, partly because one of the anticipated delights, a Cézanne water color estimated to be worth at least $116,000, had been withdrawn from the sale the night before.

"It was one of my favorites," said Mrs. Metcalfe. "I could not bear to let it go." Her sentimental explanation shielded the unsentimental fact that there were serious doubts about its authenticity. A London critic had privately pointed this out twenty-four hours before it was due to go under the gavel, so that there was no alternative but to take it out of circulation.

It would not be surprising if he were right. The art boom has resulted inevitably in bringing a flood of forgeries, mostly concocted in workshops in Paris and Rome, on to both the American and European markets. More often than not, they are sold at auction, though unscrupulous dealers and confidence tricksters have a hand in disposing of them, too. One British authority, John Berger, has calculated that of late nineteenth-century and modern paintings, as many as one in two may be a fake, and one in four is unquestionably so. The United States Treasury Department once quoted another British expert to the effect that four out of five "antiques" sold on the market there are something other than genuine, adding its own formal warning that this appalling proportion "holds true for all foreign antiques."

Spurious Picasso water colors are one of the favorite products of the fakers, who are helped by the fact that he is known to have produced more than 25,000 pieces of art to date, ranging from wall paintings to ceramics, and he has been known to fail to recognize his own work when confronted with it. One of the most engaging young forgers of this generation included the Spanish master's water colors and gouaches in his long list of counterfeits, though Jean-Pierre Schecroun, aged thirty-three, drew the line at oil paintings; that would "take too long," he said.

During the two active years that ended with his arrest in Paris in May, 1961, Jean-Pierre turned out more than a hundred forgeries, among them being forty-two Picassos, three Joan Mirós, Légers, de Staëls, Kandinskys, three Braques, six Hartungs, and two Jackson Pollacks, painted to order. Galleries in New York, Paris, London, and Cologne paid some $200,000 for them. They were thoughtfully provided with various certificates of authenticity, as is the custom in such instances, and, naturally enough, the certificates turned out to be forgeries, too.

It is usually a dealer who launches a painter on a career of deception, and this held true in the case of Jean-Pierre. He got started when a dealer, Francis Manlay, urged him to copy "La Femme au Perroquet" by Fernand Léger, whose pupil Jean-Pierre had once been. With three other accomplices, the painter and the dealer had no trouble in unloading more Légers; indeed, they suffered their only profitless day when they tried to sell a genuine Léger with no certificate of its authenticity. "Forgeries," sighed the young forger later, "seemed easier to sell than authentic works."

They submitted a counterfeit pastel by de Staël to one expert, who clutched it to his heart and sobbed, "De Staël was my best friend." In exchange for the fake which he held so dear, he persuaded the gang to accept an authentic Raoul Dufy. But they had difficulty in selling it, so they went back to the expert and traded it for one of his collection of genuine de Staël pastels. With that, they had better luck, disposing of it immediately to another dealer for $1,000.

The team combined mass production with that classical formula for success which calls for giving the customer what he wants. Posing as dealers, the four accomplices would approach galleries in Switzerland, Germany, or some neighboring country to inquire what was most particularly in demand. If the dealer, for instance, replied "Picasso," they telephoned Jean-Pierre at his local hotel room and within a hour, working from memory or a catalogue photograph, he could produce another "Picasso" or anything else on order. One of the four salesmen would have the fake framed and "authenticated" so that before the end of the day, they could ring up another transaction concluded and another customer satisfied.

They stayed clear of the law until the Lefevre Gallery in London invited a French expert to authenticate a Georges Braque which had been sold on those premises. The new owners had doubts about it and its certification. The expert detected the fake, and Jean-Pierre landed in La Santé prison, where he was granted permission to continue painting so long as the signature on each work was "Schecroun."

A profound cynicism flavors most comments on the subject of forgery. A classic aphorism in the trade has it that Corot painted 2,000 pictures, 5,000 of which are in the United States alone. The same thought, somewhat enlarged, estimates that of Rembrandt's 700 canvases, there are 10,000 over here. On the other side of the Atlantic, an official French inquiry concluded that at the Hôtel Drouot, the leading Paris salesroom, at least one faked Utrillo changed hands every week.

Nevertheless, because money is the prime attraction and there is more of it available in the United States than anywhere else, Americans are the chief targets of the forgers. In one remarkable year, 1935, five of the sixty-one known copies of the "Mona Lisa" were sold to five separate Americans for a total of $1,500,000, and Jean Charles Millet, grandson of the Frenchman whose pictures led the great price boom of the Eighties, remarked in his prison cell, "The Americans have made me rich. You can sell anything to them if you make the price high enough."

Jean Charles was caught selling scores of forged paintings, palming most of them off as the work of his grandfather. He began by forging his ancestor's signature to a number of canvases which had been painted by students of Jean François Millet. Then, flushed with success, he set up shop as a dealer in Millets in partnership with a housepainter named Cazot. As their business expanded, Cazot demonstrated that he was as deft with sable brushes as at painting windowframes, and he concocted fresh canvases, first in the manner of Millet, then of Corot, Manet, Sisley, and a dozen members of the Barbizon School.

The paintings went to dealers for as much as $10,000, and the dealers passed them on for as much as six times more. One British museum handed over $97,000 for an "authenticated" Millet which Jean Charles boasted was a fake and, when put to the test, proved it to experts who had certified it. He and his colleague in crime received only short sentences. Most of their ultimate customers had been foreigners, and French law, which frowns on art forgery to the point of giving every artist the legal right to destroy personally any fake which bears his name, takes no cognizance of such crimes when only foreigners have been duped.

Abroad or at home, the American buyer is compelled to rely largely on his own acumen for protection. Though every work of art taken out of France may leave only with the consent of a commission appointed by the Louvre, the commissioners' concern is to prevent the export of objects of national importance, not to question the authenticity of what is submitted. Forgeries, therefore, are automatically granted export permits, which unwary foreigners accept as a pedigree. On this side of the Atlantic, works of art are allowed in free of Customs duty, so that there is seldom any official obstacle to the fakes being sold.

The salesrooms of France, while charging anything from sixteen to twenty-three per cent commission, offer the buyer a measure of protection which he receives nowhere else in the Western world. Though he is also subjected to a ten per cent sales tax, all auctions are supervised by the government. Official experts, whose names are listed by law on the catalogue, assist the auctioneers, and works that are sold must live up to their authentication or the buyer is guaranteed a full refund, and he has thirty years in which to claim it.

In the United States and Britain, it depends on the auction house's whim whether or not buyers of fakes get their money back in part, in full, or at all. All houses in their conditions of sale specify something to the effect that neither they nor the seller "warrants or represents, and they shall in no event be responsible for, the correctness of description, genuineness, authorship, provenance, or condition of the property." They often take out a bit more legal insurance in their own favor by adding that "no statement contained in the catalogue or made orally at the sale or elsewhere shall be deemed to be such a warranty or representation or any assumption of liability." In other words, the risk they assume in handling fakes is zero.

The would-be buyer may look for protection in the opinion of experts, but they are not to be relied on entirely. The wise ones who had attested the genuineness of Jean Charles's forged Millets had to confess, once they had been discredited in court, that they could not tell a fake from an original, so how many fakes he had sold was anybody's guess. Bernard Berenson, the benign and bearded sage of Florence, who was probably the most respected international authority of our era, allowed that he changed his mind from time to time for fifteen years about the pedigree of da Vinci's "La Belle Ferrionière" hanging in the Louvre, finally concluding that it showed no trace whatever of the hand of Leonardo.

William Goetz, the California collector, whose home is hung with the work of Monet, Cézanne, Matisse, Roualt, Dufy, Daumier, Manet, and Picasso, spent $50,000 in New York on a Van Gogh which he was assured was worth twice as much. Dr. Jacob Baart de la Faille, the Dutch art historian who has written five books about Van Gogh, vouched for its authenticity. Van Gogh's nephew, Vincent Wilhelm van Gogh, who owned the bulk of the paintings of his uncle which made up a Metropolitan Museum exhibition in the Fifties, declared it to be a fake. Three experts called in as jury by the Metropolitan agreed with him. At last hearing, five more experts in Europe had re-examined the painting and voted in favor of Dr. de la Faille.

To offset that vindication of judgment, the doctor could remember one monumental blunder, when in an *oeuvre* catalogue of all Van Gogh works he included thirty paintings placed at his disposal by the Galerie Otto Wacker of Berlin, whose proprietor was a former exotic dancer and partner in a taxicab company. International collectors, including Chester Dale of New York, were content to accept de la Faille's authority and snap up the pictures, some of which showed a slightly uncanny resemblance to each other, such as three "Olive Trees," four "Cypresses," and four "Self-Portraits." It was a "Self-Portrait at the Easel," Number 523 in the catalogue, which went to Chester Dale, vouched for by de la Faille as an "authentic and characteristic work by Van Gogh, painted by him while at Arles in 1888."

A subsequent announcement by de la Faille left the happy owners dumbfounded, while the Berlin police instituted some discreet inquiries. In the third person, he declared that he was "compelled to append a supplement" to his catalogue designating thirty works previously described as genuine as "dubious forgeries." The conclusion had been reached "only after exhaustive study" and the error was acknowledged "with deep regret."

His self-served slice of humble pie left art experts amazingly divided, with a good half-dozen roundly declaring that the doctor had been right the first time and was wrong now, that the paintings should be accepted not as spurious but as genuine. Some purchasers demanded their money back and got it; others were less fortunate. Wacker announced that he would sue de la Faille and anybody else who spread the doctor's opinions. He also took off for The Hague with nine of the suspect pictures, where Dutch experts declared them to be Van Goghs without question.

It took almost four years of investigation to bring Wacker to trial in Berlin charged with "persistent fraud." Two dozen experts were in court as witnesses for prosecution or defense, among them Dr. de la Faille, Vincent Wilhelm van Gogh, and two art critics, Hans Bremmer and Julius Meier-Graefe. Bremmer set the ball rolling—it went round and round like a marble on a roulette wheel—by declaring that there were hundreds of fake Van Goghs in circulation, anyway. Meier-Graefe outdid him by asserting, "Anyone who buys pictures and pays enormous prices for them on the strength of expert opinions alone deserves to meet with disaster."

The painter's nephew, Vincent Wilhelm, acknowledged under cross-examination that paintings from his relative's Brabant period had been strewn around the attic of his house like wastepaper, some unsigned, some half finished, all of them accessible to eager hands and later hawked from carts in the street.

But it was the soul-searching Dr. de la Faille who produced the greatest stir. Blaming "excessive scepticism" and the temporary loss of "absolute objectivity," he testified that "in respect of five of the thirty paintings, I withdraw my opinion that they are spurious."

The thoroughly bewildered court finally sentenced Wacker to twelve months in prison, which, on his appeal, were increased by seven months more. Frank Arnau, the expert on forgery, carefully reviewed what the experts had said and noted ironically that on the basis of their testimony it could be concluded that (a) all the pictures were genuine; (b) some were genuine and some spurious; (c) all were spurious; (d) some were spurious and some genuine, but the genuine were those declared to be spurious and the spurious those certified as genuine.

There is not a single expert in the annals of painting who has not made mistakes as an art detective, which is no surprise in light of the complexity of the problem. A faked Cézanne once deceived Cézanne himself. Picasso has almost certainly, in all good faith, signed drawings which were not his. Corot, an obliging soul but the most infuriating of all painters when it comes to authentication, was happy to add his signature to the output of needy friends so that they would enjoy an immediate income boost.

There are limitless types and kinds of faking, some of them as old as the history of collecting and not all originally intended to deceive. An Egyptian papyrus in the Stockholm Museum is a how-to-do-it manual for fabricating imitation precious stones from colored glass. The Fogg Museum of Harvard University, which makes a continuing study of counterfeit art, has displayed a small statuette of Amen-Ra, created during the Saite Period (663–575 B.C.) in the style of the XIIth Dynasty (2000–1788 B.C.) and bearing an inscription which, the museum points out, is a crude copy of the writing of the much earlier period, seeming to indicate that this work may well have been created as a forgery.

The collecting mania which seized partricians like Mark Antony and Agrippa made ancient Rome a paradise for forgers, most of them Greeks, who were kept busy counterfeiting stones for jewelry and producing statues signed with the distinguished name of Praxiteles. The British Museum in 1818 committed one of the many blunders which stud its records by buying a "genuine" contemporary bust of Julius Caesar which turned out to be less than a hundred years old.

The Raphael portrait
of Pope Leo X

Faking and collecting, which wax and wane together, both faded virtually to nothing in the Middle Ages, but the Renaissance saw both activities booming again. Only the counterfeiting of coins was a crime; the concept of forgery was unknown, since the majority of paintings were executed not on canvas but on walls, and to specifications as rigid as those for building a house, which made the name of the artist for the most part a matter of small importance.

When collectors set the style for transportable easel pictures, the copying of paintings became a recommended means of teaching the craft to apprentices and students. Beyond that, a patron might commission an established painter to copy another's work, as Ottaviano de' Medici had Andrea del Sarto copy a Raphael portrait of Pope Leo X. The portrait was a shining star in the enormous Medici collection in the Palatine Palace, and Ottaviano could not bear to part with it. He had the imitation made so that he could present it to a fellow nobleman in the guise of the original.

Raphael himself was scarcely above reproach; he painted his "Wedding of the Madonna," now in the Caen Museum of Painting, so closely along the lines of "Wedding of the Virgin" by his teacher, Perugino, which hangs in the Pinacoteco de Brera in Milan, that to a casual eye they would be almost identical in content and manner.

Rudolf II, the Holy Roman Emperor, became the despair of future authenticators when he ordered two court painters to make copies of the finest pictures in Venice and Rome to start his own collection in Prague. The job of sorting out originals from imitations commissioned by him has never satisfactorily been completed.

It is hard to brand Cellini and Michelangelo as fakers, yet Cellini used to brag about his abilities—never practiced, he vowed—as a forger of coins, and Michelangelo earned himself a teen-age reputation by a bit of patently sharp practice. As an apprentice in Ghirlandaio's Florence studio, he was set to copy as an exercise the drawing of a head by an unknown master, which an outside owner had sent in for that purpose. The young man admired the likeness which he produced so well that he handed in the copy and held on to the original. When a fellow apprentice tipped off the owner to what had happened, the man demanded the original back. But not even Ghirlandaio could distinguish betwen the genuine and the spurious drawing when the two were laid side by side; Michelangelo had taken the precaution of smoking and aging his copy. Only he could tell them apart, which "brought great fame" to him, on the testimony of one of his contemporaries.

At twenty-two, he demonstrated that his hand hadn't lost its cunning by transforming a brand-new "Sleeping Cupid" into a fake antique to please a client, the redoubtable Lorenzo de' Medici. He simply buried it in sour earth, faking the apparent date of origin of the stone by more than a thousand years. Dug out of the ground, it was sent to an art dealer in Rome, who sold it to Cardinal Riariof of San Girogio, a distinguishcd collector, for two hundred gold ducats, which was a fat price for the times, keeping 170 of them for himself and returning thirty to the youthful faker.

When the Cardinal discovered thc fraud, he forced the dealer to refund his money and, so the story goes, retained the statue for his collection, while Michelangelo contrived to keep his share of the loot. What eventually became of the forgery nobody knows. There is a "Sleeping Beauty" allegedly by Michelangelo on display in Turin nowadays, but it may safely be regarded as a fake by somebody else's hands.

No satisfactory definition of art forgery has ever been written, and it is extremely unlikely that any ever can be. Vast changes have occurred over the centuries in standards of probity. A fake can be an undoubted work of art. The shading between "genuine" and "spurious" is too fine to allow more than the establishment of broad categories into which fakes, forgeries, and deceptions can be divided. The Fogg Museum defines three such categories. First, work deliberately created and sold as the creation of some other artist or period. Second, the exact reproduction of a known work; and this is tricky ground to tread, especially since artists sometimes copy their own pictures—Rubens in his old age copied his own and the work of men who had died two centuries earlier. The third category, "restored" work, is trickier still, involving the riddle of where the original ends and the touching up begins.

Correggio, for example, commanded high prices from the time of King Charles I on, when collectors imagined that there existed hundreds of paintings by him. In fact, he died at the age of forty, in 1534, after painting mostly murals, which made his easel pictures exceedingly rare. Ten of them supposedly showed up in the collection of Philip, Duke of Orleans, a fraction of which was sold at Christie's in the 1790's, but the attribution in each case is not widely accepted today. Three genuine Correggios which had certainly been owned by King Charles had been "edited" by the Duke's father, Louis. They portrayed Leda and her swan, Io, and Dana, and their fleshy attractions offended Louis's sense of morality. In the presence of his priest, he ordered his court painter, Charles Coypel, to hack them to pieces.

Coypel later reassembled the pieces and "restored" them in the style of his day, which was to attempt to erase the dividing line betwen his own inferior repainting and the brushwork of Correggio. He sold "Leda" to Frederick the Great. In 1630, she found her way to the Kaiser Freidrich Museum in Berlin, where fresh surgery awaited her: she was given a new head, leaving her no more than two-thirds intact at most, though she still passed as an undiluted original. The sister painting, the "Danaë," also mutilated and patched, was bought by a British consul in Leghorn, who carried her home with him. She sold for 200 guineas at Christie's in 1804, fetched 2,000 guineas six years later as the only unquestionable Correggio in England, then sank to a humble £324 when she returned to the same auction rooms in 1819.

Modern standards demand that restoring, retouching, and repainting should remain clearly identifiable. In the case of important pictures, the rule is usually followed, if only because the battery of contemporary scientific devices which can be brought to bear on a doubtful picture make it child's play to detect most deliberate falsification. Over the past half century, virtually every major museum in the world has acquired a laboratory equipped to employ chemistry, X-rays, ultraviolet light, microscopes, spectroscopes, spectographs, fluoroscopes, and other optical instruments which are the weapons of the art scientist. They are used mainly to investigate the techniques of early artists' schools and to help in repairing and protecting the museum's stock. Only occasionally are they put to their most spectacular function, resolving disputed identities and exposing fraud.

Wilhelm Roentgen, who discovered X-rays, was the first to turn his new seeing machine to study objects of art. X-rays indicate the density of paint on canvas and the relative thickness of layers of pigment down to the first priming coat, revealing like an unalterable signature the artist's basic working method. The Fogg Museum owns a collection of nearly 5,000 X-ray plates of paintings from most of the world's museums and private holdings.

Employed in conjunction with a binocular microscope, which magnifies paint contours to the proportions of a mountain range, or ultraviolet radiation, which is simpler to operate and gives much the same result, the X-ray represents the first step in analysis of a painting. The second is a bit of chemical detecting. The laboratory technician stabs a hollow needle, twenty-five times slimmer than a human hair, into the canvas to take out a microscopic core of pigments. Tests with water, acids, and other solvents disclose what medium—oil, albumen, or carbohydrate—was used to mix the paint. In the shape, size, and crystalline structure of the particles the picture's history can be read.

At the Fogg, the ingredients of a painting can be matched for identification against an assortment of substances gathered from around the world—pigments,

Goering took "the woman taken in adultery," and she deceived him

oils, resins, scraps of old pictures, bits of plaster, and minute fragments of wall paintings from ancient Egypt and Rome.

A microscopic spot of cobalt blue helped run to ground one of the most renowned forgers of our time, Hans van Meergeren of Holland, who has been acclaimed as a near-genius in his own distorted right for his counterfeit Vermeers. One of them, "Supper at Emmaus," which he painted in six months during the 1930's after years of experiment, was hailed as "Vermeer's most important work" and bought for 550,000 gulden by the Rembrandt Association, a society of rich Dutch art lovers, for presentation to the Boymans Museum in Rotterdam. "The Woman Taken in Adultery" sold for 1,650,000 gulden and so impressed one of Holland's temporary conquerors, Hermann Goering, that he had it added to the Nazis' wartime plunder.

To save himself from charges of having collaborated with the enemy, van Meegeren confessed to the forgeries: the painting in the Goering collection was not a national Dutch treasure but a counterfeit, he admitted, one of fourteen "masterpieces" which he had faked. At first, nobody believed him; he had carried out his deception too well, using scraped-down canvases of the correct vintage, painstakingly aging his paint layer by layer in an oven at 110 degrees, tracking down the anachronistic colors of Vermeer's own palette.

In general, Vermeer painted in yellow, red, white, and blue, the blue being made from the mineral lapis lazuli, the basis of ultramarine, which shows up under a microscope in irregular, chunky particles. They are easily distinguishable from the smaller fragments of artificial ultramarine, which came into use early in the nineteenth century along with such newcomers as cadmium and cobalt blue. Van Meergeren went to London to buy expensive, comparatively rare, and supposedly genuine lapis lazuli, sparing no effort to produce counterfeits which he wanted to stand up to any foreseeable inspection.

The original tests that Dutch art experts applied to the "Vermeers" when the forger first unloaded them on to the market cast not a shadow of doubt on their authenticity. Only when further, detailed examination was performed did the secrets of van Meegeren begin to unfold. One link in the chain of evidence was provided by the "stab" test of "The Woman Taken in Adultery." The lapis lazuli was not entirely pure as it would necessarily have been in Vermeer's day. The supply van Meegeren bought in London had been adulterated with cobalt blue.

Though, after amassing at least $2,000,000 from his work, he died in prison in 1947, his name is still reviled by museum curators and collectors. For years following his death, the outraged Boymans Museum refused even to say where it was hiding "Supper at Emmaus." The confusion was worse confounded because van Meegeren's son once boasted that still more "masterpieces" which are admired around the world were really painted by his father; and nobody knows for sure just how many paintings the indefatigable forger made.

Trade in faked Old Masters has certainly diminished as a result of the application of science to picture sleuthing, but it has by no means disappeared. Traffic in Impressionist and Post-Impressionist counterfeits is growing by leaps and bounds. In the judgment of Alfred M. Frankfurter, editor-in-chief of *Art News,* "Americans are being fleeced . . . annually of sums reaching into the millions."

One reason the forgers flourish is that their handicraft seldom gets talked about except in the Sunday newspaper supplements. "As an unmentionable subject in the art world," Frankfurter has written, "fakes rank somewhere between halitosis and B.O. on the one side and the bastard child of a maiden aunt on the other." Collectors who have been fleeced are usually too proud, or too pained, to admit it. They prefer, if they are honorable, to take down the painting and hide it in the basement rather than have it exhibited as an acknowledged fraud for the enlightenment of all. The forger, still protected from exposure, is free to find another victim.

If the duped collector is something less than a man of honor, he may try to recoup his loss and pass the fake on to some other unsuspecting purchaser. John Rewald, a German art historian who fled to the United States in 1941, has related that he had once advised a collector that one of his paintings was a counterfeit, as other experts agreed, whereupon the owner consigned the fake for sale by an auction house. Rewald felt obliged to notify the auctioneer of his judgment, but the collector threatened to sue him and anybody else who denied the picture's authenticity. It changed hands under the auctioneer's gavel for "several thousand dollars."

Dealers seldom venture opinions, whatever their doubts about a painting's pedigree. Those museums which offer free consultation services on pictures will express judgment only on works which are owned by the people submitting them for examination, and then only if the works are not for sale and have not recently been purchased. This extreme reticence is understandable in view of the legal hazards involved. The laws of libel allow the owner of a fake to sue anybody who volunteers an unfavorable opinion about it, a prospect which permits many a collector to enjoy his possessions in ignorance if not in bliss.

Disparagement can be an expensive business for any critic, as the damages claimed and sometimes collected in court prove. The purchaser of one of van Meegeren's superb concoctions, "The Last Supper," for which he had paid 1,600,-000 gulden, filed suit for damages from one of the experts who had disclosed the deception on the grounds that his picture was a genuine Vermeer in spite of everything that had been said. The expert was fortunate in not losing the case.

Duveen's career as an international art dealer was studded with lawsuits, in four of which he had to defend himself for "defamation of property." The old Anderson Gallery, forerunner of Parke-Bernet, figured in one foray, when a collector, Carl Hamilton, found himself without a customer for either his little "Doria Crucifixion" by Piero della Francesca or a "Madonna and Child" by Filippino Lippi. The explanation, he complained when he brought action, lay in the fact that Duveen had publicly described the paintings as "worthless, retouched, and ruined" before their sale day arrived and passed on his doubts to Andrew Mellon, Mrs. John D. Rockefeller, and William Randolph Hearst, among others.

The case never came to trial; Duveen settled out of court for a considerable, undisclosed sum. He could afford to, of course, since through a middleman he picked up the "Madonna and Child," which later went to the Metropolitan, for $50,000, and the "Crucifixion" for $65,000. That was the last time a Piero della Francesca appeared on the market. Who was the customer that Duveen found for it? Andrew Mellon, who bought it for some $500,000 for the National Gallery in Washington.

It is usually safe, within limits, to criticize the pedigrees of paintings owned by the very rich, by museums, or by dealers so patently crooked that any schoolboy with a collection of museum picture postcards could testify against them. Paul Getty listened silently from afar while a painting for which he paid more than $560,000 suffered a drubbing at the hands of an English art scholar, Michael Jaffe. "Diana and her Nymphs Departing for the Chase," attributed to Peter Paul Rubens, was nothing more than a product of the school of Rubens, according to Jaffe, to which the master himself added a few finishing touches. The original "Diana," in Jaffe's view, hangs in the Cleveland Museum of Art, which bought it for $350,000 in 1959.

Of all the Old Masters, Rubens is the most hazardous when it comes to attribution. There was no clear line of demarcation between pictures he painted entirely himself and those to which subcontracting specialists added animals, still life, or bits of landscape after he had completed the main figures. Other pictures begun with his sketches were finished by his pupils, then touched up by him. His factory-style studio also turned out copies of his paintings made by his assistants with little or no participation by the master.

"Madonna and Child" by Filippino Lippi: neither worthless nor ruined

Jaffe staked his argument principally on what art experts call *pentimenti,* spontaneous alterations to a painting made by the artist while he works. Getty's "Diana" is amply endowed with these. One of her nymphs has two right arms, and one greyhound has a double tip to his nose, both instances of dualism caused by bits of overpainting beginning to emerge through the top layers of pigment as an effect of old age. They are evidence, according to the English authority, that Rubens had doctored clumsy workmanship by his assistants.

But Professor Julius Held, an art historian at Columbia University and Barnard College, who vouched for Getty's "Diana" against Cleveland's, took exactly the opposite view and regarded these *pentimenti* as vital testimony that the oil man's painting was the work of Rubens alone, while the museum's was a workshop copy, possibly with a few master touches. "An artist often changes his plan as he works," said Dr. Held. The Cleveland painting, while "handsome and valuable, has no *pentimenti;* it shows the smoothness that comes from copyists' work."

With forbearance unusual in such cases, neither J. Paul Getty nor the Cleveland Museum had a harsh word for the other. The argument was conducted with scholarly enthusiasm and without a single writ, though one party or the other had clearly been noticeably overcharged in buying "Diana."

An impressive price is, of course, essential to persuade knowledgeable collectors of a painting's authenticity. Only rank amateurs regard the salesroom as a bargain basement, which makes them easy prey for the unscrupulous sellers. Bargains seldom exist in art. One Manhattan attorney, Ralph F. Colin, who combines the practice of law with the study of painting, rates the odds at 999,999 to one that any cut-price picture purchased outside the better-known auction houses or from reputable dealers is sure to be a fake, and auctioneers and dealers will do their experienced best to get from a customer at least what they believe the painting is really worth.

Ralph Colin, along with John Rewald, Theodore Rousseau of the Metropolitan, Alfred H. Barr, Jr., of the Museum of Modern Art, and the Better Business Bureau of New York City collaborated a year or so ago to shut down one Manhattan gallery which had been importing fakes and studio sweepings in wholesale lots from France and selling them as originals, on which the two proprietors set an estimated worth of $25,000,000. Their catalogues listed Rembrandts, Gauguins, Van Goghs, Renoirs, Roualts, Manets, Dufys, and two spurious Picassos offered at $175,000 apiece. It was two phony paintings by Chaim Soutine which proved to be the gallery's undoing.

In its window there had been placed a discreet card saying that works were available by Soutine, a Lithuanian whom collectors discovered in Paris in the 1930's, buying for roughly $100 paintings which have sold ("Girl with Ducks," for example) for as much as $45,000. It also happened that Ralph Colin collected Soutines, and the card caught his eye. He went into the gallery, was shown the "Soutines," and wasted no time in making a report to the Better Business Bureau.

Yet only pressure brought to bear by the art critics and legitimate dealers compelled the gallery to close. No conclusive legal action could be taken, because fraud is exceedingly difficult to prove in court, and the laws covering the purchase of art encourage debate, not decision.

While the scientific laboratory is astonishingly effective in testing the age of purported Old Masters, its battery of instruments are virtually useless in authenticating Moderns, whose history is recent and paint raw. X-ray methods can tell when a painting is not chronologically genuine, but beyond that they cannot venture. Attribution depends in the last analysis on human skill however fallible, taste, and perception. Only close study can educate the eye to detect the hallmarks of spontaneous creation which the forger can never copy.

Exhibitions provide an important defense against the fakers. Any opportunity to examine pictures—on display in a gallery, a salesroom, a museum, or a home—helps the would-be customer. Museum shows explicitly arranged to expose forgery amount to a college course in detection, with the chance to compare good with bad, false with true. Then, when the time comes to buy, quality will speak for itself.

XII

FOR LOVE OR RANSOM MONEY

A work of art creates its own environment. It produces its own circle of admirers moved by its passion, who worship or covet the stone, the bronze,
the paint on canvas. It stirs aspirations and greed. It exercises its powers over
saints and rogues alike, tempting both into believing that whatever may be done
under its influence is justified.

The legal code of Italy concerning antique works of art is as strict as any in
the world, prohibiting their export from the country even on loan. Yet in 1948 the
Metropolitan Museum serenely handed over to M. Knoedler & Company a check
for $200,000 in payment for a portrait of St. Sebastian, painted in the fifteenth
century by Andrea del Castagno, which was hot off the boat from Italy. The first
word that the government in Rome had of the transaction came in a copy of the
American magazine *Art News*.

When an official protest was lodged, Knoedler produced a completely valid
export license. A round of investigations ended with the arrest of a Florentine attorney and two staff members of the civil-service office responsible for the control
of art exports, all three charged with smuggling. Their operation was a refinement
of what police recognize as the old "gypsy switch." They had tagged "St. Sebastian" with a forged license certifying that it was an import, brought in for cleaning
by fine Florentine hands. They then exchanged the import tag for an authentic

183

export permit, jeopardizing themselves upon their capture to the extent of fifteen years' imprisonment and fines, of $4,200,000—2,100 per cent of the painting's value.

Neither the New York dealers nor the Metropolitan were in on the plot. There is nothing in international law to command the return of works of art which have been illegally exported, so Knoedler kept the check and the Met held on to the picture.

Another respectable New York dealer borrowed an idea put into practice by Ambroise Vollard, Renoir's agent, who used to cut up into neat rectangles the painter's canvas sketch pads and have him sign each morsel for sale as an original. The American paid $28,700 for a similar piece of sketchily-painted canvas when the Kirkeby collection of Impressionists and Post-Impressionists arrived at Parke-Bernet. For $5,000, he engaged the firm of Julius Loewy, specialists in restoration, to carve out eight small scenes and frame them as Renoir sketches in oils. They were put on sale in the dealer's gallery for a total of $55,000, though at least one of them—a rather nebulous but rosy blonde removing her chemise—remained unsold four years later.

The Metropolitan Museum once got entangled with another dealer and another nation's export laws, those of France, in what one outraged deputy described as "a veritable crime committed against the national artistic patrimony." The artist involved was Georges de La Tour, an enigmatic seventeenth-century painter from Lorraine, whose work was forgotten for nearly three hundred years after his death in 1652. Then, at the beginning of the present century, the art historians were fascinated by the Caravaggesque quality of his paintings, their monumental stillness, the drama of his lighting. There are no more than twenty reliably attributed pictures to admire, six of them in the Louvre. All of those are in his nocturnal mood; of his "daylight" style, only two canvases are known. It was one of these, "The Fortune Teller," that was the cause of Franco-American crossfire.

It first came to light in 1948 when a monk in the Benedictine Monastery of Solesmes, France, discovered it in the possession of what the records name only as "a good family" in the region. The news was dutifully passed back to the Louvre, whose chief curator of paintings and drawings, René Huyghe, scurried off to the house and was delighted with what he saw. On the strength of his report, the Louvre directors were on the verge of acquiring the painting out of their annual purchasing budget of some 50,000,000 francs to add to the museum's collection of more than 10,000 other pictures when the de La Tour was whipped away from them.

How many people had heard about the monk's discovery could be anybody's guess, but certainly Georges Wildenstein knew of it in his elegant home at 57 Rue la Boëtie, just off the Champs Elysées. Wildenstein, a slim, taciturn dandy, has often been described as "the world's greatest art dealer," which he may well be; he is unquestionably its shrewdest. His father, Nathan, tutored him as a schoolboy; at seventeen, Georges started building up his office archives, which at last count contained 100,000 photographs, 300,000 books, and 100,000 auction catalogues.

He runs a black Rolls-Royce limousine; some racing periodicals; *Arts et Spectacles,* which is a weekly newspaper devoted to the subject of its title; and *La Gazette des Beaux-Arts,* a scholarly journal dating back to 1859, which he took over during the Second World War and temporarily published in New York. He has also controlled for the past several years, at the invitation of the Institut de France, which is the lawful owner, the ancient Musée Jacquemart-André.

His Gallic critics, of whom there has seldom been a shortage, allege that he uses this state-owned establishment as a kind of business annex, charges unduly high admission fees, hangs uncatalogued paintings there which he hopes to sell, and has gone so far as to encourage the sale of soft drinks during exhibitions. Nobody has denied that he cherishes good friends in high places and conducts an information service second to none, made up of agents, scouts, runners, and government officials strategically located around the world.

Only Wildenstein and his informant in this case would know how soon he learned about the newly-found de La Tour, and only Louvre insiders could explain what held up their decision to offer an even remotely satisfactory price. The first skinflint offer led the owners to reply that "another party," who happened to be Wildenstein, was willing to pay more. The Louvre then inched up its bid, to perhaps 5,000,000 old francs, which was its ceiling price. The dealer did not hesitate to top that. He acquired "The Fortune Teller" for something less than $20,000, a "derisory" figure in the view of his detractors, whose research showed that $50,000 had been paid for the artist's work even before the current boom began.

All of this happened when the museum's directors were on summer vacation away from Paris. René Huyghe was hamstrung, since only the board could approve the expenditure of additional funds, and the directors were unlikely to take up the subject before October. But he warned the owners that even if they sold to anyone else, the painting would never be permitted out of France. French law makes the export of original paintings subject to the approval of the Louvre and gives that state museum the right to "pre-empt" them for the same price at which they would be sold abroad.

But by this time the painting had passed to Wildenstein. When he applied for an export visa, the Louvre blocked that. He tried again, specifying that he wanted to put "The Fortune Teller" on exhibition in New York and requesting a temporary permit for this purpose. Unlike the Italian code, French law gives the Louvre no grounds for opposing temporary departures, though when permission was granted to Wildenstein, the specific request was made that the painting should be returned to French soil. This was now 1949, and Huyghe left the Louvre to take up another appointment. The picture arrived back safely in France some months later.

Its whereabouts over the next years can only be guessed at. Since it never did appear in any exhibition, it may be assumed that it was stored for safekeeping most of the time on Wildenstein's Paris premises, part of the time in his New York vaults, which have contained as many as 250 Picassos at a go, seventy-nine Fragonards,

Left to right: Marcel Gromaire, a buffet view of Paris, Andre Malraux

ten each of the works of Cézanne, Van Gogh, Gauguin, and Corot, along with five Tintorettos, one of them twelve feet tall. Outraged French art critics later claimed that Wildenstein "hid" the painting so that their countrymen might forget it ever existed, while by carefully placed suggestions in New York he roused officials of the Metropolitan "to a state of high excitement."

On one of the rare occasions when he was questioned privately about the so-called concealment, the dealer countered with, "What do you mean, I kept it hidden?" And why had he not allowed the painting to be photographed during that period? "Just because I own something as personal property, that doesn't mean I have to consent to its being photographed, does it?"

He took the opportunity to say that he didn't know the Louvre was after the picture until it was too late and that the museum could have had it from him for "between two and five million francs" (old currency) if they had asked for it. "Never, when I have known that the Louvre was negotiating for a painting, have I attempted to outbid them." He also suggested that too much publicity about the storm that had blown up "would not be in the interests of American museums."

The most interested of those, the Met, had just announced that it had acquired "The Fortune Teller" from Wildenstein. Its export "conformed to all the legal requirements, which include the Louvre's approval," reported *The New York Times*. The painting for which the dealer had paid no more than $20,000 had fetched something between $600,000 and $800,000 from its new proprietors, according to the word in Paris, where experts calculated that at auction it would

Andre Malraux (here with President and Mrs. Kennedy
and Mme. Malraux at the Mona Lisa ceremonies) attempted the answer

probably have gone for no more than $150,000. The Met, they grumbled, was "not following an intelligent buying policy."

That was the least of their complaints. The de La Tour should never have been allowed to leave the country permanently, they said. Their outcry produced a spate of letters to Paris newspapers and art journals and demands in the Chamber of Deputies for an investigation of how a painting could be removed when it was "part of the national patrimony." André Malraux, the Minister of Culture, attempted some of the answers.

The picture, he declared, had received a temporary export visa (its second) two days before Christmas, 1957. That was the year when Wildenstein, who sports the red rosette on a silver ribbon denoting a commander's rank in the Legion of Honor, donated to the Louvre one of the three panels comprising Monet's "Le Déjeuner sur L'Herbe," not to be confused with Edouard Manet's earlier painting with the same title. But the panel that Wildenstein gave the Louvre would be valued at only a fraction of the de La Tour. It was gratefully accepted. The new curator of paintings who had succeeded Huyghe, Germain Bazin, was in the throes of reorganization, and he wanted, he said, to put added emphasis on such Impressionists as Monet. He apparently succeeded—Monet's work is fashionable today.

On the strength of the second temporary permit, against which no objections were raised, "The Fortune Teller" was now secure in New York. The following year, Wildenstein applied for export clearance. Lacking any opposition from the Louvre, the permanent visa was issued, as called for by law, by the Finance Min-

The Louvre lost the "Mona Lisa"

istry's office on receipt of a letter from the Education Ministry authorizing the action. The dealer always could wield a lot of power.

The license, André Malraux found, "seems to have been accorded as compensation" for the approximately one-third of "Déjeuner sur L'Herbe." As soon as the facts were out, a storm broke about Wildenstein's sleekly barbered head. He shrugged it off. It was all, he said, the reaction of ambitious, jealous people frustrated by their own errors. Didn't he think that the price the Met had paid was exorbitant? Hardly. He considered "The Fortune Teller," he said, no more important than many other works exported from France since 1945. "Old masterpieces sell for nothing these days by comparison with Moderns and Abstracts. If one pays $160,000 for a Braque, for instance, then a price of $300,000 would be a gift. The prices paid for Moderns are crazy. Thus the price paid for the de La Tour is not exorbitant in this context." (He was speaking in 1960, before "Aristotle" appeared.)

One of his critics, Alfred Daber, who conducts a gallery on the Boulevard Haussman, accepted the inevitability of the situation with a mixture of outrage and fatalism. "As early as 1950," he said, "I predicted that the painting would leave the country some day. It is scandalous to have allowed it to escape. It was certainly the most important painting to have left France since the end of the war. But Wildenstein's role was to look out for his own business interests. This he did. The role of the Louvre was to insure that, in the interests of the history of French painting, 'The Fortune Teller' remain in France. This the Louvre did not do." As for the Metropolitan, it was "merely doing its job, too," said Daber. There was some idle talk about the possibility of the museum's offering to return the de La Tour to France, but as in the case of "St. Sebastian" the Met retained the painting and the dealer kept his money.

"The Duke of Wellington" by Goya

Somewhere along the line, ethics may have suffered, but there was no question of laws having been broken. Yet it is well within the power of a great painting to persuade its admirers that any crime can be condoned for its sake. An Italian workman once lifted the "Mona Lisa" from the Louvre to avenge Napoleon's looting of art treasures from Italy. Irish nationalists, moved by similar patriotic sentiments, raided the Tate Gallery in London and took "Jour d'Eté" by the French Impressionist Morisot to Ireland on the ground that it belonged there under the disputed will of Sir Hugh Lane, a Dublin connoisseur who went down with the *Lusitania* in 1915.

But the oddest of all recent thefts involves the portrait that Francisco Goya painted of the Duke of Wellington, derived from a sketch of the victor the day after he clashed with Napoleon's armies at the Battle of the Arapiles River near Salamanca. The condition of the Iron Duke, 25 inches by 20½ inches of wood panel in a four-inch black and gold frame, was described as "delicate" by the time he was consigned by his owner, the Duke of Leeds, for sale at Sotheby's. He made a startling $392,000, knocked down to Charles B. Wrightsman, the Texas oilman and good friend of President Kennedy.

Immediately, British Members of Parliament set up a hullabaloo to prevent the painting's being shipped to the United States. Wrightsman promptly offered it to the National Gallery in London at the record price which he had paid. It was bought back without further fuss and hung in a place of honor on a red-draped screen in the main vestibule. One evening soon after, on the fiftieth anniversary of the Italian workman's temptation by the "Mona Lisa," a gallery guard on his way downstairs to brew a pot of tea noticed that the Goya was missing from the screen. But he guessed unblinkingly that the painting had been removed to be cleaned or photographed or for something equally innocent. Not until the next morning did the alarm go out, alerting Scotland Yard, Interpol, the FBI, and police and customs offices throughout the world that somebody had made off with a precious bit of British history in the most spectacular art robbery in half a century.

Wrightsman, vacationing on an Aegean island owned by a fellow collector, Stavros Niarchos, expressed his shock. "This last month they were stealing airliners," he said. "Now these crazy people are raiding museums. What is the world coming to?"

Christie's, eager to be heard from though they'd had no role anywhere in the Iron Duke affair, sagely said, "A portrait such as the Goya is to all intents and purposes unsaleable, unless the thief knew beforehand where it could be placed . . . There is some evidence that people will go to any lengths to possess paintings at any price." Sotheby's, having a material interest in the picture, issued a guarded plea for the thief to treat it "most carefully."

He soon set everyone's mind at rest on that point. While art critics, feature writers, and amateur sleuths everywhere were blaming insane connoisseurs and mysterious rings of thieves—and Sir Kenneth Clark, a former director of the gallery, was saying obliquely, "I wouldn't be at all surprised if the painting wasn't already out of the country on its way to one of those very, very private collectors in the U.S."—the real thief mailed the first of a series of letters to Reuter's News Agency, written in the block capitals prescribed for kidnap notes. "Query not that I have the Goya," he said anonymously, demanding that its purchase price be paid as ransom to charity "in the interests of humanity as a whole" and designating a nuclear disarmament organization.

A later note to the same addressees guaranteed that "The Duke is safe—his temperature cared for—his future uncertain." It enclosed a label which had undoubtedly been removed from the back of the inflexible wood panel on which the portrait was painted. A torrent of anonymous letters and telephone calls plagued the investigators of the crime, including one threat to shred the Goya strip by strip and steal another masterpiece unless the ransom were paid, but there were serious doubts about the reliability of any of these. Only nominal rewards were offered for the safe return of the Duke or for information leading to the capture of his captor, and they brought no useful clues. The National Gallery eighteen months later still was without its Goya, though hope had not been abandoned. "I think the painting will come back when all the fuss dies down," said its director.

Serge Bogouslavsky didn't
like the retouching

"It's too embarrassing for anyone to keep. I think the crooks who took it are not sadistic and are not likely to destroy it."

Whenever an art theft hits the headlines, there is a great deal of speculation about the skill of the thieves in evading the protective devices and precautions which museums, warehouses, or galleries rely on for security. Readers are regaled with accounts of guards who patrol every inch of the premises and electronic alarm systems wired to every door and window. But "Mona Lisa's" plebeian captor found his task was child's play—he took her out of her frame and slipped her under his smock—and his successors in crime have seldom run into any particular trouble.

A Russian art student, Serge Bogouslavsky, stole Watteau's "L'Indifférent," which is no larger than a sheet of notepaper but valued at $100,000, from the Louvre after two weeks spent snipping at the wire from which the frame hung. He returned it two months later, considerably retouched to demonstrate how poorly, in his opinion, the museum had previously performed the job. He was sentenced to two years in prison and barred from living in any French city for five years more, but he turned the time to advantage by writing a book on restoration, including a chapter entitled "Why I Stole 'L'Indifférent.'"

On the night that the Goya vanished from the National Gallery, the burglar alarms in the building, which cover every skylight and trapdoor as well as every exit and are tied in direct to Scotland Yard, had been conveniently disconnected so that the twenty charwomen, workmen, and attendants in the place could go about their chores without setting the bells pealing.

Sir Gerald Kelly, president of Britain's Royal Academy of Art, once stole an absolutely authentic Holbein which would have to be valued at a minimum of

$500,000, and it was the property of King George VI, too. The king had lent his Windsor Castle collection of Holbein portraits to a London gallery for exhibition. Kelly, to prove how simple it would be to make off with one, had an amply proportioned woman friend of his smuggle in under her dress a reproduction of the painting which Kelly had decided to purloin. While two children, who were also his accomplices, diverted the guards' attention by caterwauling in the adjoining gallery, he switched the reproduction for the original, undetected.

One of the safeguards designed to discourage theft which museums used to practice consisted of instructing guides not to cite the market value of works of art to the sightseeing public. To do so, the directors felt, would be to provide would-be crooks with unnecessary encouragement. Well-publicized auction sales have rendered this reticence out of date, and even a casual reader of the tabloids knows that paintings are worth fortunes. The inevitable result has been a marked increase in stealing pictures; art thefts are as fashionable as million-dollar nights with the gavel.

The mad collector may safely be regarded as a figment of fevered imagination. But not the kleptomaniac, or the calculating amateur, or the twisted idealist, or the gang which considers a high-priced painting a good investment, just as many a businessman does. Since the art boom began to bubble, thieves have robbed museums and private collections of millions of dollars' worth of masterpieces, minor and major, most of them being stolen, alas, not for love but for money.

The principal target area has been the French Riviera, a habitat of the rich which abounds in small, poorly protected museums and private collectors of the order of Somerset Maugham, until he concluded that he had best sell out before he was robbed. During one recent period, paintings were disappearing at a rate close to a million dollars' worth every month from this blighted territory.

On All Fools' Day, 1960, twenty paintings were removed from the walls of the Inn of the Golden Dove in St. Paul-de-Vence. Their sole protection had consisted of a dozing watchdog and chairs jammed under the knobs of the outside doors. The thieves' haul included works by Picasso, Matisse, Chagall, Utrillo, and Dufy, with an estimated value of $600,000. Their owner, young Francis Roux, received a series of telephone calls from persons unknown offering to unearth the loot for $200,000. He reported the messages to police headquarters in Marseilles, hoping that the thieves could be traced and refusing to pay any ransom. Ten months later, the pictures were back on the walls of the inn. The public explanation was that a conscience-stricken thief confessed to his priest and gave him a baggage check for the Marseilles railroad station covering packages which contained the stolen pictures; the priest had telephoned the police. In fact, Roux had paid up a few days earlier, after getting a call which warned him that this was his last chance to save his collection from destruction.

Threats to destroy or damage a stolen picture are as commonplace as the medieval custom of sending a prisoner's ear home to his relatives and friends as an inducement to paying ransom. Gainsborough's doubtful, dismal "Duchess of

Devonshire"—the portrait which repelled Millais when it appeared at Christie's—was stolen from Agnew's Bond Street gallery in London on the very night that Junius Spencer Morgan, the New York banker, suddenly made up his mind to buy it for his more celebrated son, James Pierpont, at a cost, including U.S. customs duty which was collected at the time, of roughly $75,000.

It was stolen by an American, Adam Worth, who hid behind a curtain until the place closed, then carried it through a window and hid it in the mattress of his lodging-house bed. He tried to blackmail the gallery's owner, Sir Christopher Agnew, by sending him bits of the picture with notes asking how many more inches dare he receive before the knife reached the Duchess's over-painted face.

Worth was trying to raise enough money to bail out an accomplice who was in jail awaiting extradition to the United States. When Sir Christopher did not respond and the subject of Worth's solicitude was unexpectedly freed, the "Duchess" became a positive embarrassment. She was smuggled out of England in a false-bottomed trunk and concealed in a Chicago warehouse. Nothing was heard of her for twenty-five years, during which time Worth and all but one of his gang died. Then Pinkerton's detective agency, which still keeps a sharp eye on the world and underworld of art, got in touch with Agnew's, reporting that the one ailing and impoverished survivor was ready to return the picture for a mere $7,000.

Sir Christopher's son, Thomas, went to New York for the handover, which took place according to prearranged plan. Three adjoining rooms were booked in a Manhattan hotel, the middle one of which accommodated a Pinkerton's man, with Agnew as one next-door neighbor and the thief as the other. The painting was passed by the detective to Agnew, who identified it, kept it, and handed the cash to the thief by way of the middleman, so that the dealer and the crook never set eyes on each other. After her triumphant homecoming to Agnew's, J. P. Morgan felt honorbound to buy the poor Duchess, at a probable price of $150,000.

The contemporary crop of Riviera bandits have not had to resort to lopping off bits of the paintings they have stolen. The second richest haul of recent date—from the Annonciade Museum of St. Tropez—saw three men with a stolen key load fifty-seven pictures into a van and cart off overnight $2,000,000 worth of Matisse, Bonnard, Derain, Vlaminck, Utrillo, and others—and none of them insured. At first it seemed that nobody but summer people in the fishing village cared a hoot about recovering the canvases. Then three anonymous art lovers began to tremble at the thought that the paintings might be damaged or destroyed. They clubbed together to offer a reward, promising that no embarrassing questions would be asked provided the pictures were returned. Perhaps the offer, an unimpressive $2,000, was too small, but for a year and a half it produced not a clue, either about the pictures, which made up two-thirds of the museum's stock, or the thieves, whose taste, though they had worked in darkness, had led them to the pick of the collection. They'd had an easy night's work—keys to the museum could be counted in dozens, and the place had no alarm system. Then in November, 1962, an anonymous note to Culture Minister André Malraux sent police to an abandoned farm near Paris. There they found all of the pictures virtually unharmed.

Some bizarre theories to explain the rash of robberies began to circulate around the auction houses, dealers' galleries, and the columns of some American magazines. The "mad collector" made his usual appearance as a subject for speculation, this time being described as an unnamed Brazilian millionaire, which made a change, since he had previously been an anonymous Texas oilman. There were even guesses that he was an Arabian sheik, who presumably had grown tired of counting his Cadillacs as a hobby. One newsletter, enthusiastically supported by a national picture magazine, guessed that stolen paintings were being smuggled behind the Iron Curtain, not because the natives had suddenly taken to modern art but, so the fable ran, because Communist currencies were weak and canny Communist investors wanted to sink their money in something more durable.

The fantasies were still being spun, as flimsy as silk in a spider web, when the South of France was struck again, this time in Aix-en-Provence, birthplace of Cézanne, where a loan exhibition of his work was being held in the town's Pavillon de Vendôme. While an aged custodian and a deaf watchdog slept, one thief inched his way up the side of the old building, which a governor of Provence built for his mistress in 1664. From a second-floor balcony, the intruder crawled through a transom and opened a window to admit his less agile accomplices. Taking their time to choose only the cream of the sixty items on display, they chose a masterwork, "The Card Players," which was on loan from the Louvre and is valued at $1,200,000, and seven other paintings for a total haul worth well over $4,000,000. A group of Austrian insurance companies which had written policies for $4,480,000 covering the whole exhibition immediately announced a reward of $28,000.

Hope of ransom probably provides the key to most art theft. Paintings as a rule are easy to steal but virtually impossible to dispose of. If they are worth taking, they are widely recognizable, and no dealer or honest collector would touch them at any price. But the thieves are obviously not dim-witted, and they continue in their labors. They work in nine cases out of ten for reward money, which most insurance companies in Britain and the United States indignantly deny is ever paid.

The Home Insurance Company has proved to be one of the few American firms willing to comment on the hazards and purposes of art insurance. "The industry," a spokesman said, "now frowns on using fences to get stolen works returned. We don't pay any percentage of the total insurance value to get things back. We think that by doing that we would encourage more thefts and would defeat our own purpose. There is an unofficial agreement between the insurance companies, the police, and the FBI that binds the companies not to give bonuses for the return of stolen goods." The FBI enters into the investigation of any art theft where the loss exceeds $5,000 on the assumption that at this figure the stolen property has automatically become an item of interstate commerce.

European insurers are less discriminating than their American and British colleagues, which probably explains why there are more thefts and more recoveries of stolen work. Given time, paintings purloined anywhere on the Continent are

"The Card Players" by Cezanne

usually found, often under circumstances worthy of a TV script writer; the police profess to know nothing; arrests are seldom made. The eight Cézannes looted in Aix reappeared eight months later in an abandoned car on a Marseilles backstreet. "Dramatic" and "baffling" were the tired adjectives employed most frequently in newspaper stories, which faithfully reported the customary mysterious tip to the police that sent detectives to the spot. The insurance companies said nothing.

The fact is, however, that the best possible buyer for a stolen painting is its original owner. He may be contacted direct or, more usually, through the insurance company, which is seldom unwilling to fork out, say, $100,000 with no questions asked in preference to paying out on a $500,000 policy. The company inevitably finds that the less said about it the better, since payment of ransom can be interpreted as abetting a felony and any pledge not to prosecute as the compounding of a crime.

An American collector who suffers losses is likely to be forced back on his own resources. That was the fate of G. David Thompson, a retired Pittsburgh steel man, who returned home with his wife from a dinner party one evening to find that six Picassos, two Légers, one Dufy, and one Miró had been ripped and torn from their frames. The combined act of theft and vandalism amounted to the biggest art theft in the history of the United States, a country which has had a certain degree of immunity, probably due to the abysmal illiteracy of most native hoodlums. The Pittsburgh millionaire guessed what was in store when he announced a reward of $100,000, no questions asked. The pictures were returned to him, but how or precisely when was never disclosed.

Insurance rates for fine art are extremely low, so long as the premises on which it is kept are reasonably secure. A painting valued at $50,000, for example, may be insured for $58, far below the rate for furs or jewelry. One company's spokesman explained, "People don't carry their paintings to parties with them and lose them the way they do mink and diamonds. Over the years, the insurance of works of art has become a very profitable business. The rates on a collection worth as much as $1,000,000 remain very low. The Kress collection is insured for over $20,000,000, the Frick for over $25,000,000. The rash of thefts should not affect rates immediately, for they are predicated on five years' experience."

A Washington company which insures New York's Museum of Modern Art took a different view. "We are looking a lot harder these days," an official said, "at where the work is hung, and by whom, and what it is, before we insure it." Some European firms were saying much the same. One Paris company allowed that "we wouldn't touch most Riviera insurance requests with a forty-foot insulated barge pole."

Any important art dealer or auction house carries protection against every conceivable misfortune, including theft, damage, and fire. Astonishingly enough, some museums and many private collectors do not, museums because they prefer to rely on their own guards and security devices, collectors because rates can be ruinous if they fail to meet safety standards set by the companies. One paradoxical complication is that precautions taken against theft are apt to increase fire hazards, since paintings bolted to walls behind barred windows are virtually doomed if fire breaks out. There are no recorded cases of an auction house being robbed of a major painting, though a light-fingered patron at the Rovensky jewelry sale did manage to make off with a $20,000 pearl-and-diamond pin. The auctioneers are alert to the danger that publicity about the skyscraper value of art may have sunk into the skulls of American criminals, so security is tighter now than ever. Besides banning umbrellas in the crowd, armed Pinkerton guards keep an eye on the bidding.

A crime wave followed by stiff increases in insurance rates could have an unfortunate effect on opportunities for anyone to see pictures outside the museums and salesroom bastions. Museums and collectors are more and more reluctant to let their paintings out on loan for exhibition, knowing that risk of loss multiplies the moment a picture leaves its owner's hands. The ambitions of assurers and policemen on one hand and museum directors on the other are almost exactly opposed. Conscientious curators like to have the world see their paintings, if that is possible, but the best protection is provided if the pictures are kept under heavy guard in one or two comparatively small rooms, to be inspected by a hand-picked audience. Conditions on a big night at an auction house meet the prescription almost exactly.

The fate of one painting on its way to auction, a minor Renoir landscape worth perhaps $14,000, shows that not every loss is a crime committed with thought of ransom. It vanished from the trunk of Peter Wilson's car one night. A reward of $14,000 was offered, and Scotland Yard men spent a week looking for it. But it happened that the trunk of the car had been bounced open and the picture jolted out. It was run over by two London bus drivers on their way home in a 1948 car. "We got out and saw the picture," one of them said later, after they'd been persuaded by a friend to deliver it to the police. "It looked like junk. I took it home and saw this name Renoir, but it didn't mean a thing to me. I slung it in the firewood cupboard because I thought it would burn well."

XIII

ALL THINGS BRIGHT AND BEAUTIFUL

OLD Mrs. Stanton was as fond of her jewels as if they were favorite playthings of her Victorian childhood. One of the first pleasures every day, when she woke in the giant bed that Marie Antoinette once had slept in, must have been the moments spent considering what to wear among the rings, the ear clips, the necklaces, the bracelets which she had been collecting for twenty years. Through her bedroom windows, she could hear the scream of peacocks parading on her lawns and the play of the fountain surging around the Canova statue of Venus that stood at the entrance of the house. If the wind was right, she could catch the special scent of the Colorado mountains.

May Bonfils Stanton collected all manner of things. The bedroom, like the nineteen other rooms in the white marble mansion, was crammed with fantastic furniture and bric-a-brac of any period but the present. Across the room, on a tufted chaise from Louis XV's Petit Trianon, sat her first doll, in a faded silk dress, staring at her from faded blue eyes, a relic from the same era that produced the gilded chair with the carved crest of "Victoria Regina" from which Mrs. Stanton addressed her guests when she entertained in the grand salon.

Those were the evenings when the diamonds, pearls, rubies and sapphires of her pieces glittered in their glory, hundreds and hundreds of carats of them. Even for the dressiest occasions, she had a dozen things to choose from, to go with the

199

May Bonfils Stanton

gowns which she bought unfailingly from Fontana of Rome. There was the pendant made of eighty-six diamonds supporting the "Idol's Eye," seventy carats of brilliant blue stone that first saw the light of day in the Golconda mines of India. For 300 years it vanished from history, until it was rediscovered as the eye of an idol in the temple of Benghazi. It ranks with gems like the Hope and Jonker diamonds; Mrs. Stanton bought it in 1947.

She owned a diamond ring of comparable splendor, the 39.80-carat "Liberator I," cut from the huge parent stone of 155 carats that was unearthed in Venezuela and named in honor of Simon Bolivar. She had 153 more carats of diamonds, and 107 of emeralds bought from the treasure of the Maharajah of Indore, combined in a necklace, with more matching stones in a pair of ear clips. In another necklace, diamonds and sapphires gleamed in support of an extraordinary oval sapphire weighing some 173 carats, a multifaceted thing approaching a silver dollar in size. She could take apart or put together the diamond bracelet, center clip, and two pairs of smaller clips made of diamonds and cultured pearls which combined as a necklace or divided into a parure, that serviceable treasure of dowager queens and duchesses.

All in all, the pieces amounted to what was probably the most dazzling collection in America. Some came from Europe, but most arrived by plane on the person of Harry Winston, the Manhattan jeweler who has never allowed his face to be photographed. Showing the taste, settings, and cutters' skill of today, which are far superior to those of yesterday, they were the only contemporary objects that Mrs. Stanton held in affection. She loved her jewels enough to put on a selection of them before she ate breakfast and keep them on until she went to bed at night.

From the paintings, marble statues, and bronzes that filled her library, to the tapestries and vases in the halls—everything else she loved dated to the Victorian age or earlier. "Belmar," the house, was a copy of the Petit Trianon itself, the retreat that Louis XV built for Marie Antoinette, and like the French king's fancy, May Stanton kept deer, sixty of them, on her 750 acres. She imported furnishings from the palaces of Rome, Paris, Vienna, London, and Edinburgh. She had a little chapel built off the foyer of "Belmar" and went to mass there. Among her prizes was a gauntlet that Napoleon wore when he was crowned Emperor in 1798.

"The twentieth century," she once remarked, "never existed for me." Armchair psychiatrists would probably find no difficulty in tracing her anachronisms back to her childhood and her painful relationship with her father, Frederick Gilmar Bonfils, the swashbuckling adventurer who built the *Denver Post* into the most raucous, ruthless newspaper in the Rockies during the first three decades of this century. "Little Napoleon" was one of the kinder descriptions applied to the fiery man with the waxed moustache who claimed to be descended from the emperor; in point of truth, the only link seemed to be that Bonfils' grandfather had been a boyhood playmate of Buonaparte back on the island of Corsica.

Bonfils kept May and her younger sister, Helen, in medieval seclusion in the great stone museum piece which he built in Denver when the newspaper prospered—he had picked it up for next to nothing in partnership with Harry Tammen, an ex-bartender—and the millions started flooding in. Bonfils used to storm into the office and fire everybody within hearing distance if something in the paper displeased him, and he was as strict a disciplinarian at home. Lights went out there by 9:30 P.M. at the latest. His daughters were allowed no beaux because he was sure that any men who wooed them would only be after their money.

May put up with it until she had finished school in Denver and New York, then promptly eloped. She found herself, a strong Catholic, tied to another man whom she could not tolerate. On the record, the union lasted for forty-two years until it was annulled in 1946 with her maiden name restored. But in fact she had begun living apart from her husband soon after they were married. Her feelings toward her father could not have improved after his death in 1933, when one of the provisions of his will directed that she would receive $25,000 if she consented to a divorce and only $12,000 if she refused. His widow, Belle, and her two daughters broke the will, Belle electing to take half the estate, and May's husband began suing for money.

When her mother died two years later, May inherited some $10,000,000 and a fifteen per cent interest in the stock of the *Post*, which she surprisingly sold later to a rival publisher. Now that she could afford the luxury of life as a recluse, she started work on "Belmar." When the place was completed, to the last swan on its sixty-acre lake and the last Napoleonic crest on the statuary, she ventured from the grounds only to travel to Europe to shop the galleries there for new relics of yesterday.

The jewelry collection was started seriously in 1940, sixteen years before she married Charles Edwin Stanton, a tall, almost handsome Denver architect and interior decorator, best identified for his work in restoring the "ghost town" of Central City. She was, he said, "the last of the city's Victorians," but he broke down her seclusion. They worked together in building up her collections, though her jewel buying tapered off, and crossed the Atlantic every year, once to Rome where in St. Peter's the bride, who was close to eighty, and the groom, who was some thirty years her junior, renewed their marriage vows and received Pope John's blessing.

On March 12, 1962, May Bonfils Stanton died at "Belmar," with her husband at her side. She left him half her estate of more than $10,000,000, while the other half went to the Franciscan Fathers. The jewels were reserved for a different purpose. They were to be sold, she directed, and the proceeds distributed among various charitable institutions which she had been supporting. There had been several of them, including the May Bonfils Clinic for Ophthalmology at the University of Colorado Medical Center and Seeing Eye Dogs for the Blind Association. Toward the close of her life, her eyesight had started to play tricks, but then the glowing, smooth feel of precious stones at the throat or on the wrist is as much a pleasure as being able to see them.

Something close to 1,000 people saw the jewels, divided into twenty-five lots, when they were displayed one by one in the floodlit dark blue velvet box which is reserved for that job at Parke-Bernet. "If you see anybody smoking, throw 'em out," one guard muttered to another in the jam-packed salesroom.

"What's the matter?" said the second uniformed sentry. "Diamonds don't burn."

The galleries had hopes that the "Idol's Eye" would bring $500,000 and break the record set by the 213-carat Rovensky diamond necklace, sold for $385,000 in 1957. They could count on at least $250,000 from Harry Winston, who had promised to make that opening bid as he sat, a rosy-cheeked little man, on one of the hard folding chairs, directly in range of the little dark blue box.

Earlier, he had spent some time reminiscing about Mrs. Stanton. "She was a very definite woman, and you couldn't tell her much. She even wanted her emerald and diamond bracelet, which we made two and three-quarters inches wide for her, to be two inches wider than that, but I convinced her not to do it that way. I arrived one morning at 'Belmar' at nine-thirty, and she met me at the door in full evening dress, wearing most of her jewels. She thought of her jewels like children, loved them, looked at them constantly." Winston, who was only sixteen when he started out for himself as a freewheeling dealer, had a certain parental feeling for the "Idol's Eye" necklace, which he sold her in 1946—he designed it himself.

Louis Marion gave him a big Irish smile as the auctioneer threaded his way to the rostrum, shaking hands with old acquaintances on the aisles. Promptly at

1:45 P.M., he knocked for attention. "Now, ladies and gentlemen," he grinned, "you can all do your Christmas shopping right here." To his left, straining his eyes against the glare of television floodlights, stood Leslie Hyam, and on Hyam's left, ready to bell out the bid, was Marion's grown-up son John, who is in training to follow his father's calling.

"We've got more photographers than customers," Hyam whispered to a friend. Marion was bothered by the blaze of television lights, which unaccountably flared on and off, half-blinding him. "I'm more concerned about a successful sale than about being on television," he said, and he was not joking. Things were proceeding tamely, with the bidding concentrated in no more than a dozen hands. "It's like a dentist pulling teeth," he grumbled to the crowd over his bank of microphones. "That's what I am today—a dentist."

It was not a happy afternoon for him. When Lot Number 15, the "Idol's Eye," was put with its orange tag up into the display box, Harry Winston gave a nod to open the bidding as promised. In a matter of seconds, the price was up to $375,000 twice—two bids of the same figure made simultaneously by Louis A. Green, a grocery-chain magnate who is a collector and also a director of the auction house, and by Harry Levinson, a white-haired Chicago dealer who sat with his wife. Where the two bidders sat turned out to be vital: Green was thirty feet away from Marion and Levinson perhaps ten feet closer.

Neither bidder would budge—Green because his wife was against his offering any more, Levinson because he felt that any break in the deadlock could have jumped the price up to $500,000. Marion's voice rose a tone or two in perplexity as both men sat tight. "Let's get it organized," he pleaded. "Won't one of you try an extra $500?" Neither of them would. "It's murder!" yelled one of the dealers who stood in a cluster at the back of the room.

There was only one thing to be done, and that was to invoke a seldom-used rule, which Green later said he didn't know about, while Levinson said he personally did: in an impasse, a disputed lot is traditionally knocked down to the bidder who is closer to the auctioneer. "You wouldn't think it possible," Marion said nervously. "I hate to make this decision." But continuing silence left him no choice. The "Idol's Eye" was knocked down to Harry Levinson, and press photographers clustered around like moths besieging a candle flame.

Harry Winston did not leave empty-handed. He helped set one more record which the day brought in spite of the auctioneer's frustration by taking back, for $185,000, the "Liberator I" ring that he had sold to Mrs. Stanton in the first place. It brought the total take to $1,242,940, more than any jewelry auction had ever earned before.

On the opposite side of the Atlantic, the closest thing to the elegance of the Stanton sale had taken place three years earlier at Sotheby's. The arrival under the hammer of the Westminster tiara, for disposal along with the ducal pictures to meet eighty per cent death duties, created almost as big a stir as May Bonfils's diamonds and sapphires, though it fetched far less than the American collection.

The tiara's 1,240 stones outnumbered any single piece that May Stanton owned, but two of them, pear-shaped and weighing together approximately fifty-seven carats, came from the same land as her "Idol's Eye"; the two Arcot diamonds owned by the Rajah of Arcot until Clive of India defeated him early in his campaigning to wrest control of the territory from the French. The confiscated diamonds were presented by Clive to Queen Charlotte, then sold under the terms of her will so that her daughters could collect the cash.

In 1837, the Marquis of Westminster (the dukedom came later) bought the Arcot stones for £11,000 as a birthday present for his wife. He planned to have them made into drop earrings for her to wear at the first tea party given by Victoria, who had been crowned in Westminster Abbey that summer. But the marchioness fell ill, and her husband had to go alone to take tea with his brand new sovereign.

By the time the tiara arrived at the auction house, it had been designed, with the usual aristocratic regard for obtaining maximum wear from heirlooms, to be split into two diamond ear drops, while a third large stone could form the heart of a brooch. It took only three minutes of bidding to take the price to $308,000 and knock down the piece to Levi Cohen, a London jeweler acting for Harry Winston.

Whether this was a mammoth, medium, or modest price is impossible to judge, since the market in diamond jewelry, or any other variety, over the last two hundred years is notoriously tricky to estimate. Until the middle of the Victorian era, size was valued more than quality in any important piece, with the result that well-nigh perfect stones would be set next to flawed ones. It was the carat count that mattered, not much else. Nowadays, cutting, matching, and color are all weighed in the balance in evaluating diamonds. Since any modern jeweler will not hesitate to reset and, if necessary, recut stones, very few accurate comparisons exist even over recent generations.

A different story is told by antique gold and silverware, which have risen steadily under the pressure of public demand, without keeping pace with the climb in paintings. This is decidedly a London market, in which rings of dealers remain active, though some individual traders are allegedly such lovers of their acquisitions that they cannot bear to part with them to any customer.

Gold reigned unchallenged as the stuff for emperors, and commoners rich enough to afford it, until the Spanish conquistadores seized the mines of Mexico and Peru and shipped tons of silver ore back to Europe. Only then was there enough of the metal in circulation for silversmiths to make the great dinner services, toilet ware, pots, bowls, and candlesticks which set new standards of sophistication for the world when Paris created them for her Sun Kings.

Because it was almost too easy to melt down and turn into coinage, silver and silver plate had a precarious existence. At the end of the seventeenth century, court extravagance had burdened France with a government debt so tremendous that Louis XIV turned to using china on his table; any citizen who refused to follow suit and deliver his silver to the mint was liable to arrest, by decree.

The Paris craftsmen, presumably reconciled to seeing their finest work constantly converted into currency, had to pin any hopes of posthumous fame on customers from overseas. Fortunately there were plenty of them, from William of Orange to Catherine II of Russia, who was forever commissioning specially massive pieces to present to her favorites, like Count Gregory Orloff, who wound up with a table service for his part in a conspiracy which led to the murder of her predecessor and husband, Peter III.

One silversmith she patronized was Jacques Nicolas Roettiers, whose father worked in the Royal Mint, not as a furnaceman, happily, but as an engraver. Young Roettiers had been in business for himself for only two years—he was twenty-eight—when an order arrived from James, Third Earl of Berkeley, for a silver dinner service, apparently intended as a coming of age present for his son Augustus, who two years hence would be twenty-one. Berkeley did not live to see the day; some twelve months after the order had been placed, he died at the castle of his father-in-law, the Duke of Richmond, at Aubigny. Augustus, the suddenly elevated Fourth Earl, rapidly had Roettiers expand the order to bring the service up to a total of 168 pieces.

The last of them was delivered in 1738 to Berkeley Castle, Gloucestershire, where it stayed while the guillotine rose and fell in France and all but two other dinner services from Roettiers's workshop vanished into the melting pots. The 168 pieces remained in the castle, unrecognized and insured for a mere $15,000, as one earl succeeded another until the score reached eight. The Right Honorable Randal Thomas Mowbray, Eighth Earl, was the last member of the family to possess the Roettiers silver. In 1961 it was handed over to Sotheby's, a shining array of plates and platters, tureens and flatware, the finest Louis XV service in the world. Cautious staff members concluded that only by dividing it into several lots could it be disposed of at a price it deserved, but Peter Wilson's decision was against that. When the gavel finally fell, Frank Patridge & Sons, London dealers, had bid $579,600, which is a record likely to stand for quite a while.

Silver—English, French, or early American—would appear to offer as good an opportunity as any for a salesroom visitor to begin collecting with minimum

Onehundredsixtyeight pieces of silver for $579,600

risk of error. A single piece of plate has fetched as much as the $75,600 paid at Christie's by the Minneapolis Institute of Fine Arts for one of the only two known wine cisterns by Paul de Lamerie—it weighs a staggering forty pounds—when it turned up from the Duke of Sutherland's collection. De Lamerie was another eighteenth-century French craftsman whose work fell victim to the fires of war and revolution.

One teaspoon has been known to bring over $5,000, but this was an even greater rarity, dating from the fifteenth century, and it needed a special providence to have escaped history's burning breath. But these survivals from the centuries scarcely represent the average Wednesday morning's business in a London sales-room. Lots that go for sums between $40 and $50 account for a good-sized share of the turnover, and a single session may see the gavel fall at $25 one minute and at $100,000 a little later. The surest bargains are likely to be discovered on the less expensive side of the halfway mark between those two extremes, and the price rise over recent years may be spectacular.

Paul de Lamerie silver is a case in point. In 1944, a set of his George I candlesticks sold for $2,200; in 1960, they made $15,700. The following year, a set of silver tea caddies from the same hands went for $18,500, which was $17,200 more than they had fetched in 1954. Apart from the de Lamerie, a retired British army colonel consigned to Sotheby's a wax jack which he understood Charles II had given to one of the officer's ancestors. It went in 1930 for $1,300; but resold in the 1960–1961 season at $10,100. And a set of silver chessmen dating back to the reign of George III writes its own graph of ascending prices in a series of four sales: $400 in 1936, $1,000 in 1946; $1,400 in 1956, and $7,600 four years later.

In the London rooms, almost anything that man has ever set a value on can be tucked into a day's turnover somewhere, usually either as an "object of virtue" or a "work of art," a category which in one cataloguist's words "embraces furniture, porcelain, glass, carpets, musical instruments, firearms and armor, antiquities." It covers buttons (a French collection of them fetched $18,500), tapestries, scent bottles, chandeliers, and more recondite items like posset pots, finials, and tazzas, most of them moving up in value as the cult of collecting spreads.

A Pennsylvania collector shipped over to one London house an accumulation of Japanese netsuke, which are little toggles, carved from anything that comes to hand, used to tie the girdles around kimonos. To some unsympathetic Occidental eyes, they have the stamp of an Oriental dimestore, but other people are fascinated by them, to the extent of gladly handing over $500 for a particularly good specimen. That was the best price made during the entire morning that was needed to dispose of the Pennsylvania netsuke; it was bid on a carving of a snail perched on a mushroom.

Two gleaming, five-inch figures of Russian peasants, one evidently waiting in line to take a sauna bath, the other a drunken mujik, earned $39,200, which is a stupefying sum until it is considered that the first was made of purpurine, quartzite, amazonite, aventurine quartz, Kalgan jasper, and nephrite, while jasper, agate, purpurine, and aventurine were the ingredients of the second. Both were the work of Carl Fabergé, the master jeweler of Tsarist Russia whose Imperial Easter eggs are every auctioneer's delight.

One of the most specialized and most profitable items which has grown in collectors' esteem over the past thirty years is the glass paperweight, French, English, or American. What used to amount to little more than an excuse for poking around in little antique shops has become a sharp, competitive search for rarities from the classic manufacturing period, 1845 to 1860, when the three great French factories of Baccarat, St. Louis, and Clichy were in full swing. "Exquisite" is the only word for the flower patterns and bouquets sealed in the hearts of the imported weights; glassworks in London, Birmingham, Boston, Cambridge, and Cape Cod soon began to copy them. Trade talk among connoisseurs nowadays deals with double overlays, sulphides, millefiori, pastry molds, and a dozen other means of distinguishing one period from another.

Collecting them has attracted a lot of American devotees, among them the late Colonel Robert Guggenheim of Washington, D.C., who had 750 weights; it took three separate Sotheby sales to handle them, and they brought his estate $166,200.

It used to be fashionable, in Europe, anyway, for the possessors of dusty pictures, old silver, and faded manuscripts to pretend that the stuff was really a bother to care for and probably worth very little at that. The auctioneers have changed things considerably. It is fashionable now to pack off the heirlooms to the salesrooms and confess that the aim is to raise as much cash as possible.

Everybody who is anybody has answered the siren song of "What am I bid?" Lord Home, Britain's Foreign Secretary, recently got rid of some family silver this way. Princess Marina picked up $7,000 from the auctioning of a three-and-a-half-inch Fabergé flower basket. A descendant of Sir Francis Drake consigned to the gavel his seafaring ancestor's will and twenty-three other documents, including the royal letters patent and seal of Queen Elizabeth sending him off from Plymouth to raid Cadiz and "singe the King of Spain's beard."

The will, signed "Fra: Drake" by a trembling hand, was witnessed by six crewmen the day before the explorer died of dysentery aboard the good ship *Defiance* as she lay anchored in Portobello harbor, Panama. His estate was made up of the rich landholdings which were his reward from the Virgin Queen for repeatedly singeing King Philip's whiskers by raiding his treasure galleons. Childless, Sir Francis left almost everything to his brother Thomas, who sailed on most of the voyages. The will was preserved for 366 years by the family, living on Devonshire acres inherited from the admiral. The Drake Museum near Plymouth got the will for $9,520. A New York dealer bid $10,080 to obtain the royal raid permit and seal, but the city of Plymouth strongly objected to its leaving England, and the dealer consented to donate the document to the museum.

The demand for important books, manuscripts, maps, and letters outstrips the supply. The shortage of material in the auction business is felt acutely in these categories, with the effect of producing more and more unlikely items in the sales. The original manuscript of Tennessee Williams's *The Glass Menagerie,* passing through Parke-Bernet, made $6,000. A copy of Thomas Gray's *Elegy,* which sold for sixpence when it first appeared at a Paternoster Row bookstall in London in 1751, went for $6,200 in 1962. Christie's extracted $18,200 for E. M. Forster's manuscript of *A Passage to India.* Hodgson's, the London book auctioneers in Chancery Lane, knocked down for $4,060 the scientific records of the proceedings of Britain's Royal Society from 1832 to 1947, a sign of the big bidding that goes on for scholarly books of comparatively recent vintage these days. A faintly scato-logical eight-line poem, "The Age Demanded," written by Ernest Hemingway in 1925, was sold in 1963 to a San Francisco collector for $1,300. Even a file of mili-tary records said to have been picked up in Hitler's bunker in the garden of his Chan-cellery in Berlin was assigned for auction by a Canadian archivist.

Bits and pieces of correspondence signed by Astronaut John Glenn, dealing with earthbound troubles like battery failure in his little foreign car, were bought in New York (as "historical souvenirs" for $450) on the same day that letters from Albert Einstein on the Unified Field Theory brought in $19,000. Christie's disposed of a·fifteenth-century Book of Hours for a near-record $89,600. Sotheby's obtained a record $64,400 for a French-English Vocabulary and Conversation Book from the library of Ripon Cathedral, both produced in the fifteenth century by William Caxton, one of the godfathers of printing.

A run-of-the-mill book auction has an atmosphere peculiarly its own. The audience can usually be counted at two or three dozen well-groomed, secretive men. These dealers circulate among the ten houses that handle or specialize in books. Bidding proceeds at almost the speed of sound as pencils tap, forefingers rise, and catalogues flutter. In these subdued circles, television has intruded only once or twice, most recently when John Glenn's scribbled notes and postcards turned up.

Rare, recondite, or just plain remarkable papers flutter through these sales-rooms continually, the least impressive in appearance of all the hoards of civilized man: the autograph letter of George Washington, written to acknowledge his com-mission as lieutenant colonel ($2,800); an 1860 pamphlet ($60) entitled "The Thrilling Narrative and Extraordinary Adventures of Miss Madeline H. Everett," who was abducted from a ladies' seminary and consigned to the Havana slave market; Beethoven's correction to the *Archduke Trio* ($7,600); one of the two known copies of a 1507 map of the world, bearing for the first time the name "America," the choice of cartographer Martin Waldeseemuller, who later wished that he'd called it "Prisilia" ($35,000).

Occasionally, a pulse of excitement quickens in the rooms as when the pre-cious battered manuscript with a Romanesque binding appeared—it happened to be a miracle of survival, a gospel dating from the twelfth century worth well over $100,000. Or it may be something much less awe-inspiring but more lightly ro-

To Ianthe. Oct Sept: 1813

I love thee Baby! for thine own sweet sake:
Those azure eyes, that faintly dimpled cheek
Thy tender frame so eloquently weak
Love in the sternest heart of hate might wake;
But more, when on thy fitful slumber bending
Thy mother folds thee to her wakeful heart,
Whilst love & pity in her glances blending
All that thy passive eyes can feel, impart:
More, when some feeble lineaments of her
Who bore thy weight beneath her spotless bosom
As with deep love I read thy face, recur,
More dear art thou o fair & fragile blossom
Dearest, when most thy tender traits express
The image of thy mother's loveliness.—

Evening — to Harriet. Sep. 1813

O thou bright Sun! beneath the dark blue line
Of western distance that sublime descendest,
And gleaming lovelier as thy beams decline
Thy million hues to every vapour lendest,
And over cobweb lawn & grove & stream
Sheddest the liquid magic of thy light,
Till calm Earth with the parting splendor bright
Shews like the vision of a beauteous dream,
What gazer now with astronomic eye
Could coldly count the spots within thy sphere?
Such were thy lover, Harriet, could he fly
The thoughts of all that makes his passion dear,
And turning senseless from thy warm caress
Pick flaws in our close woven happiness
July 31st 1813.

A page from Shelley's notebook

mantic, like the notebook of poems by Percy Bysshe Shelley, probably the only one left outside museums.

This roan-colored book contained fifty-three poems, with perhaps as many as three-quarters never published. It was the first of its kind—twenty-seven more were written in his lifetime—and rated by scholars to be the most valuable original source of study that had yet come to light. Several of the poems were dedicated to Harriet Westbrook, a school friend of one of Shelley's sisters, whom he married a matter of weeks after their first meeting, to rescue her from "persecution" at home and at school, when she was sixteen and he three years older. Five of the poems had been written in by her during the little time she lived. Above one of them she had inscribed, "To Harriet."

The marriage was already breaking up, though two children had been born, when Shelley fell deeply in love with Mary Godwin, who was two years younger even than Harriet. He abandoned his wife and children for Mary. On a December day two years later, Harriet drowned herself in the Serpentine, the ornamental lake that winds through London's Hyde Park. Shelley promptly married Mary, denouncing the tyranny of priests and judges when the courts ruled that the children by Harriet could not be left in his care. Mary Shelley, of course, is usually remembered for her first novel, the hardy perennial "Frankenstein," which she wrote soon after their marriage, but she hadn't her husband in mind as the monster. She was left a widow at twenty-five, when the passionate poet was drowned while sailing in the Mediterranean.

There was a certain element of suspense involved when the notebook was consigned to Sotheby's by Mrs. L. A. Worrall, a great-granddaughter of his. The auctioneers could sell the book but not the rights to publish its 3,000 lines of verse. Those were to appear in a freshly printed volume in the near future, and the auction house wanted to find a buyer for the notebook before then so the manuscript would bring a better price. They succeeded. On July 1, 1962, a London dealer bought it—at $28,000—for a private collector so desperate for secrecy that he would not allow even his nationality to be made known.

An extra attraction of manuscripts and printed works as collector's items is that they are almost impossible to forge successfully, because the only way to imitate old, handmade paper is to follow the same time-consuming, profit-killing procedures originally employed for its manufacture. An exception has to be made for ancient maps, prints and engravings, which are quite commonly faked. On the other hand, furniture as a whole is much more suspect. Soaring prices, as always, lure the faker, and throughout Europe there are workshops devoted to turning out new "antiques" in endless supply to meet the demand on both sides of the Atlantic.

The danger seldom lies in buying classical cabinetwork, which makes the top prices, since this is a true connoisseur's study. Tests can be applied to the pieces down to the last joint, nail hole and hinge to identify the hand of the maker, and exact imitation is prohibitively expensive. But the growth of collecting results in the entry on to the market of less knowledgeable customers at the levels of medium and lower prices. Enough old beams are snapped up by furniture makers, especially in France, for the American buyer, as ever, to beware. The apple of his eye may have been "revalued" by the addition of an unwarranted trade-mark masquerading as that of an eighteenth-century French master *ebeniste,* or have been doctored by the addition of new components, or amount to nothing more than an honestly produced reproduction deliberately tinkered with to convert it into a spurious antique.

The United States Treasury Department once applied an actuarial test based on figures of population, number of wealthy families of the eras concerned, chance destruction by breakage, fire, old age, and flood, and concluded that not one-tenth of the imports from the British Isles could by any stretch of hope be termed genuine. That was in the late Thirties. Demand, market values, and supply have tripled since then.

The bull market is nowhere more bovine than in eighteenth-century French furniture, which appreciated 150 per cent in the single year of 1959, according to an economist's calculations. At Christie's, one small Louis XV writing table appeared on the block, a handsome enough thing, undoubtedly made by Jean François Oeben, the royal cabinetmaker. It boasted the usual secret drawer, but that was empty. It went for a record-shattering price of nearly $100,000.

Really rare and fine pieces have taken off into the wide blue yonder, out of the range of predictable price. After the Thelma Chrysler Foy accumulation of French antiques was shown to interested dealers and museums, Leslie Hyam and his staff had a last-minute consultation before the auction to estimate what it would make. "We told the executors of the estate that the collection would go for $1,750,-000," he had said. "In reality, it fetched $2,600,000, which represented an undervaluation of nearly fifty per cent. So you never can tell."

His people failed in similar happy fashion when a Sèvres blue service came into the house and was appraised at $30,000. By the time the bidding had ended, Rosenberg & Stiebel, acting supposedly for Benson Ford, had gone to twice that sum. Louis Marion has sold a satinwood and mahogany commode not even guaranteed as the work of Thomas Chippendale for $70,000, a Louis XV lacquer table for $25,500, a Louis XIV carpet for $30,000, coaxing up the figures to the point where furniture, rugs, and objects of art were a category accounting for more than $3,000,000 in the $14,127,516 business of Parke-Bernet in 1962.

The same relative story applies in London, and for the same reason—the style, size and daintiness of French furniture match today's tastes and economy-size living rooms. Over there, I. O. Chance studiously noted, "There's always a 150-year lag in the popularity of furniture, so that we can be expecting Victorian pieces to come into their own soon." Signs in the 1962–1963 season were that he was right, and bigger sums were being paid for smaller sizes of Victoriana, particularly when they were well-made copies of eighteenth-century items.

Most good furniture has been a good bet for a collector since the early Twenties, so long as he stayed clear of oversized and heavily carved pieces, the Spanish Renaissance, and the Italian. At the Judge Gary sale in New York in 1928, a marquetry table from the dazzling days of Louis XV, another Oeben piece, was carried off at $71,000. In the desperate days of 1932, a *secretaire* built for Marie Antoinette was quoted in France at $220,000, which was ten times its cost fifty years earlier.

The ceaseless, if not always reliable, tide of imports from across the sea goes on pouring into the United States, some of it to return for "planting" when a rich enough customer is involved. It has been reported, for instance, that one New York millionaire who does his buying in London has not yet caught on to the fact that choice pieces from Manhattan dealers cross the Atlantic with him, to be put on display in London so that he can have the satisfaction of discovering them there.

The supply of authentic pieces may be running low, but there are enough left in French mansions and English castles to provide any customer who has an impressive bank account with some more happy times waiting for the sweetly anxious moment that comes just before the gavel falls. There is a story about the Duke of Buccleugh's visit to the Louvre, where he was greeted by a curator who had crossed the Channel and seen what the Duke had in the way of French tables, chairs, chaises, beds, bureaux and cabinets.

"M. le Duc," he said forlornly, "I apologize to you for the furniture we have here."

XIV

A KIND WORD FOR VIRTUE

A STRANGER attending a white-tie-and-television auction for the first time has been known to feel it was he and not the paintings that were going under the hammer. The impact on ears, eyes, nerves, and possibly bank account can be strenuous, and the beginner may become as emotionally bruised as while watching a close finish at Aqueduct. There is precisely the same atmosphere of hazard, of men facing odds, of big money riding on a chance.

The salesroom audience has the worldly air of wanting to enjoy the pleasure of seeing and being seen. The visitor may be unable to resist the temptation to crane his neck to spot the couple who regularly visit with the Kennedys, John, Robert or Edward; the Greek shipping magnate whose yacht is anchored off 79th Street; the movie producer who had to sell half his pictures when his wife walked out; the actress who imagines that Modigliani once played opposite Sophia Loren; the dealers whispering together behind crumpled catalogues; the Ivy League attorneys, impassive behind thick spectacles and representing who knows whom; the dark eyes of café-society courtesans; and white beards of the *cognoscenti*.

Here they sit, the élite of the art market, in an aura of perfume, hairdos by Mr. Kenneth, sables, crisp linen, and stainless-steel brains. A newcomer to the scene can only be impressed and try to remember not to wave to anybody under any circumstances. To be admitted, he has to have a ticket which no broker can provide, making the white or colored card that arrives by mail from the auction house one of the status symbols of the New York, London, or Paris "A" groups. Waiting for the start produces the same symptoms—an increased shrillness, a shuffling of feet, a brightened look in the eyes—that ripple through the crowd at the Sands in Las Vegas when the word spreads that Sinatra is coming in to deal a few hands of blackjack.

The salesroom congregation on evenings like this represents the apex of a pyramid of buyers which grows continually taller and broader, like a sand castle built by many hands. The base of the pyramid spreads farther and farther as literally millions of people, prompted by the manifestations of the art boom that appear in newspapers, magazines, books, and department stores, make their first purchases of a framed print, a volume of reproductions, a facsimile of "Aristotle" or some other master work bought at a museum counter.

Anyone who has gone so far as that may well continue. The slopes of the pyramid rise higher as the builders turn to collecting in a modest way. At the $100 level or below it, they can begin buying modern ceramics, Japanese prints, bits of silver, Chelsea plates, or paintings by young unknowns hung from the railings in the Washington Square annual show. At this stage, they will probably peek in at their first auction: the private house sale which promises something they can afford, the weekly or monthly sales held in a thousand suburbs across the land.

As their interest carries them up from one level to another, the mass pressure of their buying starts to take effect on market prices. They acquire somewhat more expensive pictures, putting away out of sight the earlier things which no longer appeal to them. There are the exceptions where taste and luck combine to give a beginner something of lasting importance and value, but usually there is nothing to be done with past purchases acquired at the foot of the pyramid but give them away or push them up into the attic. It is not advisable to pay storage in the majority of instances, though warehouses in every big city have rooms crammed with unframed canvases which customers have bought in the hope that someday their children or grandchildren will have a fortune on their hands. The odds against windfalls of this nature are enormous, but many collectors, against the advice of those who perhaps know better, persist in believing that pictures are like mint coins or good wine, automatically increasing in worth as the years go by.

An important altitude is passed on the climb up the slope when the collector buys his first $1,000 painting. Even at current prices, this qualifies him as a serious customer at all but the biggest sales. He might pick up some Old Master drawings, good bronzes, rare editions, or modern paintings with a reasonable expectancy of future gain at resale. For example, Francis Picabia, who has hung in the Armory Show and once produced a Cubist portrait of Gertrude Stein which made her look "as if she had been shaved for the last mile," could be bought in the 1960's at Sotheby's for well under $1,000. Bernard Buffet, another Frenchman whose reputation is still climbing, sold at the $1,000 mark a dozen years ago, yet his canvases are currently rated at ten times that figure. The Modernist, Marc Chagall, whose work was banned in Nazi Germany, sold for $50 at Christie's in 1939; by 1961 a painting of his was up to $43,000. It may also be remembered that Renoirs by the dozen hung unsold on the walls of Ambroise Vollard's shop for years, and Cézanne still lifes could not originally find a buyer at 600 francs.

Once the climb toward the top of the pyramid has been undertaken, the collector discovers himself increasingly in the competitive company of curators from the smaller museums and institutions, shopping at figures close to his. Somewhere along the path, the characteristics of his interest in painting will probably undergo a sea change. The novice who lays out a comparatively few dollars for something at the start of his career is prompted purely and simply by admiration for what he buys. As his outlays increase, price occupies a bigger place in his thinking, and it may eventually become a case not so much of art for art's sake as art for investment.

Every salesroom has its lists of clients who have clambered up the slopes, from the $1,000 purchase to one costing twice as much, then up to the $10,000 mark and so on. There is always room at the top for more recruits to the bidding where the sky seems the limit. It has been estimated that no more than 500 men and women make up the peak of the international market, those customers willing to pay $50,000 and more for a painting. The majority of them live in the United States, with the rest to be found in Switzerland, France, Germany, Italy, Great Britain, and South America, but they follow the auctions on both sides of the Atlantic, ready to bid in person or through their agents. Add a maximum of perhaps 200 museums with endowments big enough to allow them to keep this high-flying company, and you have considerably fewer than 1,000 potential buyers for the very finest and most expensive works.

It is only toward the summit that price fluctuations are important. At the pyramid's base, the supply of goods is steady. Most of them—art books, prints, reproductions—are manufactured for the market. At the lower levels fluctuations are insignificant because the intrinsic value of most of the items is small. At the $1,000 stratum, price begins to count more heavily, and a great proportion of buyers—possibly even a majority of them—think at least as much in terms of profit as of beauty.

The idea of paintings as a source of financial gain is no older than the history of the merchant classes; the original patrons of arts had no thought of it. Painting then was done, to specifications, in fresco with the pigments applied to fresh mortar. Only when artists turned to their smaller pictures, the so-called easel paintings, and worked in tempera and oils on wood panels or canvas was there anything that could serve for commercial speculation as it passed from one owner to another. Even so, centuries went by before trading in pictures established itself, mostly because they are awkward and fragile objects for sale or barter compared with precious stones or metalwares.

The wild extravagances of the French sovereigns in building palaces and hunting for art treasure to fill them gave impetus to the speculators. The Marquis de

Coulanges in a letter to his widowed niece, Madame Marie de Sévigné, expressed a seventeenth-century viewpoint that might serve as a prologue to the latest Wall Street guides for art investors. "Pictures are so many bars of gold, there have never been better acquisitions," he wrote. "You can always sell them at twice their cost whenever you want. So never get bored with having new ones at Grignan [where she lived with her son-in-law], and cover all your halls and passages with them as soon as the rooms are full."

As Maurice Rheims has pointed out, Madame de Sévigné passed on the investment advice to her friends, as one of the early booms in art got under way. It lasted for the better part of a century, pushed along by competition between Paris merchants and the courtiers of Versailles. The royal collection alone numbered 2,000 pictures, 546 of them of the contemporary French school, and a sizable share of the 12,000,000 livres that Louis XV squandered on Madame Pompadour went for French "Moderns," too.

The Revolution and Napoleon knocked the bottom out of the French market, demonstrating the usual effect that wars, domestic turmoil, and financial collapse have on prices in general. From a speculative standpoint, the French school sank into a decline. The market now was in Gainsborough, Reynolds, Romney, Lawrence, Constable, and the rest of the eighteenth-century Englishmen whose paintings were in demand to adorn the stately halls of the nabobs' mansions which were mushrooming across their native land on the proceeds of trade with the Indies.

It took another hundred years, and the arrival in the marketplace of the American millionaires, for pictures to become symbols of affluence, and for sale prices, usually of the same painters that the New World rich had bought from the Old, to find a place in the newspapers. But the first million-dollar paintings were bought out of income and for personal pleasure of one kind or another, not for investment. In the J. P. Morgan era, a man founded a collection not to sell but to keep or to bestow upon the nation for posterity's sake.

The change in attitude among many of the élite is directly traceable to the growth of taxation since the 1930's. Investment has been steered toward works of art, which offer one of the few havens where a rich man can enjoy himself without incurring anybody's particular displeasure. Paintings which were formerly regarded as priceless have emerged as something rather like State lottery bonds whose value is spelled out in dollars and cents. The lucky winners of them are regarded with the same esteem as a 1950's investor who cleaned up on uranium stocks.

Unquestionably, art produces handsome profits, as newspaper headlines proclaim. By most standards of comparison, an investor in paintings has been receiving a better return on his dollar than an investor on Wall Street for years now. This held true long before the securities market sagged in the summer of 1961 and failed to make anything like a complete recovery. *The New York Times* industrial stock average stood at 693.95 at the end of that year compared with 595.15 on December 31 of 1960. The rise of 16.6 per cent couldn't compare with the increase that occurred in broad categories of works of art.

Dr. Franz Pick, a New York financial expert, found that eighteenth-century Baroque sculpture rose some 150 per cent in the same twelve-month period, the biggest upward movement of any category. The Old Master market went up about fifty per cent, but the figure was heavily weighted by the "Aristotle" transaction. French Impressionists continued to gain—roughly forty per cent in Dr. Pick's arithmetic—and the work of one painter, Chagall, doubled in value, perhaps because of the favorable publicity he received from the magical stained-glass windows he did for a synagogue in Israel.

"To sum up," said the doctor, sounding like a modern echo of Coulanges, "all these objects of art gave much more protection against monetary risks than gold, platinum, or any currency, not to speak of most other 'investments' in the printed form of so-called securities."

The auctioning of "Aristotle" was promptly followed by a flurry of pamphlets, brochures, newsletters, and tipsheets devoted to the beguiling theme of speculating in pictures. The publishers of one New York guide advertised its merits by proclaiming in approved commercial style, "How to make super-profits in the art market now . . . Art market up 975 per cent versus 241 per cent for stock market." There was no indication of how either figure was arrived at.

French & Company, art dealers of Madison Avenue, published a plain-spoken brochure entitled "Taxes and Art"—a Gobelin tapestry depicting "The Toilette of Esther" was reproduced on its cover—which proved so popular with lawyers, museums, and certified public accountants that a second printing had to be ordered within the space of a month. Some attorneys and CPAs wanted copies as a basis for pep talks to clients, presumably urging them to get out of blue-chip stocks into sounder prospects like Picasso's blue period.

"Taxes and Art" set out the approved means of giving away art objects while still keeping them for the giver's lifetime, citing the illuminating case of a "Mr. Roberts," who has a gross income of $200,000 and a painting valued at $80,000, which he employs to collect "a charitable deduction right now in the amount of $38,424." If there was any real criticism about a certain cynicism in the tone of the brochure, French & Company reported that no harsh words had come to its ears.

Money, and money alone, has always been the primary concern of the auction houses, with considerations of taste and beauty subordinated to the demands of the marketplace. Scholarship in an auctioneer or dealer is important to the extent that it enables him to judge commercial value. "Turnover . . . the high level of prices . . . the rare and valuable lots . . . percentage increase . . . record-breaking season. . . ." This is the sales talk of the auction rooms and the language that studs their annual reports, which are quite openly designed to attract fresh business for the next season.

Peter Wilson talks price at Sotheby's: "We can usually get what we estimate pictures will fetch." I. O. Chance talks prices at Christie's: "The auction room is a gamble. No work of art has any basic value. It's a question of a buyer backing his own fancy." Louis Marion talks price at Parke-Bernet: "Art has had nothing but a bull market for the past decade. As a result financial counselors are sending more and more investors to the auction block to seek capital gains as well as aesthetic appreciation."

There was, in fact, some uneasiness and a moderate falling off in prices on the art market after the 1962 declines on Wall Street. In London, the usual March sale was postponed for a month in 1963 to give dealers and collectors an opportunity to regain the courage that had ebbed away. The deliberate delay proved to have been justified when Sotheby's, opening with a bang, put up a dozen Impressionists owned by the late Alfred Wolf, another refugee from Nazi Germany who went to live in South America. They made a reassuring $794,640, and the dealers, who had looked upon the sale as a test of things to come, agreed that confidence had been restored. It was not a dealer, however, who came up with the best price of the day but Francis Taylor, who used to conduct an art gallery in Beverly Hills, California. He paid $257,600 for a van Gogh landscape, "Vue de l'Asile et de la Chapelle de Saint-Rémy," on behalf of his daughter Elizabeth, regarded in some circles as something of a landscape herself.

The question of gain, though not of capital gain on resale, may well have motivated every major collector of the American era of titans. Henry Clay Frick, the steel and coke emperor, was a pioneer in his willingness to talk about the prices he paid and his need for assurance that he had not been unduly extravagant. He became the dealers' delight when his purchasing reached an annual rate of between $2,000,000 and $4,000,000 before the First World War, as he picked up for $1,250,000 the Fragonard Room of J. P. Morgan; bought Frans Hals's "Old Woman" for $150,700 after Knoedlers had acquired it at a New York auction for some $30,000 less; paid Duveen $1,250,000 for the third choice of Morgan's fabulous porcelains.

But it seems to have been a Velásquez portrait of Philip IV of Spain that fretted Frick most, after he had handed over $410,000 for it to Thomas Agnew & Sons, the greatest sum that the work of this painter had made to date; Arabella Huntington went him $35,000 better two years later for "The Duke of Alvarez," which hangs in the Huntington Library in San Marino, California. Frick learned that Philip IV himself had paid the artist only the equivalent of $600 when his portrait was painted in 1644. To calculate whether or not he had been overcharged by Agnew's, Frick worked out the total compound interest at six per cent over the intervening 267 years and found, to his delight, that the Spanish king would have done better investing his money than paying the painter.

More recently, the dealers Rosenberg & Stiebel of East 57th Street sold Charles B. Wrightsman the Vermeer "Portrait of a Young Girl," an 18 by 16 inch canvas of an ageless beauty with a smile as enigmatic as the "Mona Lisa." It had changed hands in Rotterdam in 1816 for three florins, or $1.80 in contemporary United States currency. The Texas collector paid $350,000. If the Dutchman's three florins had been banked at three per cent compounded quarterly, his account today would stand at roughly $80. But the market value of the Vermeer had grown by 19,000,000 per cent. Soon after Wrightsman had it, a London dealer told a visiting American that he had a client who might be prepared to pay $1,000,000 for the young woman.

Despite the fact that a painting retains some minimal value however much it depreciates while stocks may not, the securities markets and the salesrooms used to act in the past like a married couple, prospering or declining hand in hand. The troubled half-century after 1790 brought hard times for most people and rock-bottom prices for every kind of painting. Even Gainsborough (1727–1788), who had been well favored by Britain's merchant princes in his lifetime and whose "Portrait of Mr. & Mrs. Robert Andrews" fetched $364,000 in 1960, was bringing a skinflint $30 for a full-length "Duke of Gloucester" eleven years after the artist's death. Starting in the 1840's, the market as a whole climbed fairly steadily until it suddenly zoomed under pressure of American buying at the end of the century and stayed up for years, at least in the United States. But prices went over the precipice along with everything else during the Depression, dropping by an average of fifty per cent between 1929 and 1933. The boom figures of the Jazz Age did not return for another two decades.

But when accountants recommend art as an investment nowadays, they can quote portfolios full of statistics to support an argument that the salesroom and Wall Street have been divorced, that the cyclical recessions following the Second World War have not interrupted the impressive climb on the art market. The French auctioneer Maurice Rheims, who is no Philistine, can add his voice to the stock exchange chorus and say, "A work of art is the best investment over a length of time."

It is possible—the auction houses do it consistently—to interpret works of art in the vocabulary of Wall Street. Today's "blue chips" would be the Old Masters of virtually any school or century, should they be available; they seldom are because they are the backbone of museums everywhere. The "growth stocks" are the Impressionists and Post-Impressionists, particularly Cézanne and Gauguin, whose work has been the basis for the most spectacular speculations of modern times. Eight years before his death at the age of forty-seven, one of Cézanne's still lifes was offered for sale in Paris for a few hundred francs to help finance the return of Gauguin, who lay seriously ill in Tahiti. The Cézanne was of the kind that a critic derided as "crooked fruit in tipsy bowls," and no buyer could be found until an expensive carved frame had been added, free of charge. As for Paul Gauguin, he had suggested shipping out fifteen pictures a year from Tahiti for an annual pittance of $480; it was one of these, "Te Tiai Na Ve I Te Rata" (I await the letter), as brilliant and haunting as tropical bird song, that made the record price for a Gauguin in 1959—$364,000.

Pursuing the Wall Street parallels, Contemporary painting has been classified as the "speculative" element in the art market, to be bought in hope of appreciation but at the risk of loss. The degree of danger varies, of course, with the reputation of the artist. Picasso qualifies as the most popular painter of the age. However, he has lived through so many style periods and produced such a volume of work that his prices fluctuate broadly, despite the careful control which his agents exercise (under an agreement signed as far back as 1912) over the flow of pictures available for sale. Until recently, only the finest examples of his earlier painting commanded impressive figures. A turning point was reached in 1959, when a group of American buyers offered a fantastic $1,960,000 for "Guernica," his massive, tortured reminiscence of the Spanish war. Since then, as less and less of his work remains in circulation, almost anything of any significance from his hands may bring close to $100,000, like the best of the twenty-nine drawings and paintings included in the sale in 1960 of the New York collection of Jacques Sarlie, the financier.

Matisse, Braque, and Léger have to be included with Picasso as the safest bets among the Contemporaries, in the judgment of investment counselors who are knowledgeable on the subject. They are followed close, in the opinion of Richard Rush in a singularly cool-blooded book entitled *Art as an Investment,* by Chagall, Derain, Dufy, Modigliani, Roualt, Segonzac, Utrillo, and Vuillard. An artist who qualifies as being every bit as attractive for future profits is Andrew Wyeth, a Contemporary American working, usually in tempera, in a vein of neorealism that is all his own.

Born in 1917 in the Pennsylvania community which is still his home, he is remembered among New York agents as the lad who used to deliver the commercial pictures of his father, a leading magazine illustrator of his day. In 1950, a Wyeth could be found for $3,000, but the people who bought them seldom let them go, and the auction record of his work is virtually nonexistent. Today he accepts only three or four commissions a year for fees as high as $75,000, and his "That Gentleman" made $58,000 in 1961, when the Dallas Museum of Fine Arts came up with this highest-ever price paid by a museum for a work by a living American artist.

Wyeth runs counter to the rules of the marketplace in more ways than one. His characteristic mood is melancholy. That consistency is one factor that helps make him a gilt-edged bet, since the big prices always go for work that is "typical" of the artist. A melancholy air, on the other hand, normally operates to a painter's disadvantage. Skulls, skeletons, blood, disfigurement, or broken bones in a canvas depress a salesroom audience. In the case of Old Masters, who worked in an era of less queasy stomachs, charnel-house details are often painted out before the pictures are offered. A bright palette is worth more than a sombre one; experience shows that bidding will be brisker for vibrant, sunny colors.

The fact that Wyeth's "That Gentleman" should have scored so well is unusual, too, in that its subject is a gaunt old man, sitting brooding in a bare room. Except for Rembrandts, studies of old men cannot compete with portraits of young women or children for auction-house attention. This disparity was never more clearly marked than at Sotheby's in the 1959–1960 season when a matching pair of Gainsborough portraits arrived under the hammer from the collection of Sir John Leigh. The pale "Anne, Countess of Chesterfield," pensive by a pillar in a garden, made $95,200. Her handsome husband, "Phillip, Fifth Earl of Chesterfield," fondling his dog in presumably the same *al fresco* setting, was good for only $39,200.

Dead fish, no matter how pearly their scales, are hard to sell as subjects. Dead game makes a better impression, possibly because fur and feathers are prettier. Flowers have it over either porgy or partridge, especially nowadays if the bouquets are one of the many insipid flower pieces by Henri Fantin-Latour, which leapt from about $100 in the 1890's to a booming $42,000 in 1959. Odilon Redon's enchanted gardening is enormously successful, too, perhaps because of his choice of blossoms. Even among flowers there are salesroom likes and dislikes, as Christie's discovered when some Fantin-Latour hollyhocks went for $2,145 compared with roses at $14,300. That was thirty years ago and more. A Fantin bouquet recently made $58,000.

When it comes to animals, dogs and horses stand about equal. A George Stubbs, "White Poodle in a Punt," from the Earl of Shrewsbury and Waterford, sold for $47,600 in 1960, and a pair of frieze pictures, "Stallions," by the same dependable Englishman brought $51,600 a year earlier. Other domestic creatures are not so reliable in performance, especially the sheep and cattle of Rosa Bonheur— sheep for $191.40 and cattle for $176.40, both at Christie's in 1954.

The sheer dimensions of a painting play a major part in determining its commercial value. The classical rule of the bigger the better, and more costly, does not apply in an age when many collectors live in economy-size city apartments with limited wall space and the stately homes with fifteen-foot ceilings have long since fallen to the demolition gangs. The average auctioneer figures that anything larger than thirty-six inches in width or breadth may slow down bidding, unless the work is of Old Master quality. A full-length, full-size portrait of nobody in particular à la Rubens which, with enough clouds or drapery, can run to eight feet tall, may be disappointing at any sale. Yet "Adoration of the Magi" by the tireless Sir Joshua himself brought $771,000 when it was put up at Sotheby's, even when a hole had to be cut in the floor to hoist the 12 by 6 foot giant up from the basement.

Part of the explanation for the remarkable price lay in the picture's unbroken pedigree. It was unquestionably a Rubens, its previous owner was undoubtedly the Duke of Westminster, and its proprietorship could be traced clearly back to the artist. A celebrated owner helps the price of any item from his collection that goes to an auctioneer, as Somerset Maugham well realized when he wrote about his pictures for Sotheby's catalogue before they went on sale. A famous name draws other famous names in as bidders. "The interest in an illustrious pedigree," Professor Julius Held of Barnard College has noted, "may reflect a rudiment of fetishism, a subconscious belief in a charisma transferred on such objects from their previous owners." It may, on the other hand, reflect the purchaser's knowing that a good pedigree improves his own chances on future resale, besides giving him something to talk about at the dinner table meantime.

A clean bill of health in a painting's attribution is important whether or not any previous owner rates a column in *Who's Who* or the *Almanac de Gotha*. In the case of Old Masters, reliable attribution may be difficult to determine. In these high-priced days, when many collectors buy famous names rather than intrinsically fine pictures, a reconsideration of a painting's pedigree is likely to be a serious business in terms of dollars and cents. "Cupid and Psyche" by Jacques Louis David, the great and influential eighteenth-century French portraitist, sold in Paris in 1961 for $42,882, an unusually good figure for this artist. It would not have made a tenth of that sum if this David had been discovered to be the work of Madame Charpentier, virtually unknown in the annals of art, who certainly painted another "David" which the Frick collection bought for an appreciable sum.

Petrus Christus and Jan van Eyck are two Flemish realists whose work is almost indistinguishable. A Van Eyck drawing, "Man with a Falcon," was reattributed to Petrus Christus recently on the evidence of the look in the fellow's eyes. That switch made partial amends for a "Christus" panel of "St. Jerome in his Study" which the Detroit Institute of Arts bought for $18,000 before having it cleaned and restored. It turned out, in expert opinion, to be a Van Eyck, with some additions by his less-esteemed compatriot, and therefore to be valued at probably $750,000.

The physical condition of a picture obviously has some bearing on its value, even if the London houses are something less than meticulous in mending holes in canvas before the gavel rises and falls. A grimy painting in a battered frame, however, may well be a better purchase than a much-restored and possibly overpainted job which has been to the cleaners too often.

The final and most fundamental factor in determining salesroom price is the immemorial law of supply and demand. Every museum's storage space contains pictures—as high as ninety per cent of inventory—that do not merit hanging because only scholars are interested in seeing them. Every major dealer is in something like the same boat, with stock he cannot sell at any worthwhile price, which he holds on to in the hope that taste will change and drugs on the market like the Barbizon School will be acceptable again. The auctioneers face no problem like that; theirs is an in-and-out trade with a fast turnover.

Demand must outdistance supply for a painter's work to climb to the breathless altitudes. The still uncertain market in Gainsboroughs—Peter Wilson has judged it as problematical, though some of his competitors think it is on the rise—would be adversely affected if Queen Elizabeth, for example, were suddenly to dispose of the set of fifteen matched portraits of the British royal family which the artist produced by commission of George III. She could similarly pull down the market for Leonardo da Vinci, Michelangelo, and half-a-dozen other Old Masters if it were decreed that she must unload the royal collection, as happened to Charles I. Since his dire day, that collection has accumulated 4,500 paintings and 20,000 drawings, including an incredible 600 Leonardos.

For an artist's price to keep climbing, there should be enough of his work in circulation for several sales figures to be established in each decade, so that all his work benefits. If too many years elapse without a recorded sale, an Old Master can fall out of the running by comparison with the Moderns, who are continually resold. A work of art needs publicity, just like the auction house that sells it.

For all the publicity that attends the disposal of a first-class Old Master, it is

The universe in paint on canvas

the Impressionists, Post-Impressionists, and major Moderns which have shown the most phenomenal inflation over recent decades. There are Cézannes and Renoirs that have soared up in price a stratospheric 6,000 per cent. In the five years ending in 1960, Post-Impressionist values were multiplied by an average of more than seven times, making them the prizes of the salesrooms today.

So far as anyone can judge, there is no visible limit to the potential price inherent in any sought-after painting that appears at auction. "Aristotle" represented a break-through when the figure exceeded $2,000,000 for the first time. Theoretically, there are plenty of pictures in existence—Raphaels, Leonardos, Botticellis, more Rembrandts, and any easel painting of Michelangelo, if one could be found—that could go to the $3,000,000 mark. And under the relentless pressure of cold war and sizzling tax rates, conditions exist for new generations of multimillionaires to club together and pay $4,000,000 or $5,000,000 for some prestigious work and write it into their wills as a bequest to the Metropolitan, or London's National Gallery, or an institution yet to be built in a brand-new African nation.

Farther down the slopes of the pyramid, the millions of collectors spread around the world represent a demand that is virtually insatiable and so broadly based that it is proof against anything, short of world-wide calamity. In older days, a comparative handful of people could stop buying, as the European rich did after Napoleon scared them, and the American rich after 1929—and they could drag the whole market down.

Excluding the unobtainable Old Masters, the best buys have always been the modern painters of each generation. The trick that can accumulate a fortune is to decide who is the artist whose work will survive. The years destroy 10,000 reputations for each one that they make. The Landseer that went for $25,000 in 1880 sells for $200 half a century later. A Van Gogh that could be picked up for $150 or less makes $200,000 nowadays . . . but nobody bought him while he lived.

Because nobody can outguess time and what havoc it wreaks or heaven it brings, the only possible answer is to buy not a school that's in vogue or a fashionable name, but quality, provided the buyer has any thought of collecting rather than of reselling for a dollar profit. If the peak prices of this era are largely dependent, as they may well be, on the tax laws of the Federal government, then any drastic revision of those laws could bring a turn in the market as supply outstripped demand in the very schools—Abstract and Contemporary—where bargain hunters look most hungrily for profits today.

Quality—or virtue, to use an old-fashioned but long-respected word—survives. It gives pleasure to a painting's owner no matter how often the auctioneer's gavel is pounded over it, or whether the school is in or out of esteem, or if the market is high or low.

What is *virtue?* There are as many answers as there are artists, living and dead. But it may be measured in terms of how completely and subtly the painter expresses his belief in himself, in his fellow men, and in the nature of the universe they share.